MOBILE TECHNOLOGIES AND THE WRITING CLASSROOM

Mobile Technologies and the Writing Classroom

Resources for Teachers

Edited by

CLAIRE LUTKEWITTE
Nova Southeastern University

National Council of Teachers of English
1111 W. Kenyon Road, Urbana, Illinois 61801-1096

Staff Editor: Bonny Graham
Manuscript Editor: Josh Rosenberg
Interior Design: Jenny Jensen Greenleaf
Cover Design: Pat Mayer
Cover Image: KrulUA/iStock/Thinkstock

NCTE Stock Number: 31961; eStock Number: 31978
ISBN 978-0-8141-3196-1; eISBN 978-0-8141-3197-8

It is the policy of NCTE in its journals and other publications to provide a forum for the open discussion of ideas concerning the content and the teaching of English and the language arts. Publicity accorded to any particular point of view does not imply endorsement by the Executive Committee, the Board of Directors, or the membership at large, except in announcements of policy, where such endorsement is clearly specified.

Every effort has been made to provide current URLs and email addresses, but because of the rapidly changing nature of the Web, some sites and addresses may no longer be accessible.

Library of Congress Cataloging-in-Publication Data

Names: Lutkewitte, Claire, editor.
Title: Mobile technologies and the writing classroom : resources for
     teachers / edited by Claire Lutkewitte, Ph.D., Nova Southeastern
     University.
Description: Urbana, Illinois : National Council of Teachers of English,
     2016. | Includes bibliographical references and index.
Identifiers: LCCN 2016018949 (print) | LCCN 2016031818 (ebook) |
     ISBN 9780814131961 (pbk.) | ISBN 9780814131978 (eISBN) | ISBN
     9780814131978 ()
Subjects: LCSH: English language—Rhetoric—Study and teaching. |
     English language—Computer-assisted instruction. | Creative writing—
     Computer-assisted instruction. | Mobile computing.
Classification: LCC PE1404 .M627 2016 (print) | LCC PE1404 (ebook) |
     DDC 808/.0420711—dc23
LC record available at https://lccn.loc.gov/2016018949

CONTENTS

INTRODUCTION

*The possibilities are numerous once we decide to act
and not react.*

GEORGE BERNARD SHAW

Several years ago, when my writing students first began turning in assignments composed entirely on mobile devices, I jumped at the chance to study their work. Intrigued by how and why students chose to use these devices rather than their laptops or desktops, I embarked on several research projects to understand what made mobile technology unique and different from technologies of the past. Through case studies, interviews, and textual analyses, I discovered that students enjoyed working with their mobile devices and found that in doing so, they were more engaged in the class. At that time, writing scholarship devoted to mobile technologies was scarce, so I turned to other fields for insight, mainly the mobile learning research field. Excited and encouraged by what I saw, I began crafting assignments and activities that had students thinking about and using mobile technologies.

As time went on, I began to see a growing interest at writing conferences among scholars and academics who were taking mobile technology seriously. When I attended the Conference on College Composition and Communication Annual Convention in 2015, for example, I witnessed several informative presentations on teaching students about and with mobile technology. However, even with mobile technology's growing presence at conferences, there is still a lack of resources to help faculty implement a pedagogy that takes advantage of what mobile technologies have to offer, even if only on a limited basis. That is the motivation for this book. This book is meant to offer up strategies to writing instructors who want more than just a conference presentation or a journal article as a guide. It is also meant to champion the need for faculty to responsibly bring mobile technology into the classroom, whether that is just by discussion or by having students compose with it. We cannot nor should we ignore the power of mobile technologies and what they offer students and faculty.

Nevertheless, defining mobile technologies is not a simple task considering they mean different things to different people at different moments in time. In one sense, we can draw from Asi DeGani, Geoff Martin, Geoff Stead, and Frances Wade and define mobile technologies as handheld connected devices that mediate the user's environment. We could use the term *handheld* rather than *portable* because portable, as David Menchaca explains, "is in contrast to mobile" and "suggests that you can move your computer from place to place," while "mobile suggests that you can continue to compute while you are doing so" (319). This could help to distinguish what was once considered mobile (e.g., heavy laptop) from what is now considered mobile (e.g., smartphone).

Furthermore, because mobile technologies are handheld, we can characterize them as *intimate* and *personal*, which as DeGani et al. note, can lead to a sense of ownership of not only the device but of the learning that takes place with mobile devices (6). Mobile technologies are intimate and personal in that users hold them close to the body because they are small and require users to keep them close in order to operate them. Because technologies are "known through the body," we are able to "develop a feel" for them (Nye 4). When we develop a feel for them, we also develop the skills necessary to use them and we come to expect a certain ease in using them. In addition, mobile technologies are intimate and personal because, as de Souza e Silva and Frith write, they can be used as an individual way of filtering a user's experience with space (156).

Mobile technologies are often called smart devices because their software and applications enable users to do more than just basic functions like make a phone call. Now, more than ever, we need to see mobile technologies as more than just a substitute textbook that relies mainly on print in a digital format. In other words, mobile devices can do more than just house our class's textbook. Applications, or apps, can help us filter our experiences as do other functions such as GPS, which heightens our awareness of location in time and space. Smart devices can capture data, communicate with a network, provide entertainment, and so forth. Their software and applications can even provide users with information to make smarter decisions in the moment at hand.

Yet, in order to understand what mobile technologies are, we also need to consider how mobile technologies have and will affect us even if we don't own them. Referring to the entire mobile industry, Tomi Ahonen calls mobile the seventh mass medium of the world and notes that "during the past decade, mobile became the fastest-growing major industry on the planet, and by 2009, mobile passed the $1 trillion level in annual income, becoming one of the biggest industries on Earth" (30). Never before has there been a technology that has been adapted more quickly by more people than mobile technology. One only needs to visit a public place to observe that many people's lives are regularly mediated by mobile technologies. According to the 2015 Ericsson Mobility Report, "During 2014 alone, 800 million smartphone subscriptions were added worldwide. It took over five years to reach the first billion smartphone subscriptions, a milestone that was reached in 2012, and less than two years to reach the second billion, illustrating the strong growth" (Cerwall 3). In the United States, the Pew Research Center's "Mobile Technology Fact Sheet" reports that as of January 2014, "90% of American adults have a cell phone, 58% of American adults have a smartphone, 32% of American adults own an e-reader, 42% of American adults own a tablet computer." To further illustrate just how big mobile is, Ahonen explains that "mobile today is far bigger than broadcast media (television and radio combined), far bigger than the computer and information technology industry (magazines, books, and newspapers)" (30).

Because of its magnitude, mobile has impacted education in many ways. Colleges and universities across the country have instituted mobile initiatives, from offering mobile-only courses to providing incoming students with iPads to developing workshops for instructors who are interested in teaching with mobile technologies. In 2012, for example, the dean of the College of

Arts and Sciences where I teach gave all faculty an iPad and told us to explore how to use it. And so, for a semester, faculty met in groups to discuss how to use iPads in the classroom, whether or not they would be useful, and so forth.

Now, such initiatives have led many institutions and organizations to invest more time and money into studying mobile technologies. Research suggests that this investment is warranted as mobile technologies have proven to be good for students and students prefer to use them. For example, studies show that students are learning with mobile technologies:

◆ According to Jon Mason's 2013 study in *Global Mobile*, "Usage of mobile devices within the classroom was shown to promote *inquiry-based learning* and *collaborative learning*" (202).

◆ In their study, "Bringing It All Together: Interdisciplinary Perspectives on Incorporating Mobile Technologies in Higher Education," Christina Partin and Skyler Lauderdale found that "students are more genuinely engaged in the classroom if they are able to incorporate their mobile devices into their learning" (101).

◆ In a survey on students enrolled in courses that utilize mobile technologies, Ronald Yaros found that "compared to the learners in other blended courses without mobile devices, [students gave] consistently higher ratings for effective learning, access to content, engagement with peers, orientation to the blended format, use of online tools, the ability to review content for a mobile quiz, meeting workload requirements, allocation of time, self-pacing for study and self-directed learning" (70–71).

◆ Investigating a postgraduate development studies program in which students used mobile technologies, Elizabeth Beckman concluded that mobile learning allowed students to maintain and build connections and make commitments within communities (160).

In specific ways, mobile technologies have changed the way students write. As I mentioned at the beginning of this introduction, I've witnessed many students in my own classes using mobile devices to compose their assignments. But my students are hardly unique in this regard. While earlier studies like the one Moe Folk mentions in Chapter 3 show students' reluctance to using mobile technologies in academia on a deeper level, more recent research concludes the opposite is becoming true of today's students. For example, in a survey of more than thirteen hundred first-year writing (FYW) students at seven colleges and universities, Jessie L. Moore et al. found that "while they use cell phones for expected genres (e.g., texts (SMS/cell)), for example, students also report using cell phones to write academic papers, reading notes, and lecture notes" (9). As the scholars in this book attest, writing students can and are willing to write about, analyze, reflect on, and use mobile technologies for academic purposes with great success.

Nevertheless, despite their impact, mobile technologies can pose daunting and frustrating challenges for instructors. Many of the authors in this book mention that colleges and universities do not necessarily have the infrastructure in place to take advantage of mobile technologies. After the dean at my institution gave all faculty iPads, a colleague and I studied how faculty used them to teach, to conduct research and scholarship, and to serve the university. In doing so, we discovered that faculty face many challenges trying to incorporate iPads into their pedagogy. These challenges included, among others, not having a course management site that is mobile friendly, not having the funds to purchase specific apps, not having hardware in the classroom to connect iPads, and not having instructional training to use iPads (Lutkewitte and Vanguri).

So, this book comes then at a time when instructors are pressured to be innovative at their colleges and universities (often for the sake of attracting higher enrollment) but are not provided ideal circumstances to do the innovating. While this book does not solve all the problems instructors face when using mobile technologies, what this book can offer is (1) a starting point for those who haven't used mobile technologies before in the classroom, (2) a reassurance that you are not alone for others who have been trying, and (3) a call that we can do more with less.

The book is divided into two parts, Part I: Writing *for* and *about* Mobile Technologies and Part II: Writing *with* Mobile Technologies. Not every institution provides the necessary support for instructors to engage students in writing with mobile devices, especially those institutions that are print-centric. Likewise, not every student or instructor has access to mobile devices. However, as Rodrigo has argued, access, for example, should not be an excuse for not doing. Faculty and administrators need to be creative in their approach, and this book shows how many instructors have done great things in spite of not having ideal circumstances. For readers who do not have enough resources or support, you might begin with discussions, activities, and assignments *about* mobile technologies rather than those with them. After all, technology as a subject is not new to our field. We have long ago recognized that a technology is "a text that can be analyzed and placed in a cultural context" (Nye 4). So, perhaps, you could begin with how students read their mobile devices and the texts they contain. For example, writing instructors can help students understand the rhetorical moves readers and writers make when text messaging as well as help them to critically examine the places and spaces in which their actions with mobile technologies occur. A discussion of mobile technologies could even include a discussion about composing conventions, what is appropriate and what is not. For instance, when I taught a QR assignment similar to that described in Chapter 3, my students and I engaged in discussions about appropriate conventions for composing visuals for mobile technologies.

While Part I is about reflecting on the use of mobile technologies, thinking critically about society's view of technology and analyzing rhetorical decisions, Part II is about writing *with* mobile technologies and features chapters that demonstrate how instructors and students can use their mobile technologies to compose texts. In Chapter 7, which begins this part, Jessica Schreyer writes about how first-year composition students can use mobile devices during their writing and research processes. Working to understand what it means to be a part of a university's community, students in her class research their campus while utilizing their mobile devices' functions, like the camera function, to gather and keep track of research notes. Students then use this research to construct a multimodal project. Part II also features chapters about making writing instruction better, using mobiles for portfolios, getting students outside the classroom, and seeing mobile technologies as identity texts.

Many of the chapters follow a similar organizational structure to make accessing information easier for readers. And many chapters provide practical pedagogical strategies along with examples of assignments and student work. The authors not only describe how their assignments and activities can be implemented, but also ground their discussions in theory. While the technologies mentioned in this book may change over time, the authors also provide strategies for how such assignments and activities can be adapted so as to ensure that students will continue to learn the necessary skills to succeed as writers.

Readers need not be tech experts to experiment with mobile technologies in the classroom. After all, a willingness to try out and work with technologies puts us in a better position to inform and assist administrators who are responsible for making the tech decisions on our campuses. And it is imperative that instructors work with administrators and decision makers on campus to figure out how such changes in technologies can be best met productively. Not doing so is not an option as there is too much at stake to leave decisions about technology to those who are not tied directly to our writing classrooms.

Works Cited

Ahonen, Tomi. "Mobile and Megatrends." Bruck and Rao 29–45.

Beckman, Elizabeth A. "Learners on the Move: Mobile Modalities in Developmental Studies." *Distance Education* 3.2 (2010): 159–73. Print.

Bruck, Peter A., and Madanmohan Rao, eds. *Global Mobile: Applications and Innovations for the Worldwide Mobile Ecosystem.* Medford: Information Today, 2013. Print.

Cerwall, Patrik, ed. *Ericsson Mobility Report on the Pulse of the Networked Society.* Mobile World Congress Edition. Stockholm: Ericsson, 2015. Print.

de Souza e Silva, Adriana, and Jordan Frith. *Mobile Interfaces in Public Spaces: Locational Privacy, Control, and Urban Sociability.* New York: Routledge, 2012. Print.

DeGani, Asi, Geoff Martin, Geoff Stead, and Frances Wade. *Mobile Learning Shareable Content Object Reference Model (m-SCORM) Limitations and Challenges [N09-35]*. Cambridge: Tribal, 2010. PDF file.

Lutkewitte, Claire, and Pradeep Vanguri. "Assessing iPad Use by Arts and Sciences Faculty." *Academic Exchange Quarterly* 19.2 (2015): 39–44. Print.

Mason, Jon. "Mobile Education." Bruck and Rao 197–211.

Menchaca, David. "Terms for Going Wireless: An Account of Wireless and Mobile Technologies for Composition Teachers and Scholars." Ed. Amy C. Kimme Hea. *Going Wireless: A Critical Exploration of Wireless and Mobile Technologies for Composition Teachers and Researchers*. Cresskill: Hampton, 2009. Print.

Moore, Jessie L., et al. "Revisualizing Composition: How First-Year Writers Use Composing Technologies." *Computers and Composition* 39 (2016) 1–13. Print.

Nye, David E. *Technology Matters: Questions to Live With*. Cambridge: MIT P, 2006. Print.

Partin, Christina M., and Skyler Lauderdale. "Bringing It All Together: Interdisciplinary Perspectives on Incorporating Mobile Technologies in Higher Education." *Increasing Student Engagement and Retention Using Mobile Applications: Smartphones, Skype and Texting Technologies*. Ed. Laura A. Wankel and Patrick Blessinger. Bingley: Emerald, 2013. 83–114. Print. Cutting-Edge Technologies in Higher Education. 6D.

Pew Research Center. "Mobile Technology Fact Sheet." *Pew Research Center*. Pew Research Center, 27 Dec. 2013. Web. 22 Mar. 2015.

Rodrigo, Rochelle. "Mobile Teaching versus Mobile Learning." *EDUCAUSE Review* 29 Mar. 2011. Web. 2 May 2014.

Yaros, Ronald A. "Effects of Mobile Devices and Text Messages: A Multi-Study Design to Explore a Model for Mobile Learning in Introductory Journalism." *International Journal of Cyber Behavior, Psychology and Learning* 2.3 (2012): 59–72. Print.

I

WRITING *FOR* AND *ABOUT* MOBILE TECHNOLOGIES

As discussed in the introduction to this book, mobile technologies have impacted the way our students write, leaving educators to figure out what to do in the classroom. While research shows an increase in the number of people who own mobile technologies, students need not own mobile technologies to talk about them. In fact, helping students develop a critical awareness of them and their impact on how they experience the world is vital to the writing classroom now and in the future. As Amy C. Kimme Hea warned many years ago, "an uncritical perspective on space-less and time-less technologies leads to an erasure of history, place, context, and agency" (204). Harking back to Rochelle Rodrigo, I recognize that every institution is different in terms of what resources are available to faculty. But faculty members have to make the most of those resources, even if they are scarce. And they cannot let a lack of access to mobile technologies be an excuse for ignoring them. As Rodrigo explains, "Instructors and institutions will need to help students be creative in finding access to different mobile multimedia production devices." In my own classrooms, for example, not all students have mobile technologies. However, I have found ways to work around this by having students share with one another, by bringing in devices to use in the classroom, and by sharing my own devices with students. Doing so has proven worthwhile.

For instance, in my first-year writing courses, students participate in an activity that has them reimagine a paper brochure as an interactive app. In Chapter 5, I have provided the instructions for the activity, but here I want to explain what we do as a class. Our classes are held in our campus's library, a four-story building that houses artwork in addition to books. To help visitors navigate the artwork in the library, the library created a paper brochure. As a class, I ask students to reimagine what this brochure would look like as an app.

As a class, we discuss their answers, talking about the rhetorical decisions they make when reimagining the brochure as one that could take advantage of other modes of communication. They need to figure out how a text could be transferred from one medium to another. In doing so, students pay attention to the affordances of mobile technologies. What is lost? What is gained? For example, they are keenly aware of the GPS capabilities of smartphones and often talk at length about incorporating an interactive map of the artwork. Such an activity has garnered deep conversations about technologies, their limitations, their invasion of privacy, their usefulness, and so forth. But, more than anything, it has brought to light the principles of rhetoric and has led students to understand why writers, even those who work solely with mobile technologies to communicate, need rhetoric. The rhetorical skills that students gain in doing this activity, from understanding their audience to developing a clear purpose, will help them in the future even as their technologies evolve, which they will. As more and more institutions embrace Bring Your Own Device (BYOD) initiatives, classrooms will be filled with students who have a variety of mobile devices; the need for a rhetorical foundation in which to work from will remain.

In another one of my courses, an upper-level writing course that is also described in Chapter 5, the same held true. In an assignment, I asked students to design their own mobile apps. While they did not write code for them or physically make them, they did come up with a concept and design. Students considered, among many things, how the design and content of their apps would be shaped by the notion that users would use them in a variety of places. For example, one of my students came up with the idea to create a study app that lets users find locations for studying. In the description of her app, she talks about how users can use the app to find out if a location is available, how many outlets there are available for computer and smartphone hookups, if there is access to coffee and snacks, how far users have to travel, and how users will get there. She explained later that the assignment helped her develop an awareness of audience. She made decisions about the colors, the text, and the locations she wanted to include in the app, all based on the interests of her audience. Instead of thinking about me, the instructor, she thought about a real audience, and because she did, the assignment was more meaningful to her.

While this description of what takes place in my classrooms is brief, it represents the type of assignments and activities described in the remaining chapters of Part I. As the authors of these chapters demonstrate, implementing a pedagogy that utilizes mobile technologies can be successful and meaningful for both teachers and students. Readers will witness how instructors can help students make the most of their experiences with mobile technologies in the writing classroom and how that experience is ultimately tied to student learning.

In Part I, readers will learn how to help students create a mobile composition kit by researching apps based on how useful they would be in a composition course. In the first chapter, Christina Moore argues that such a project can lead to a practical discussion about applying rhetorical skills when using mobile technologies and how writing and research are impacted by such technologies. But she also sees her project as a way for students to reflect on what they learned throughout the semester in their composition class.

In Chapter 2, Ann Amicucci offers a way for instructors to help students analyze public arguments about mobile technology use by rhetorically reflecting on their own uses. Drawing from Cynthia Selfe, Amicucci argues for the need to be critical of mobile technologies and the social contexts in which we use them. Her assignment and activity sequence calls for writing about, observing, analyzing, and discussing mobile technology use.

Not only will readers find assignments in Part I that have students reflecting on their use, but they will also read about assignments that ask students to compose for mobile technologies, even if that composing isn't done on a mobile device. Examples of such assignments include Moe Folk's QR assignment, my mobile app assignment as discussed in the book's introduction, and Melissa Toomey's rhetorical analysis of an app assignment.

The authors in Part I take on a rhetorical approach to considering the multimodal choices we make as writers, whether that be understanding the needs of our audience or being aware of our context and purpose for composing. They also highlight the importance of teaching students about the affordances or capabilities of mobile technologies, about developing an awareness of time and place, and about being critical of public documents, such as terms of service and privacy policies, that govern the use of mobile games, as discussed by Stephanie Vie in the final chapter of Part I.

Works Cited

Kimme Hea, Amy C. "Perpetual Contact: Re-articulating the Anywhere, Anytime Pedagogical Model of Mobile and Wireless Composing." *Going Wireless: A Critical Exploration of Wireless and Mobile Technologies for Composition Teachers and Researchers*. Ed. Amy C. Kimme Hea. Cresskill: Hampton, 2009. 199–221. Print.

Rodrigo, Rochelle. "Mobile Teaching versus Mobile Learning." *EDUCAUSE Review* 29 Mar. 2011. Web. 2 May 2014.

CHAPTER ONE

Making a Mobile Composition Kit: Project for Testing the Waters

CHRISTINA MOORE
Oakland University

The technology policies in our syllabi show how technology can both promote and impede the learning experience within our classrooms. While most student work relies on computers, we might ban them in the actual classroom. And our contention with mobile technology—tablets and smart devices, usually phones—is even more complicated. It gives our writing students an audience through social media but often distracts our captive audience in the classroom. At the same time, mobile technology could make our captive audience less distracted by providing immediate feedback and customizing content to each learner's pace (Ciampa). We may understand the potential for mobile technology to engage students in new types of writing and rhetorical situations but ultimately dread seeing cell phones in our students' hands. We might also have an inkling that mobile learning (m-learning)—learning that takes place through the use of tablets and smart devices—is a fad that will fade away soon enough. While educators are still excited and optimistic about the possibilities, "the iPad's status as an educational fad or revolution remains to be determined" (Scharber 71).

Fortunately, instructors of writing and rhetoric need not have this contention and challenge resolved before bringing mobile technology to the classroom but can instead use this issue as a study in rhetoric. The Mobile Composition Kit Project calls on students to consider how to use mobile technology to carry out the work of their composition class. In teams, students evaluate the app market and choose a bundle of twenty apps that would be most helpful to students in the course. Through such a project, students discuss how technologies have changed how we write, evaluate what apps best fulfill the work of the course, and reflect on the ways in which mobile technology could be useful in achieving the course objectives.

Theoretical Grounding for the Assignment and Activities

For all the promise of m-learning, there are reasonable concerns regarding mobile technology's place in formal learning spaces. While app technology evolves rapidly, it is lagging as far as tools and apps that work smoothly in the classroom. Scholars began their inquiry into how mobile technology could affect learning with the release of Apple's first smartphone (iPhone in 2007) and tablet (iPad in 2010). This time period produced studies that not only imagined mobile technology's learning possibilities but also how teachers at all levels might go about determining the place for mobile technology in their curricula. This literature ranges from general education in elementary school (Murray and Olcese in 2011) to teaching writing and rhetoric in higher education (Kimme Hea's 2009 *Going Wireless* and Lutkewitte's 2012 *Web 2.0 Applications for Composition Classrooms*).

When looking at mobile composition (writing composed through tablets and smart devices) from this starting point, the technology opens up exciting opportunities, "greatly favoring constructivist and collaborative approaches to learning, and flexible and adaptive approaches to teaching" (Manuguerra and Petocz 61). Smart devices have the capacity for these learning approaches but are less obviously compatible with formal learning contexts. Mobile composition and learning are so ubiquitous in our informal, everyday lives that we will likely learn unintentionally, and we won't recognize learning when it happens (Pachler, Bachmair, and Cook 273; Pigg et al.). Like the relationship between print books and ebooks, perhaps "mobile learning will find its niche in formal education settings, and will remain ubiquitous in informal settings" (Dennen and Hao 21). The challenge comes in implementing mobile learning into an intentional, metacognitive learning context such as the classroom.

This challenge is amplified by the small percentage of mobile apps for classroom use. Like Manuguerra and Petocz, Murray and Olcese recognize the potential of mobile technology's hardware to promote collaborative learning experiences but see its shortcomings in the software. The app market largely consists of "productivity applications and some games" that are "principally individual-based" (45). Mobile apps tend to encourage individual consumption rather than collaborative production. Based on Murray and Olcese's evaluation of the app market for education, they conclude that most apps "are woefully out of sync with modern theories of learning and skills students will need to compete in the 21st century" (48). This is still a hurdle today when teachers and educational technologists believe the app market is still conducive to consumption rather than production (Dikkers 115): "while we can download the daily news, the latest video, or an augmented explanation of an environment, the richness of a remote learning experience is often lost through the delivery of electronic media" (Hokanson 43). The most optimistic educators speak of mobile learning in near-future terms of the changes mobile learning "are about to cause" (Dikkers 104), and some predict we are still five years away [ca. 2020] from an app paradigm designed for mobile learning (Dennen and Hao 21; Russell and Hughes 293). Perhaps this is why many of us may see smartphones as the texting-posting-sharing device that pulls students away from class rather than the device that draws outside places into the classroom.

In this place between potential and practice, what is a good entry point for mobile learning in the composition classroom? How do we move our classes into mobile-based writing without proficient knowledge on mobile learning, perhaps even while harboring doubts and concerns about its place in our courses? Even when we recognize the relevant place for mobile technology in writing, it is challenging to find this entry point with variables such as

1. availability (Do all students have the mobile tech required?),

2. proficiency (Do I know how to use mobile tech well enough to promote learning outcomes and course objectives?),

3. timing (When and where would mobile tech not only best fit in course content, but also better promote learning outcomes?), and

4. budget (Would mobile composition require paid apps?).

These considerations can be enough to overwhelm an instructor who hasn't yet tested the waters.

Some educators have tested the waters by evaluating how well current mobile apps meet their teaching and learning needs. In concluding that the app market does not meet twenty-first-century learning practices, Murray and Olcese provide a "framework" and "guideline" for inquiring what is possible for mobile learning. They analyze the app market with specific criteria of what characterizes learning, arriving at four categories—tutor (providing instruction and content), explore (students uncover content), tools (students can create or manipulate content), and communicate (share ideas with others) (43). Murray and Olcese have begun the work FitzGerald calls for: a framework for considering how to implement mobile technology based on learning objectives. They set up a simple criteria based on their needs and reviewed apps accordingly, finding many more apps that fit the "tutor" criterion than any of the others (explore, tools, communicate). Teaching guidelines on mobile learning continue to follow this framework for evaluating apps and planning pedagogical possibilities. Dennen and Hao created a similar "paradigm" based on the categories of Tutor, Information Source, Simulator, and Collaborator (22). Each class can come up with its own framework based on its needs and objectives.

This chapter's Mobile Composition Kit Project puts this evaluation framework in an applicable, practical assignment for composition students. Using a similar app market evaluation model, the project enlists students to research the app market and assemble a bundle of apps that best accomplishes the work of the course with a small hypothetical budget. Inspired by other educators' evaluative design (Murray and Olcese; Dennen and Hao), student teams decide which categories should frame their app research. They then organize their "kit" by selecting apps that fit in each category, and then present the results in a table format.

This project serves as an entry point for a range of tech comfort levels, from hypothesizing the use of mobile tech in a course to actually using mobile tech in the course. This chapter breaks down the components and outcomes of this project, which ultimately succeeded in starting a practical discussion on mobile composition specifically and how technology influences writing in general. It also revealed student misunderstandings of mobile composition and the writing process at large. Some Mobile Composition Kits students produced neglected revision tools or failed to seize the opportunity to write on location. As a cumulative end-of-the-semester assignment, this exercise also challenges students to consider how writing and rhetorical skills translate to mobile media.

Description of Assignments and Activities

The Mobile Composition Kit Project (see Figure 1.1) instructs teams of students to choose twenty apps that would be most helpful to students in the course (in my case, the second of two required first-year composition courses at a four-year university). Once the team determines the four categories they will use to research their apps, they select apps based on a hypothetical fifteen-dollar budget. In a table format, they arrange descriptions of each app based on their categories and explain how the categories and apps were chosen. The full project directions and a sample of one team's kit are offered in this section.

This project was completed at the end of the semester as a way to review the course's learning objectives. The project spanned one week, which included a pre-project discussion on writing technologies across decades and a post-project discussion on mobile technology's place in a college composition course. The Mobile Composition Kit Project has the following goals:

1. Discuss with students transfer for writing, pre- and post-project.

2. Reflect on the cumulative composition skills of the course.

3. Assess how students perceive the work of the course and composition generally.

4. Build a Mobile Composition Kit for future use in composition courses.

5. Evaluate how mobile composition could work in course content.

1. Discuss with students transfer for writing, pre- and post-project. Holding discussions before and after the project prepares students to consider how composition technology affects their writing process and more broadly how to choose the tools they use for writing and research tasks. This project specifically targets not the building of new skills and knowledge but the application of these writing skills in two contextual considerations: the context of tools and the context of place (Ehret and Hollett; Hokanson 45), training their "procedural and tacit knowledge" (Pachler, Bachmair, and Cook 278). For instance, students might realize that they can apply their fluency in Twitter to create an account dedicated to a class project. These discussions train students to recognize this knowledge and deliberately plan their writing process accordingly.

Before the project, students write a response and then discuss two questions:

1. How has the writing and research process changed in the past thirty years?

2. How will the writing and research process change in the next ten years?

These questions focused on "writing and research" due to the course objectives, which were primarily to equip students with university-level research skills. The time frames help students think about how much technology has changed the process of consuming and producing text, taking them far back enough to imagine writing and research without ubiquitous computer and Internet access and far forward enough to imagine less-popular technologies, such as wearable technologies, being widespread. Such considerations prepare them to plan for the future of writing by evaluating their writing needs, asking the question, "Is there an app for that?" (Lutkewitte 2), and evaluating the app market accordingly. In the process, the instructor also asks these questions

The Mobile Composition Kit:
Applying Class Concepts to Future Composition

Research and writing is hard work, but if you ask older generations about their process writing papers, you'll hear a narrative of a lot of extra work involved due to technological advances not yet realized. For this assignment, we will look into a possible present and future for research and writing through mobile computing. Applications or "apps" found on smartphones and tablets isolate websites, tools, and tasks to a single location, working under the assumption that this better reflects the way we use computers in the first place.

Background. Curious as to whether iPads were ready for elementary and secondary education, Murray and Olcese researched the app market and used potentially useful apps. In doing so, they created their own categories of apps based on their needs as educators: tutor, explore, tools, and communicate (43). While they concluded that software developments were not ready for K–12 education, this exercise in imagining education through mobile development is a step toward advancing the learning experience. This evaluation model is still in use as educators determine how to use mobile tech in their classrooms (Dennen and Hao).

Assignment Directions. In this group project, we will follow Murray and Olcese's lead and research the app market to find fifteen (no more than twenty) apps that a first-year college writing student would need in order to carry out the work of this class. Determine what "categories" best characterize the writing and rhetoric of this course. Think of this as a twenty-first-century take on the "books you would want on a deserted island." You will have a fifteen-dollar hypothetical budget, so be sure your choices do not add up beyond this amount. Through this project I will look for the way in which you understand the writing process based on this class. *For example: Since primary research is part of the research writing process, what apps would help you conduct and record this research?*

1. Choose categories to plan the kinds of apps you would need.
2. Research the best apps that fit these categories and the needs of a writing student.
3. Narrow down your choices by using the app and considering their class application.
4. Format your choices in a table of contents format offering categories, descriptions, prices, and explanation as to how each app contributes to the Comp II classroom.
5. Post your group project to Moodle by attaching the table of contents and writing a post that explains your group's process and approach.

You will have all of class time on Monday and Wednesday to work on this. During this time you should decide how to complete the project and coordinate responsibilities. Feel free to work as a group outside of the classroom if you want everyone to have computer access, but I will always be in the classroom to answer questions and discuss choices.

How Does This Fit in with Composition II? This team assignment reflects what you have learned as far as the components of research writing, the writing process, researching (both primary and secondary) resources for future writing applications, writing in a digital, multimodal environment, and writing collaboratively. These writing and research principles should translate to any future school and work environment.

FIGURE 1.1. *Description of the Mobile Composition Kit Project.*

through the lens of writing and rhetoric: In what new type of composition work should we engage our students? What does the app market offer composition teachers, and what is left wanting?

Student teams (three to four students each) are given two one-hour class sessions to create a Mobile Composition Kit that would allow them to do the work of our course. They determine what categories of apps best reflect the needs of this course and find fifteen to twenty apps accordingly (see Figure 1.2). They are given a hypothetical budget of fifteen dollars, an amount that gives them the freedom to buy one or two excellent apps or multiple good apps, while paying close attention to free apps as well.

After the project, I ask students to reflect on their findings to consider these questions:

1. What advantages and disadvantages does mobile composition hold compared to a laptop?

2. What writing situations best fit mobile devices rather than laptops?

Most often, students' answers to these questions revolve around location, which is fitting for mobile tech, but more on the "anytime, anywhere" mentality (Kimme Hea 215) rather than the importance of writing in specific contexts. They were quicker to evaluate mobile tech on the criteria of battery life, ease of typing, portability, and usability on the move rather than focusing on the locations and situations in which they could actually use the technology. Within the frame of primary research practices, students recognized that mobile tech allows them to collect visual and aural data more feasibly than with a laptop, but the decontextualized nature of the assignment thus far limited their ability to identify place-based advantages to mobile composition.

Students more easily identify the disadvantages of mobile composition because such a writing context is unfamiliar and not considered "academic." If students do not stretch their imagination of how writing will change in the next decade, they will rely on aged skepticism that claims "serious writing" cannot take place on the same device they use to text, chat, and play, or a skepticism that blinds them from the productive mobile composition they already do. They look at academic composition only through the white-and-black of written text and, therefore, find value in tech that allows them to write copious text in a word processor.

Student App Bundles

Article Search (Free)
The Article Search app allows iPad users to search through and access many scientific papers, journals, articles, and magazines by using built in search engines and databases. This app makes it possible for WRT 160 students to readily search and find useable research material for class assigned papers.

Wikipedia Mobile (Free)
The Wikiview app allows iPad users to navigate and browse through Wikipedia articles without having to go through the actual website. This app makes it possible for WRT 160 to find research for assignments, when professors allow the reference to it or just to get a sense of the topic before searching for research.

iTunes U (Free)
The iTunes U app gives iPad users access to many courses of other universities and more than 500,000 lectures, videos, books, documents, and presentations that are all free. This app would offer WRT 160 students a different way to find research or visual media pertaining to a certain subject.

iSSRN (Free)
The iSSRN app provides scholarly research to anyone interested with over 260,000 articles to choose from. This app would give WRT 160 students an easy way to search and find scholarly articles for secondary research.

TED (Free)
The TED app allows iPad users to play and view over 1,000 talks from remarkable people around the world whether they are in the field of business, music, technology, etc. This app would be helpful for WRT 160 students who are looking for video presentations that would help add to their research.

FIGURE 1.2. *This sample from a student team's project shows the format in which students delivered their app bundle decisions. "Research" was one category among five others: Books, Notes, Writing Guidelines, and Other.*

This understanding of how technology is used for school does not coincide with technology currently used for work. In a 2013 Gallup poll of future knowledge workers sampling more than one thousand recent college grads age eighteen to thirty-five, 86 percent said they often used computers or technology for school projects, but only 14 percent used the online collaboration tools that they deemed important to their current or prospective careers, such as video conferencing (Levy and Sidhu). While students will need to write reports and conduct forms of traditional research, mobile composition should focus on the broad ways in which we produce ad hoc and carefully crafted texts meant to cultivate collaboration at the right place and time.

2. *Reflect on the cumulative composition skills of the course.*
The Mobile Composition Kit Project assembles an app bundle meant to be used over the entire course. The categories reflect what the students consider integral actions to the work of the class as a whole rather than any one particular project in our course. They were put in the rhetorical situation of considering what tools a composition student would use for the whole course, which helped them think back to the beginning of the course and review the semester.

3. *Assess how students perceive the work of the course and composition generally.*
By asking student teams to come up with categories for their apps and choosing each app, the instructor gains insight into the basic work of composition as their students understand it. For instance, more than one student team included a dictionary app in their bundle, which surprised me since our reading strategies often called students to define meaning through context. It made me question whether they generally use dictionaries in their writing, or if educational apps made them automatically think of dictionaries. Choices like this reveal that guidance on how to reflect on their composition process might help them make more analytical, theory-in-use choices.

4. Build a Mobile Composition Kit for future use in composition courses.

For the instructor who is not yet ready to plunge into a class that regularly uses mobile composition, I suggest using this activity as a cumulative review at the end of a course. Based on the app bundles their student teams generate and the ideas the class produces, an instructor may then consider how to implement mobile composition possibilities at the beginning of the course. An instructor could offer these app bundles to a new class the next semester and ask them to test, analyze, and adjust the app kit accordingly. As the comfort level grows, it will become easier to implement mobile composition into assignments.

5. Evaluate how mobile composition could work in course content.

Both of these suggestions produce generalized app bundles. Creating an app bundle for a single project rather than an entire class may afford more interesting, contextual choices specific to the students' needs and perhaps engage them in more immersive, creative projects. If teams of students are inquiring about a campus-based issue, starting the project with a Mobile Composition Kit might tap them into the campus's social media presence, maps, emergency protocols, along with app tools that allow them to snap pictures and videos that relate to their inquiry. Few changes would need to be made to the assignment description to cater to a variety of learning contexts.

Results of the Assignment

The Mobile Composition Kit Project helped navigate planning elements of mobile composition mapped out earlier in the chapter: availability, proficiency, timing, and budget. The assignment provides enough flexibility to work among many higher education class environments and demographics.

- ◆ **Availability** – At the university where I conducted this activity, about half of the students brought laptops to class, and more than 90 percent had smartphones or iPads. Although my students were self-equipped with this technology, I did permit teams to work anywhere in order to not limit anyone's ability to participate, such as campus computer labs or the technology center. Students used laptops to search apps on the app market, and many searched and discussed apps on their phone. My iPad, which belongs to our department, was available for students to use, but most students opted not to use it. Our student technology center offers iPad loans, but availability was limited.

◆ **Proficiency** – While this project works well for composition instructors with no prior experience with mobile technology, I would suggest instructors complete this assignment themselves to gain a base knowledge of what is available on the app market and what they consider important criteria, tools, and capabilities of mobile composition. This provides a clearer comparison once student teams have assembled their own mobile composition kit. This assignment also worked well for students of all mobile tech proficiencies due to the team component. Those who were more comfortable with searching and evaluating apps took a lead role in that process while other students could provide input on composition skills and tasks that should be included in the app bundle.

◆ **Timing** – As the previous section explains in more detail, this assignment works well as a cumulative review project at the end of the course. For more implementation throughout the course, it can also be done at the beginning of the semester or with specific projects.

◆ **Budget** – While students were given a hypothetical budget of fifteen dollars, they were encouraged to not actually purchase these apps since I did not want students to feel compelled to spend money for a project. They felt the app amount and budget were perfectly reasonable. The budget guideline affected their choices well; they researched whether cheaper or free apps could accomplish the same task, but also recognized apps that were worth part of the budget funds. One group only used four dollars of their budget.

Discussion: Emphasizing the Importance of Place

This assignment's intention is to generally discuss and investigate how mobile technology can be integrated into college composition classes, but we should also beware of looking at mobile technology in the same lens as we would older stationary technology.

After students briefly shared their Mobile Composition Kits with the class, we held a post-project discussion on the advantages and disadvantages mobile technology afforded the work of our composition course. Students were clearly thinking of mobile composition in terms of the technological capabilities rather than how it would change their occasions for and ways of writing. While students could go anywhere to complete the project, place was not integral to this project. Therefore, most carried out this assignment in the classroom only with devices in hand. Although the post-assignment discussion questions would get at this consideration of place, I did not ask them to consider *where* writing should take place. While students should think about how new technology can change the way they execute their current writing tasks, we miss the larger points of mobile composition's potential if we limit their perception of what type of writing takes place with this technology. Within this assignment, we should remember to "embrace and articulate the literacy rationale rather than the omnipresent technology rationale" (Scharber 71) and guide our students to do the same. For instance, we could ask students to explore how writing on a device that takes pictures influences how they use written text and how they archive, communicate, or publish multimedia texts.

When students consider where writing happens, they can move toward how location influences their writing. We can think of the link between text and place as meaning-making contexts (Pachler, Bachmair, and Cook). If we restrict mobile composition to traditional spaces, such as the classroom and library (Bjork and Schwartz 225; Pachler, Bachmair, and Cook 279), we will "homogenize the same material difference that instructors are trying to underscore" (Bjork and Schwartz 225) through mobile composition. In other words, using mobile technology should be intentional, used for distinct rhetorical situations and purposes rather than "anytime, anywhere" access alone (Kimme Hea 215).

While students in this assignment occasionally referred to mobile tech's ability to conduct better primary research data collection, other benefits and shortcomings evaluated mobile technology within the same context as a laptop: copious typing, word processing, and browser window display. In "Old[er] Women Writing Teachers Learning New[er] Technologies," Jacqueline

McLeod Rogers admits to first understanding the computer as "a glorified typewriter, an extension of a text production tool rather than a revolutionary source of information retrieval and communication" (10). Without proper reframing, our students will likely see mobile devices as "a glorified laptop" rather than a revolutionary composition tool.

Unless we emphasize the rhetoric of place and how this influences what people write and why, our students will likely miss this point of mobile composition. This assignment in its general form does not require students to consider different writing contexts, from specific locations to writing beyond the research paper. Instead of mobile composition as a place-based activity, students considered mobile composition to be place-less, reinforcing old writing norms rather than considering how mobile technology will change our expectations of writing and rhetoric, how these devices will change the way we produce text rather than merely consume it (Turnley 99; Lutkewitte 2). Mobile learning can "totalize rather than localize technology" (Turnley 99). The more the Mobile Composition Kit Project is implemented for a place-based writing situation, the more their composition will benefit from mobile technology.

If we want students to think of mobile composition as more than a difference in tools—as a mode for specific rhetorical situations and purposes—students have to be prepped for this mindset. It would be best for students to actually practice writing in the field itself. Instructors can apply the framework of the Mobile Composition Kit Project to a place-based assignment, such as guided tours (FitzGerald), geo-mapping (Schmidt; Edwards and Nyquist), and adventure learning (Henrickson). If the assignments do not clearly call upon place-based writing, instructors should challenge students to come up with a place-based, mobile tech version of a decontextualized assignment. This is an opportunity for students to better understand how they already consume text and imagine what is possible in composition that wasn't possible when they were in elementary school. This activity framework can be used for any writing technology as they may evolve, such as wearable technology or virtual reality.

This assignment is a framework for evaluating how an emerging technology will be used to do current work, but it is also a way to think about how work itself will change due to this technology. How will the writing process change? How will the relationship with our audiences change? As technologies continue to emerge, many falling away quickly while others gain momentum, we should be encouraged that the most important skill we as composition teachers bring to our students is not a proficient knowledge of technologies, but our knowledge of "rhetorical decision-making strategies" (Lutkewitte 3), the ability to evaluate how useful they are and how they will change the way we write and relate to audiences.

As composition instructors in the midst of quickly innovating technology that influences our field, we have an important charge: "To model scholarly vitality and to deeply engage student interest and imagination, we need to represent literacy and communication in a way that includes the technologies currently changing how students conceptualize and engage in writing" (McLeod Rogers 10). With our students, we must dig into the complicated issue of not how to translate tried-and-true writing methods to new technologies, but how meaning-making itself has changed because of new technologies. Instructors can use this assignment as a way to engage students, understand literacy and communication, and consider a technology's role in the literacy of their world. It is a simple project that turns tacit doubts and concerns about a new technology into a powerful way to analyze and assess those concerns.

Works Cited

Bjork, Olin, and John Pedro Schwartz. "Writing in the Wild: A Paradigm for Mobile Composition." Kimme Hea 223–37.

Ciampa, Katia. "Learning in a Mobile Age: An Investigation of Student Motivation." *Journal of Computer Assisted Learning* 30 (2013): 82–96. Web. 4 Mar. 2015.

Dennen, Vanessa P., and Shuang Hao. "Paradigms of Use, Learning Theory, and App Design." Miller and Doering 20–41.

Dikkers, Seann M. "The Future of Mobile Media for Learning." Miller and Doering 104–19.

Edwards, Nathan, and Jason Nyquist. "HotSeat: Learning and Designing on the Move." Miller and Doering 158–71.

Ehret, Christian, and Ty Hollett. "(Re)placing School: Middle School Students' Countermobilities While Composing with iPods." *Journal of Adolescent and Adult Literacy* 57.2 (2013): 110–19. Web. 4 Mar. 2015.

FitzGerald, Elizabeth. "Creating User-Generated Content for Location-Based Learning: An Authoring Framework." *Journal of Computer Assisted Learning* 28.3 (2012): 195–207. Web. 29 May 2014.

Henrickson, Jeni. "The Conceptualization, Design, and Development of a K–12 Adventure Learning App." Miller and Doering 172–87.

Hokanson, Brad. "Rich Remote Learning and Cognition: Analog Methods as Models for Newer Technology." Miller and Doering 42–55.

Kimme Hea, Amy C., ed. *Going Wireless: A Critical Exploration of Wireless and Mobile Technologies for Composition Teachers and Researchers*. Cresskill: Hampton, 2009. Print.

———. "Perpetual Contact: Re-articulating the Anywhere, Anytime Pedagogical Model of Mobile and Wireless Composing." Kimme Hea 199–221.

Levy, Jenna, and Preety Sidhu. "In the U.S., 21st Century Skills Linked to Work Success; Real-World Problem-Solving Most Strongly Tied to Work Quality." *Gallup*. Gallup Poll News Service, 30 May 2013. Web. 29 May 2014.

Lutkewitte, Claire. "Is There an App for That?" Lutkewitte 2–8.

Lutkewitte, Claire, ed. *Web 2.0 Applications for Composition Classrooms*. Southlake: Fountainhead, 2012. Print.

Manuguerra, Maurizio, and Peter Petocz. "Promoting Student Engagement by Integrating New Technology into Tertiary Education: The Role of the iPad." *Asian Social Science* 7.11 (2011): 61–65. Web. 19 Jan. 2013.

McLeod Rogers, Jacqueline. "Older[er] Women Writing Teachers Learning New[er] Technologies: Teaching and Trusting." Lutkewitte 9–26.

Miller, Charles, and Aaron Doering, eds. *The New Landscape of Mobile Learning*. New York: Routledge. 2014. Print.

Murray, Orrin T., and Nicole R. Olcese. "Teaching and Learning with iPads, Ready or Not?" *TechTrends* 55.6 (2011): 42–48. Web. 19 Jan. 2013.

Pachler, Norbert, Ben Bachmair, and John Cook. "User-Generated Content and Contexts: An Educational Perspective." *Mobile Learning: Structures, Agency, Practices*. Ed. Pachler, Bachmair, and Cook. New York: Springer, 2010. 273–95. Web. 29 May 2014.

Pigg, Stacey, et al. "Ubiquitous Writing, Technologies, and the Social Practice of Literacies of Coordination." *Written Communication* 31.1 (2013): 91–117. Web. 15 Oct. 2014.

Russell, Gregory, and Joan Hughes. "iTeach and iLearn with iPads in Secondary English Language Arts." Miller and Doering 292–307.

Scharber, Cassandra. "'Apping' Its Way into the Future? K–12 English Education." Miller and Doering 66–79.

Schmidt, Christopher. "The New Media Writer as Cartographer." *Computers and Composition* 28.4 (2011): 303–14. Print.

Turnley, Melinda. "Reterritorialized Flow: Critically Considering Student Agency in Wireless Pedagogies." Kimme Hea 87–105.

CHAPTER TWO

Analyzing Mobile Technology Use: Dismantling Assumptions through Student Reflection

ANN N. AMICUCCI

University of Colorado, Colorado Springs

The college writers I meet each semester are a varied group when it comes to mobile technologies: some sport the latest smartphones or tablets, and others can't afford them. Some don't like to use a phone at all, while others don't like theirs to be out of sight. Yet when I *read* about teenagers' mobile technology use, I hear a different story: authors of mainstream, public texts write homogenous characterizations of millennials as people with their faces glued to digital screens at all times (see Bartz and Ehrlich; Henley; Kang). In writing courses, when we focus students' reflective and analytical attention on mobile technologies, we have the opportunity to prompt students to think critically about—and perhaps even refute—the ways their use of mobile devices is portrayed in public texts.

In this chapter, I share an assignment and activity sequence through which students examine their own and others' mobile technology uses and compare these uses to published discussions of the same. Drawing on theories of reflection on situated literacy practices, I illustrate practical steps that teachers of Basic Writing, First-Year Composition (FYC), and Advanced Composition can take to engage students in critical discussion of mobile technology use. I showcase examples of student reflection and argue that guiding students to think critically about mobile technologies positions them to critically analyze public arguments about mobile technology use. In composition courses where rhetorical analysis is practiced, students following this sequence will have the opportunity to exercise their analytical abilities in relation to articles in which authors depict and forward assumptions about mobile technology uses. By teaching students to dismantle these assumptions and to support that dismantling with information gathered through reflection and observation, we can lead students to become discerning consumers of the arguments they encounter in mainstream media in which their own relationships with technology are portrayed.

Theoretical Grounding

Mobile technology use includes the ways individuals interact with mobile devices, their use of devices to perform communicative tasks, and the choices they make about when and how to use devices. This technology use is necessarily situated in many contexts, including that of a social network among users and those who come into contact with them. As James Paul Gee argues, literacy practices are inherently ideological because they cannot be removed from, or considered apart from, the contexts in which they exist (41). When asking students to reflect on and analyze mobile technology use, we have to facilitate their consideration of how such use is socially situated.

Prompting students to recognize the social contexts for their mobile technology use is only a first step—we have to prompt their critical thought about the influence social context has on their use and on the ways that use is depicted by others. Cynthia L. Selfe writes that at the same time we are utilizing digital technologies in education, we must "get teachers and students *thinking critically about such use*" (419). Drawing on Mark Weiser's argument that "the most profound technologies" are those so seamlessly merged with our daily lives that we no longer notice them (94), Selfe suggests that it is at the moment that a technology becomes invisible in users' lives that it "develop[s] the most potential for being *dangerous*" (435). Selfe's cautionary tale is focused on technology used to facilitate education, but we can extend it to mean that within any educational context, we are tasked with prompting students' abilities to be critical users of technologies. Student learning can be valuably informed by the task of reflecting critically on the affordances and limitations of mobile technologies.

Because all literacies are socially situated, studying mobile technology use as a literacy practice necessitates focusing on groups of people who engage in this practice, rather than only on the literacy practices of any individual (Barton and Hamilton 13; Gee 41). However, I argue that using the individual as a reflective starting point enables teachers to lead students to engage in critical thinking about situated literacy practices.

Descriptions of Assignments and Activities

To prompt students to think critically about their own mobile technology use and the ways that use is portrayed in public texts, I advocate for a three-part assignment and activity sequence that can be used in Basic Writing, FYC, or Advanced Composition courses. The learning outcomes for this sequence are that students will (1) reflect critically on their own and others' uses of mobile technologies and (2) analyze how messages about such uses are constructed for a public audience.

Reflection on Mobile Technology Use

First, students read and respond in writing to an "exhibit question" (Stake 97), an open-ended question that describes a scenario and asks students to write how they can or cannot relate to it. These questions showcase uses of mobile technologies, as in the following examples:

◆ Question 1: Steve jokes that he is addicted to technology. He sleeps with his phone by his side, and he sometimes wakes up at night to answer texts. He's always texting when he's walking around campus and usually texts or plays on his phone even when he's hanging out with his friends. Can you relate to Steve and his use of technology? Please explain.

◆ Question 2: Shonda is the only member of her group of friends who doesn't have a smartphone. When she and her friends are together, the others take photos and post them to Instagram or Facebook, and they frequently check social media on their phones. Shonda has several social media accounts and wishes she could access them from her phone but can only access them from her home computer. Can you relate to Shonda and her use of technology? Please explain.

◆ Question 3: Isabel has just started working as a newspaper intern. When she attends staff meetings, she notices that some people have cell phones out and use them and others don't. Each time she checks her phone during a meeting, she wonders how this choice is perceived by her new coworkers. Can you relate to Isabel and her use of technology? Please explain.

Each question prompts student reflection on mobile technology uses couched in social contexts. Question 1 leads students to consider the frequency of their cell phone use in comparison with Steve, who is "addicted" to his phone and depicted as using it frequently. Question 2 asks students to consider issues of access in light of Shonda, who is the only friend in her group without mobile Internet access. Question 3 gives students the opportunity to think about the rhetorical choices at play in utilizing mobile technologies in social settings—in this case, Isabel's coworkers may pass judgment on her use of a cell phone in the workplace. Rather than giving students explicit directions to reflect on how their use of mobile devices is shaped by social context, an instructor can use the generalized anecdotes in these questions as a starting point in students' process of considering how mobile technology use is socially situated. Depending on the level of a course, students can be asked to write between two hundred and five hundred words in response to these questions. In Basic Writing and FYC, students can respond to one question, while students in Advanced Composition can be given all three.

When students come to class with their written reflections, the instructor guides them to analyze what they have written. As a first step, the instructor can share one or two examples with the class as a whole, with student permission. Starting with these examples, the instructor asks students to categorize reflective responses by asking questions such as the following:

◆ Question 1, frequency of use: How frequently does this writer use his or her cell phone? What does the writer value or devalue about frequent cell phone use? Does the writer label his or her own use as an "addiction" like Steve's?

- ◆ Question 2, technology access: What level of mobile technology access does this writer have? What does the writer value or devalue about this access? Does the writer share Shonda's desire to access social media through mobile technology?

- ◆ Question 3, rhetorical choices: What choices does the writer describe making about when to use a mobile device? What does the writer value or devalue about mobile device use in social settings? Does the writer describe thinking about how mobile device use will affect his or her perception by others, like Isabel does?

The purpose of this categorization and analysis of reflection—both as a whole class looking at student examples and as individuals looking at their own writing—is to prompt students to think critically about their own mobile technology uses.

Observation of Others' Mobile Technology Use

In the second part of the sequence, students observe others' behavior with mobile technologies, take notes on this observation, and analyze their notes. Students can be given the following directions:

- ◆ Take something to write with and something to write on, and go to a public location on campus or elsewhere where you can observe the behavior of others without being noticed. Some good locations to visit are a cafeteria or outdoor common area. You will observe three to four individuals. Pick one person first, and write down a few words to describe this person so you will remember him or her later. Then, watch the person for a full ten minutes and answer these questions:

  1. Does the person appear to have a mobile device? If so, jot down any details you notice about it. Consider our class conversations on access to technologies and notice what access this person appears to have.

  2. If the person has a mobile device, how is he or she using it? Jot down anything you notice. Consider our conversations on frequency of mobile technology use and notice how often this person is using a device within the time you observe.

3. Is the person interacting with anyone face-to-face, or are there others near the person? If so, jot down anything you notice about these other people. Consider our conversations on mobile technology use in social settings and notice whether the presence of others appears to influence the person's use of a mobile device.

Move on to the next person. If you see a group of people, you can observe each person of the group separately, but you may also find it interesting to study people in different groups.

Students can be asked to do this observation activity in class or as homework and to take notes on paper or on a mobile device of their own.

Students' next step will be to analyze their observation notes in a manner similar to that by which they analyzed their reflections in response to the exhibit question. I suggest having students start with informal, small-group discussion of their observations, which will allow them to hear about others' findings and to get an initial sense of whether their findings are similar to others'. Then, students can engage in more formal analysis, again asking questions to categorize their findings, such as the following:

◆ Frequency of use: How frequently were the people you observed using mobile devices? Did they use these devices consistently in the time you observed, or put them down and pick them back up again? Did the presence of others appear to change their use?

◆ Technology access: What types of devices did the people you observe appear to have? Based on what you could observe, what is the extent of these users' access to mobile technologies?

Students can be encouraged to answer questions such as those above for each observed individual, then compile their findings into a summary of all individuals together.

While students can pick up some information about others' mobile technology use through observation, this information is necessarily limited. Further, students will not be able to learn anything about the rhetorical choices made by mobile technology users simply by observing them from afar. The purpose of this step in the sequence is to introduce students to observation as an inquiry method. While setting up the observation assignment and discussing the results, teachers should acknowledge the limitations of this method. In examining how technological literacy activity is socially situated, for example, students can be asked to consider contexts that are invisible in their observation of others, such as the social connections a person makes via a mobile device, the social contracts implicit in the person's relationships with friends who are present face-to-face, and the effect of the person's socioeconomic status on his or her access to mobile technology. Teachers can encourage students to identify ways to gather additional or more accurate information on others' mobile technology use. In courses involving sustained research projects, students can proceed from this activity to conduct formal interviews with mobile technology users to gather information unobtainable through observation.

Analysis of Portrayals of Mobile Technology Use

Finally, students read, respond to, and rhetorically analyze a portrayal of mobile technology use in a public text. Assigned readings can focus on frequency of mobile technology use, technology access, rhetorical choices in mobile technology use, or on all three topics; see Table 2.1 for a description of related reading assignments. When reading an article, students can be asked to respond to questions such as:

- How does the portrayal of mobile technology use in this article align with your own experience? Does it match the reflection you wrote earlier this week?

- How does the portrayal of mobile technology use align with the uses you observed among other people?

Students should be directed to refer to specific examples from the text and from their experiences or observations to support their responses.

In class, students can begin with small-group discussion of their reading responses, then move to rhetorical analysis of an article by answering questions about the article's construction of an argument. In this discussion, students can respond to questions such as:

TABLE **2.1.** Articles to Assign for Student Reading

Topic	Article Title	Article Synopsis
Frequency of Mobile Technology Use	"Texting: Can We Pull the Plug on Our Obsession?" by Susan Spencer, *CBS News Sunday Morning*	Spencer describes the perils and benefits of being glued to a cell phone. She interviews Sherry Turkle and Nicholas Carr on the ramifications of near-constant mobile technology use.
	"An Open Letter to Texting-Crazed Teens" by Andrea Bartz and Brenna Ehrlich, *CNN Tech*	The authors write to an audience of teens, offering advice to avoid texting excessively and to avoid sexting entirely. The authors advise teens to increase their practice of conversation via phone calls.
Technology Access	"A Smartphone Future? But Not Yet" by Teddy Wayne, *The New York Times*	Wayne offers brief profiles of several individuals who choose to use older-model cell phones rather than smartphones and discusses their reasons for doing so. Among those interviewed are Jonathan Safran Foer and Nicholas Carr.
	"How Half a Million U.S. Teens Are Texting without a Data Plan" by Parmy Olson, *Forbes*	Olson describes steps teens take to work around lack of access to data plans and Wi-Fi in order to send text messages. She depicts mesh networking software developed to give mobile technology users access to texting without data plans.
Rhetorical Choices in Mobile Technology Use	"Why I'm Breaking Up with the Apple Watch" by Vanessa Friedman, *The New York Times*	The author discusses her experiences of wearing an Apple Watch, likening the watch's visibility to wearing a name-brand fashion accessory, and her decision to abandon this form of mobile technology.
	"Keep Your Thumbs Still When I'm Talking to You" by David Carr, *The New York Times*	Carr addresses mobile technology use in social situations from an etiquette standpoint, addressing differing opinions on what is considered rude versus acceptable behavior with mobile devices in public.

◆ What is the central argument in this article? What does the article value or devalue about mobile technology use?

◆ Who is the audience for this article? Does that audience include the mobile technology users the article describes? How are mobile technology users positioned within the article?

◆ Who is the author of the article, and what background or expertise informs this author's position? How is the author's position constructed in the article?

Following these questions or others similar to them, students can be guided to analyze how mobile technology use, whether similar or dissimilar to their own and that of people they have observed, is constructed in a public text. In Chapter 4, Melissa Toomey presents a pedagogical approach to teaching Rhetorical Key Terms that can be applied here; following Toomey's guidelines, an instructor can guide students in their analysis of the assigned article's rhetorical construction. The purpose of this final phase of the sequence is to give students practice in rhetorical analysis while also challenging them to acknowledge how their own experiences and observed findings hold up against public texts that tackle topics of mobile technology use.

In this assignment and activity sequence, students begin by examining their own mobile technology use, broaden their perspectives to observe others' uses, then broaden these perspectives further by looking at portrayals of those practices in public texts. The sequence asks students to resist assumptions about mobile technology uses—their own and others'—by thinking critically about and observing such uses. Then the sequence asks students to move beyond their lived experience to consider how these mobile technology uses, or perhaps even assumptions about such uses, are forwarded in public texts. This sequence can stand alone to facilitate students' practice of reflection, observation, and analysis, or it can be used to lead into a larger writing or research project.

Student Examples

To show the type of reflection that can result from "exhibit questions" (Stake 97), I share in this section examples of student responses to one of the questions described previously. The examples showcased here were collected in an IRB-approved research study at a public, mid-sized, midwestern university.[1] Students responded to two exhibit questions on the survey, one of which relates to the purpose of this chapter; in it, students responded to the anecdote describing Steve and focusing on frequency of mobile technology use. In what follows, I present example responses to illustrate the types of reflection generated by an exhibit question. Because this reflection occurred in a research context, students' answers are shorter than those in a classroom setting are likely to be. Students in a course would be asked to follow certain writing conventions, such as providing examples and full explanations for their responses, whereas students responding to this question on the survey were not held to such conventions.

In the first set of examples, students who describe frequent mobile device use support this label of frequency by comparing their choices of whether to keep a mobile device nearby and whether to keep it turned on to Steve's choices. As a reminder, in the exhibit question, Steve "sleeps with his phone by his side" and is "texting when he's walking around campus." Students write:

- ◆ "My phone is with me when i sleep it's just become a habit. Sometimes i wake up in the middle of the night but rarely respond unless its important. I dont usually play on my phone around friends but I do text when im with them." (Survey 13)

- ◆ "Steve is not very different from the majority of people in our age group. I text, check stocks, check weather read email and talk on the phone while I walk to class. I sleep within 5 ft. of my iPhone and it acts as my external hardrive, remote connection for my imac and my alarm clock." (Survey 8)

- ◆ "I can relate to Steve. I find myself always on my phone, and sometimes I don't even realize it. When your by yourself it makes you feel better to have something to do. I feel uncomfortable when I don't have my phone w/me." (Survey 36)

In these examples, students' brief reflections show how they are identifying their frequency of mobile device use and considering what that use means. In writing reflections like "it's just become a habit" or "Steve is not very different from the majority of people in our age group," students are taking a first step toward understanding their mobile device uses. This understanding can be built on when students put their mobile technology uses into conversation with others' through the assignment and activity sequence described in this chapter.

In a second set of examples, students who make value judgments about frequent phone use have mixed perspectives, with some describing feelings of being lost or disconnected without a phone and others criticizing the practice of using a mobile device as frequently as Steve does. Students describe whether they can relate to Steve by writing:

- "I can, but only a little bit. I do text everyday but not very often. I try not to text too much when I am with other people and talking to them because I think it can be rude. I turn my phone off at night so texts late at night have to wait until morning for me." (Survey 75)

- "Yes, I can relate to Steve. I fall asleep while having a conversation through texts usually every night. I also use my phone while walking on campus. However I try to limit my phone usage while hanging out with friends because I feel that it is rude." (Survey 25)

- "No, I cannot relate. There needs to be a 'shut-off' at some point, or a time for one's self when technology is ignored or set aside for a short time each day. When I am with friends or family I generally don't text or excuse my self from them to do so, or apologize if I absolutely must reply. It is rude to do otherwise, and a lot of people now-a-days don't seem to be considerate of others this way." (Survey 164)

In these reflections, students are acknowledging the social situatedness of their mobile technology use. As Gee notes, in developing a literacy, an individual "is socialized or enculturated into a certain social practice" (45), and students' labeling of certain uses of a cell phone as "rude" is evidence of this enculturation. The exhibit questions described in this chapter can function as a starting point for student reflection and eventual exploration of how students' own uses of mobile technologies compare with others' uses and portrayals of those uses in public texts as shown in these student examples.

Conclusion and Further Discussion

As I describe in this chapter, use of mobile technologies can become the subject of students' reflection, observation, and analysis. Christina Moore argues in Chapter 1 that the process of prompting students' critical understanding of mobile technologies can also involve examining how we promote and police mobile technology use in our classrooms. In this vein, students' attention to the ways mobile technology use is shaped by social context could continue beyond the sequence I describe to involve meta-analysis of the social context of the classroom and technology use within it.

The assignment and activity sequence I present focuses on mobile devices, but it does not require the use of a mobile device. All students, regardless of access to mobile technologies, can participate in it. Access itself is an important component of this sequence, though, as asking students to reflect critically on the ways mobile technologies are used and the ways that those uses are portrayed in public texts requires us to have conversations with students about disparities in technology access across socioeconomic groups and among college student populations.

In generating critical thought about situated literacy practices, we have to prompt students to think about power disparities, including questions of who has access to mobile devices, what types of devices they can access, and whose discourses about these devices are valued and heard in the public sphere. As Brian Street notes, studying literacy practices within their ideological contexts must include consideration of "'whose literacies' are dominant and whose are marginalized" (77). As of 2015, an estimated 64 percent of adults in the United States owns a smartphone, and this number drops for those with lower incomes and those without a college education (Smith and Page 13). Public portrayals of cell phone use, however, obscure these realities: retail advertisements encourage customers to use coupons on their smartphones, and television shows have hashtags that direct viewers to live tweet while watching. Many flyers hanging around the campus where I teach boast QR codes, inviting students to scan the code with a smartphone to access more information. Mobile technology users and non-users alike encounter frequent messages in daily life that suggest everyone has a smartphone, and many of the public texts I cite in this article corroborate this message. As we educate our college students in their development as writers, we need to facilitate their critical thinking about and critique of the messages constructed in and communicated through public texts. As the *Framework for Success in Postsecondary Writing* outlines, student writers who aim to become stronger critical thinkers will "think through ideas, problems, and issues [and] identify and challenge assumptions" (Council 7). When we pay attention to the ways writers talk about mobile technologies, assumptions abound, making this subject ripe for students' practice of critical thought.

We know that mobile technologies are constantly evolving. There may come a time when everyone who wants to have a mobile device will have one and when all mobile devices will have Internet access. As technologies evolve, though, socioeconomic gaps that create disparities in technology access will remain. The assignment and activity sequence I describe in this chapter can be used to prompt students' critical thought about all technologies, regardless of how mobile devices evolve down the line. In our efforts to enable students' "ability to analyze a situation or text and make thoughtful decisions based on that analysis" (Council 7), we can turn students' reflective and analytical attention toward mobile technology use. Following Selfe, we can prompt our students to "pay attention" (413)—to notice and think critically about their own and others' uses of mobile technologies and to analyze the ways public texts forward arguments and assumptions about those uses.

Note

1. In this study, students enrolled in eight sections of FYC completed an anonymous survey about their digital literacy practices, answering questions about frequency of digital technology use and the audiences for this use. Among 177 respondents, 98.86 percent indicated using a mobile device daily for text messaging, with friends (for 97.18 percent of respondents) and family members (for 87.57 percent of respondents) being students' most common audiences for text messaging.

Works Cited

Barton, David, and Mary Hamilton. "Literacy Practices." *Situated Literacies: Reading and Writing in Context.* Ed. David Barton, Mary Hamilton, and Roz Ivanič. New York: Routledge, 2000. 7–15. Print.

Bartz, Andrea, and Brenna Ehrlich. "An Open Letter to Texting-Crazed Teens." *CNN.com.* Cable News Network, 1 Aug. 2012. Web. 12 June 2015.

Carr, David. "Keep Your Thumbs Still When I'm Talking to You." *New York Times*. New York Times, 15 Apr. 2011. Web. 12 June 2015.

Council of Writing Program Administrators, National Council of Teachers of English, and National Writing Project. *Framework for Success in Postsecondary Writing*. CWPA; Urbana: NCTE; and Berkeley: NWP, 2011. PDF file.

Friedman, Vanessa. "Why I'm Breaking Up with the Apple Watch." *New York Times*. New York Times, 10 June 2015. Web. 12 June 2015.

Gee, James Paul. *Social Linguistics and Literacies: Ideology in Discourses*. 4th ed. New York: Routledge, 2012. Print.

Henley, Jon. "Teenagers and Technology: 'I'd Rather Give Up My Kidney Than My Phone.'" *Guardian*. Guardian News and Media, 16 July 2010. Web. 12 June 2015.

Kang, Cecilia. "Many Teens Tell Survey They're Addicted to Social Media, Texting." *Washington Post*. Post Tech, 26 June 2012. Web. 12 June 2015.

Olson, Parmy. "How Half A Million U.S. Teens Are Texting without a Data Plan." *Forbes*. Forbes Tech, 10 June 2015. Web. 12 June 2015.

Selfe, Cynthia L. "Technology and Literacy: A Story about the Perils of Not Paying Attention." *College Composition and Communication* 50.3 (1999): 411–36. Print.

Smith, Aaron, and Dana Page. "U.S. Smartphone Use in 2015." *Pew Research Center*. Pew Research Center, 1 Apr. 2015. Web. 15 June 2015.

Spencer, Susan. "Texting: Can We Pull the Plug on Our Obsession?" *CBS News*. CBS News Sunday Morning, 12 Oct. 2010. Web. 12 June 2015.

Stake, Robert E. *Qualitative Research: Studying How Things Work*. New York: Guilford, 2010. Print.

Street, Brian. "What's 'New' in New Literacy Studies? Critical Approaches to Literacy in Theory and Practice." *Current Issues in Comparative Education* 5.2 (2003): 77–91. Print.

Wayne, Teddy. "A Smartphone Future? But Not Yet." *New York Times*. New York Times, 23 Mar. 2012. Web. 12 June 2015.

Weiser, Mark. "The Computer for the 21st Century." *Scientific American* 265.3 (1991) 94–104. Print.

CHAPTER THREE

Kairotic Aurality: Audio Essays, QR Codes, and Real Audiences

MOE FOLK

Kutztown University

One constant complaint about any institution is food quality. If, for example, students wanted to advocate for changing the quality of their dining hall experience, a traditional place for attracting attention would be the editorial section of their school newspaper. However, given the various compositional modes and delivery methods open to us today, is the letter-to-the-editor method of connecting with the primary audience the best way to effect change? What about a flier hanging inside the cafeteria itself, a flier designed to get the attention of the student body and that includes a scannable bar code at the bottom? When students scan the bar code with a mobile device, they are taken to an audio essay hosted on SoundCloud. The audio essay starts to play and asks the listeners to turn over their right shoulder and walk to the salad bar, where they point out how exactly the setup and contents could be changed. The audio essay continues to argue about other aspects of the cafeteria and food, drawing on the listeners' proximity and visual experience to make effective points. In short, an approach that takes advantage of portable audio, digital delivery, and the flexible time, space, and immediacy provided by QR codes and mobile devices is much different from writing a delayed, disembodied letter in the school newspaper. The audio essay can even conclude with a link to a petition students can click on in real time, or it can physically guide students to an office where students can voice their concerns with the dining service. As composition continues to embrace a wider view of literacy that goes beyond letteracy, more instructors are able to explore how aurality offers an important means of expression and persuasion because of the different ways writing concepts of voice, ethos, and audience are invoked. Aurality is made more powerful when further augmented with the capabilities of mobile devices. The assignment that this chapter covers attempts to reconcile all these realities by having students tackle a local issue, produce an argumentative audio essay, publish the audio essay on SoundCloud, make a flier with a QR code on it that directs the target audience to the audio essay, and then hang the flier in a perfect place for the target audience to read the flier and scan the QR code.

Theoretical Grounding of the Assignment

There are two main supports undergirding this assignment, both of which reinforce each other: considerations for embracing aurality in the FYC classroom and considerations for embracing mobile devices. To begin, this assignment is rooted in the multimodal tradition of what the New London Group argued: no single expressive modality, including print, can carry the full range of meaning in a text; the importance for instructors and students alike is to determine the affordances and constraints of different modalities given the rhetorical situation; and developing such skills in students helps them fully participate not only in other college courses but also in their ongoing social, economic, and civic lives (see, for example, Cope and Kalantzis). Further, my embrace of aurality in FYC is influenced by Cynthia Selfe, who suggests that today's teachers should "respect and encourage students to deploy multiple modalities in skillful ways—written, aural, visual—and . . . model a respect for, and understanding of, the various roles each modality can play in human expression, the formation of individual and group identity, and meaning making" (121). Toward that end, I use this project to help students explore the affordances and constraints of audio, and I want to develop my students' sonic literacy à la Comstock and Hocks, who "noticed that when [their] students create and manipulate sound files, whether in the form of a voice-over narration or soundtrack, that they develop a stronger, more embodied sense of audience and of our popular cultural soundscapes. . . . They are also more apt to see composing as an iterative process that requires listening, getting feedback, revising, and starting over again" (n.p.). Similarly, Heidi McKee points out that with spoken words—whether in person or experienced through digital delivery—"we explicitly attend to the words that are stated, but we also implicitly adhere to how those words are said" (340). In addition to what is said and how it is said, I use this assignment to help my students understand the importance of where those words are spoken.

This attention to where a composition is experienced is best realized through mobile devices. Beyond the simple portability that gives them their name, mobile devices must be reckoned with because of a ubiquity that transcends cultures and continents: the number of smartphones outstripped the number of computers in 2011 and keeps climbing. In essence, we are entering an era in which mobile learning, or m-learning, and mobile pervasive learning has enveloped us, so writing teachers need to adapt, especially considering how studies indicate that mobile pervasive learning is beneficial (Mac Callum et al.). Baiyun Chen and Aimee deNoyelles, in their study of mobile device usage on the vast University of Central Florida campus, show the deep penetration of mobile devices, but they also note how students are often not using them deeply, if at all, in their academic work. The authors advocate even more access to mobile devices, additional support for integrating mobile technologies for learning, and conclude, "Instructors must gain knowledge of these innovative technologies and integrate them into the curriculum with sound facilitation and assessment strategies, as well as be able to support the mobile practices of students." My assignment is an attempt to come to terms with such developments and incorporate ideas such as Cochrane's six critical success factors for implementing pedagogical change with mobile devices. In addition, this assignment aims to capitalize on what Parsons identifies as the top mobile learning innovations: placing learning in a specific context, augmenting reality with virtual information, contributing to shared learning resources, having an adaptive learning toolkit in the palm of your hand, and taking ownership of learning (221–23). The assignment helps to unlock, as Parsons calls it, the electronic Swiss Army knife potential of mobile device tools (221).

The mobile devices help me teach kairos and audience because they pinpoint place and allow easy access to real people. Scanlon advocates the use of mobile devices for their ability to foster location-based learning and also cites a number of positive uses of that pedagogical approach (87–88). In addition, Martin and Ertzberger demonstrate how "here and now" learning improved students' achievement, engagement, and attitude versus regular computer-based instruction. Being able to improve achievement, engagement, and attitude is essential for early required courses such as FYC that are integral in molding students' academic self, as well as molding their social self and affecting their ultimate retention.

This assignment seeks to use the mobile phone to capitalize on immediacy and its ability to connect the user fully with the present as almost no other technology can. In addition, once the end users (audience) have understood the audio essay and gauged its importance in real time, they can use the same mobile device to transcend that time and location to spread the content further. For example, the end users could post a picture of the QR code flier on Instagram, and tell their followers to visit the cafeteria and listen to the audio essay, or follow a link on the flier to sign a petition about providing more vegetarian options. As much as I want students to grapple with the rhetorical aspects of aurality, I want them to interrogate the idea of kairos and think about the opportune moment for their compositions and the choices they make within them. Delivering to mobile technologies is key because doing so provides the perfect place to practice rhetorical concepts with a technology that is not only optimally suited for such an application but will continue to evolve; students can continue to evolve from this early academic experience as well to conceptualize more sophisticated uses of mobile devices for their own purposes down the road. In the future, I would like my first-year writing students to compose more *with* mobile technologies in the ways that, among others, Jessica Schreyer and Ashley Holmes describe in this collection; however, for now, my students and I grapple with the same challenges Lutkewitte and Vanguri point out with regard to integrating mobile technologies at their institution, and this assignment offers a solid means of working toward fuller mobile integration within my writing classes down the road.

Assignment Description

In the context of my institution's sole FYC course, I use this audio essay assignment as the second project of a three-project sequence that culminates in a final portfolio. It serves as a bridge between a first assignment centered on personal writing used to create and publish a Google map and a third assignment that is a course requirement across all sections—a large research project with annotated bibliography. In the audio essay with QR code assignment, students are asked to pick a topic that has an actual physical location where the primary audience can be reached, preferably something on campus, the community, or even their hometown if they commute or go home on weekends. The flier will be seen by the target audience, and so the students have to think about how to craft it to get their audience's attention. Figure 3.1 is the assignment sheet.

A key requirement is that students must use at least four other sonic resources beyond the student's own voice; these resources often consist of background music and interviews they find on sources such as YouTube. In class, I go over how to find and edit sonic resources (you can scan the QR code in the assignment sheet to get there), and, on our CMS, I post a trove of examples of where to find such resources, as well as professional audio essay examples and audio essay examples from previous students. I encourage students to think of these sonic resources as citations (see Comstock and Hocks) that can enhance the overall ethos of their work in a way a good source enhances a research paper. I do not want students to simply add music filler to cover up awkward silence, fortify their own voice, or add to the length of the audio essay just like expanding font size fills up a paper. For students who are extremely shy or completely recalcitrant about using their voice, I do let them use other techniques such as layering sounds and interviews if they wish, but I do stress that doing so ends up being much more work. I also allow students

PROJECT TWO | AUDIOPHILE

ENTER THE AUDIO "[T]ext travels alone into the world without the context in which it was created, or with only as much context as can be included in the text itself (metacommentary, linkings, bibliographies, narratives, images)." —*Rickert & Salvo*

(From left to right: Ira Glass, Jay Z/Beatles Grey Album cover, Audacity interface, QR code example—scan it!)

OVERVIEW

For this project, we will continue to explore how new technologies contribute to new types of compositions. Specifically, you will create an argumentative audio essay of at least 5 minutes (which you might think of as a persuasive story that incorporates analysis of an issue), post that audio essay online (I recommend SoundCloud), and create a flyer that directs your primary audience to the audio essay using a QR code. While this project could cover almost any topic and be as formal/"traditionally academic" or informal/"popular" as you like, think of how you can connect with your chosen audience by harnessing the benefits of digital audio as discussed in our readings and examples. By creating an audio essay, you will continue to develop your abilities to produce and analyze both traditional and contemporary texts.

ASSIGNMENT PARAMETERS

The composing process will start with a proposal. After that, you will produce a script for the 5-minute audio essay for peer review and build your audio composition. I will go over how to use Audacity, a free program that allows you to make audio compositions easily, but you can use programs like Garageband, Pro Tools, Logic, or anything else you want. In addition to your own voice, **the audio essay should include** *at least* **four other clips/effects/ sounds/voices/interviews to back up your points** (but not overwhelm them!). Think of these sources working in the same way citations and quotations work in research papers. You can work in groups, but keep in mind I will expect groups to produce a longer, more complex audio essay. Feel free to add images if you want (e.g., synching images to the audio in PowerPoint, creating a video argument and posting on YouTube, etc.).

ASSESSMENT

Argumentative Audio Essay:	70%
Flyer:	10%
Reflection:	20%

DUE DATES

Proposal:	T 2/17
Rough Draft of Written Script for Audio Essay:	T 2/24
Rough Draft of Digital Audio Essay and Flyer:	TH 3/19
All Final Drafts:	T 3/24

FIGURE **3.1.** *The audiophile project assignment.*

to work in groups if they want to, but I stress that more will be expected from the final product in terms of depth, length, sonic resources, and overall sophistication. For assessment, I use the rubric in Figure 3.2.

PROJECT 2 RUBRIC

I. Audio Essay 70 pts.

Introduction quickly and clearly grounds topic and engages audience (10 pts.)
Perfectly.......................Strongly...............................Adequately.................................Weakly...................Barely

Uses audio resources besides own voice with purpose; the resources support instead of dominate. (20 pts.)
Perfectly.......................Strongly...............................Adequately.................................Weakly...................Barely

Offers a thorough look at a topic and provides a clear point for audience to consider. (20 pts.)
Perfectly.......................Strongly...............................Adequately.................................Weakly...................Barely

Uses an appropriate cadence, style, and tone. Vivid description and word choice pull audience in. (10 pts.)
Perfectly.......................Strongly...............................Adequately.................................Weakly...................Barely

Arrangement produces a strong narrative arc (beginning, middle, end) that engages audience. (10 pts.)
Perfectly.......................Strongly...............................Adequately.................................Weakly...................Barely

Comments:

II. Flyer 10 pts.

The flyer engages the primary audience and persuades them to go to the audio essay; the choice of where the composer deployed the flyer could not be improved.
Perfectly.......................Strongly...............................Adequately.................................Weakly...................Barely
Comments:

III. Reflection 20 pts.

The reflection is thorough in discussing both the composition process and the rhetorical aspects (Part II of assignment sheet), particularly the use of ethos, logos, pathos, as well as how the composer tried to appeal to a certain audience. The composer discusses all the choices made in the construction of the audio essay in depth. If working in groups, the author discusses how the collaborative atmosphere affected the composition process.
Perfectly.......................Strongly...............................Adequately.................................Weakly...................Barely
Comments:

FIGURE 3.2. *Audiophile project rubric.*

Technologies Used in the Assignment

If students wish, they could compose all documents for the assignment on mobile device apps (with more options for both designing the flier and audio essay available on iOS than on Android). At minimum, students could use more traditional digital technologies to craft their materials, with the final delivery to the audience shared and experienced on mobile devices. In making topics and gathering sources, I go over YouTube tricks such as how to pwn YouTube in case students need to get pieces of interviews in various formats (if you haven't tried it, type "pwn" between the period and the "y" in any www.youtube.com video URL and see what happens). I also go over Audacity, an open-source audio editing program, and I aggregate various websites on our Learning Management System (LMS) where students can gather free or Creative Commons audio resources such as sound effects and beats. Finally, I show them how to design basic fliers on a variety of sites. I also show them where to get QR code readers and generate their own free QR codes (http://www.qr-code-generator.com).

Techniques for Conducting the Assignment

As far as the technical side goes, with any assignment that draws on digital platforms, I try to allow a variety of paths for students to follow. Rather than, say, make all students use one program whose interface or abilities might be too costly, complex, annoying, or even constrictive, I pick one cross-platform, free program that I support so that students with a wide variety of backgrounds and machines can access that program but choose another option if they wish. For this reason, I support Audacity, an open-source program available at http://audacity.sourceforge.net/download/.

However, I also encourage students to use any programs they may already be comfortable with, or to use software they use (or will be using later) in their majors. For example, there is a video production major at my university, and their students use Pro Tools and audio elements within Adobe Premiere and Final Cut heavily. This way, I go over an easy-to-use software such as

Audacity that all students can access and use, but those whose passions, talents, and goals lie elsewhere still have the ability to bring their own agency into platform choice.

In addition, despite the focus on audio, I do not completely close the assignment to audio-only meaning-making. I believe giving students agency over their meaning-making modes and final products is important, and I follow through with this by allowing students to add images to the audio and ultimately make a video if they wish. The QR code can take the primary audience to any website URL, so students are able to post a YouTube or Vimeo video link instead of an audio file on SoundCloud. Students can thereby again practice making and using forms they might use in their majors, and many students from a range of majors choose to add images to the audio essays because they say they would more likely be persuaded if images were part of the argument. I do caution students that adding images will make the project harder since they're adding a whole other mode to work with. Most of the students who decide to use video are often new to it, and many of them will be working with less-robust video platforms such as Windows Live MovieMaker and iMovie. As a result, I advise them to do audio in a dedicated audio program such as Audacity or GarageBand, then import the audio file into the movie program once it is revised and finished.

Many of my students come from backgrounds where they haven't had a chance to practice multimodal compositions in a school setting, especially an English course. And even though they probably have been exposed to audio essays, many of the students claim they have never heard of such a thing until getting the assignment. For that reason, I begin the INVENTION process by playing a wide variety of examples, both professional ones and ones from former students. I often begin by giving a professional example that relies heavily on audio sources, "The World's Most Important 6-Second Drum Loop," which is a nineteen-minute YouTube video, although the video is just images from an art show—the images aren't necessarily important for understanding so much as they allow the audio essay to be uploaded to YouTube. The piece makes an important point about copyright and creativity in the Internet age, with the argument built on showing how a snippet of drumming from the Winston Brothers known as the "Amen Break" has been used and repurposed since its inception in 1969. I have students listen to the piece and write about it, usually as a long discussion post on our LMS. I ask them to consider whether the argument could have been made just as well on paper, and I ask them to identify which audio sources they felt were most crucial to furthering the author's argument.

The students intuit that a written description of the Amen Break can only go so far, but once they actually hear the break, they instantly recognize it. While the YouTube example is much longer and uses more sonic resources than I ask of my students, it doesn't intimidate them so much as inspire them to go deeper, especially with regard to delivery. I warn them the person has a rather dull voice, and I share it as an example of great audio content and argument (how exactly would you make this argument in words?), but the dry delivery is an example of what to avoid. In that sense, they see how delivery matters, and how voice and style matter, but they don't get intimidated by a "professional" audio essay because they see how they can do much better in one part. In addition to this example, I provide links and examples from "This American Life," "StoryCorps," "The Moth," and "RadioLab," examples that span a variety of topics and have an array of tones from serious to humorous as well.

FINDING SOURCES: To find and gather sonic resources, I provide a list of websites where students can find and sample sounds such as Freesound, Sound Snap, and Sound Dogs, and places where they can find Creative Commons–licensed music such as Jamendo, Audio Farm, and Free Music Archive. I also show them how to convert YouTube videos into MP3 files in case they want to use interview snippets from professionals or other resources from YouTube.

FIRST PEER REVIEW: I don't require students to draft digitally for the first peer review in any certain way. If they want to jump into the software, they can. However, I advise them it's easier to begin with a more flexible structure such as a script or storyboard first. That way, the students also start with writing, a more familiar mode they are used to editing/revising in, before they actually start editing and building digitally with new programs. For the first peer review, I break students into groups of five and have them read their scripts to the other group members (or play what they have started digitally if they went that route). In actually reading out loud, they get to practice and get feedback on delivery instead of just the static words on the page. I've found that this step lessens the anxiety of making the digital recording and also helps the revisions because they've practiced in front of peers and tested what works. Also, many of the students who are a bit shy about writing substantive peer review comments on written drafts can't hide and often give elaborate aural feedback on the scripts.

EDITING WORKSHOP: After peer review, I go over the actual software and specific editing techniques. For Audacity, the key is understanding the time shift and fade tools to make something sound more professional. I have a handout that shows students what tools they need to know and includes a variety of FAQ and troubleshooting tips.

DIGITAL PEER REVIEW: The next step is a digital peer review in which students bring and review their actual digital audio (or video) files, which are by now (hopefully) complete drafts with beginnings, middles, and ends. They also bring drafts of the QR code flier; although the final URL isn't available, they can at least test the design and writing on their peers to get feedback. Prior to this digital peer review, I reiterate the concept of kairos and provide examples of student fliers so we can discuss the visual rhetoric of the fliers and the placement of them relative to their intended audiences.

FINAL DRAFTS: After finalizing the audio files, the next step is uploading the audio files so that the student can get a URL where others can access the audio file. For the audio files, I have students use SoundCloud, and for video files, YouTube. Once they get the URL, they paste it into a QR code generator and download the JPG of the code to insert into their fliers. I collect all student work through my university's LMS, and I ask students to post the link to SoundCloud and a picture of where they actually hung their fliers. As a backup, students upload the final MP3 of the audio essay and JPG of the flier. Finally, there is also a reflection that asks students to detail their composing process and analyze their work rhetorically. The reflection helps me to grade their work and understand it better; it also helps them to articulate the intentionality in their work and mitigates happy accidents, a key for developing rhetorical capacity.

As far as assessment goes, I use the rubric above to grade their work and adapt it to fit any videos or other assignments that might include different tweaks on the standard audio essay. Traditionally, the assignments that receive lower grades seem to have an underdeveloped sense of purpose and audience in that they don't take advantage of place and the connection to mobile devices, and they also usually let sonic resources overpower their own contributions. Though I point out the importance of audio editing professionalism as it ties to ethos and persuasion, I do stress throughout the process that I am grading their content, not their overall sound quality (although editing does factor into that sometimes such as non-rhetorical use of silence or accidental overlappings). In a major devoted to sound production, hissing sounds or wind during an interview would be a grave determinant when factoring a grade, but I allow a lot of leeway since most students are doing this for the first time, and the reflection offers a roadmap for what they were trying to do in case their digital reach far outpaced their digital grasp within the time constraints of the assignment. Just as Ann Amicucci pointed out in Chapter 2 of this collection, reflection is a key part of both student understanding *and* instructor understanding.

As far as the logistics of grading these assignments, I use the rubric within this chapter as a place for indicating numerical grades and sharing important notes with students. I also add audio comments through our LMS; this allows me to say much more than I could write at any time, plus I can supplement my comments with audio aspects of my own. For example, sometimes I can mimic their sources or even their own voices to point out places where editing and mixing could be tightened for the final portfolio. Even though I am adding a separate audio feedback component to the written feedback component, the grading process is actually very manageable compared to print grading because I can make notes about, say, the introduction while the introduction is actually playing, unlike in print grading where consuming the final work and leaving feedback are always separate tasks for me.

After grading the projects, the students are able to revise them for the final digital portfolio in the course. Since their work is published online and many students share their work with friends on social media in addition to the fliers, they garner additional helpful revision suggestions beyond mine. In SoundCloud, for example, listeners can post comments right inside the audio track at the actual moment where it makes sense, which in turn allows for a richer conversation within the track itself from subsequent listeners. I sometimes add my own comments to students' tracks in SoundCloud (usually really positive ones, preferring to share negative comments only within our closed CMS). Thus, the revision process is complicated productively and also engages students because it's not just a closed student-teacher loop so much as a living, breathing document that they know others are listening to and seeing, which hopefully contributes to the impact their work is making. I also make it extra credit for students to listen to their peers' final audio essays where they are meant to be experienced and offer any additional revisions suggestions for the final portfolio. On the whole, flexibility is important when asking students to move outside of their comfort zones while contacting a primary audience who shares proximity with them; thus, my outline here should not be seen as rigid steps but as ways to help what is to many a more familiar writing process to support their work while still allowing for creativity, individuality, and revision.

Student Examples

On campus, students have tackled many quality-of-life issues such as smoking near building entrances and hogging library computers for social media while other students wait to do academic work. The cafeteria food example used earlier in this chapter is a popular option as well. Given such a wide variety of opinions and potential topics, students rarely have trouble coming up with ideas, and it is helpful to assist them in considering how the actual topic can be acted on and accessed by the local target audience.

Knowing that they will ultimately have a concrete place where they will contact their audience, and also that their audience will use something they almost all have in common, a mobile device, to access their content, helps them consider how to craft their work. If students decide to develop a topic related to their hometown instead, I try to help them the best I can. For example, one student was dismayed that his high school was considering cutting the theater program that he had been so heavily involved in. He used his audio essay to make a plea for the importance of theater programs in schools, and he included research showing it helps students stay in school and interviews with former teachers and students about the impact of the program. He made a flier to hang in the hallways before an important school board meeting where the issue would be discussed. That way, the people voting on the issue, as well as the general public who had a forum to voice their opinions before the vote would take place, became his target audience. His SoundCloud numbers reflected the fact that many people used their mobile devices to listen to his audio essay before the board meeting, and, ultimately, the high school did retain the theater program. As a result, the student was pleased to see his work being used beyond the school walls and to play a role, no matter how small, in the actual vote.

Another student example shows the tricky nature of an assignment that deals with actual places. The student tackled the national issue of overprescribing depression medication and wanted to hang her flier right in the health center, because she felt the campus health services also overprescribed such medications. Her goal was to warn students, especially first-year students, of what might happen if they sought help, why it's a problem, how to resist, and where to seek other alternatives. The student could not hang fliers directly in the health center, so the student decided to meet her target audience by hanging the flier right on the health center sign outside the building. Sensing that might cause conflict, I said it was okay to take a picture of the flier there as her chosen connection point with the audience but to remove it right away in case it caused problems; that way, she could hand the picture in for the project, but it didn't remain there to alienate the health center or her potential audience. Instead, she supplemented her target audience by publishing the link to her SoundCloud file on her graduating class's Facebook page. In such cases where the best place to hang the flier and contact the audience might be illegal or problematic in some other way, I allow students to contact their target audience online as long as they make and deploy the flier so they have that connection to space. I would prefer students to identify and develop topics they are passionate about, rather than just selecting something that works completely within the parameters of the assignment.

Conclusion

As the introduction to this collection shows, mobile devices are an integral extension of our students' academic and social worlds. This assignment allows students to use that familiarity as an anchor to try what is often new for them, especially in a writing class: crafting an audio essay and a flier with a QR code. The familiarity helps root them to a place where they can picture others using the device to access their content in a location where that content is paramount. Aurality is a powerful meaning-making mode, and the immediacy with which we rely on digital composition and delivery should make us, as instructors, more cognizant of ways in which we can have students work in real settings with real audiences to explore the power of immediacy and opportune moments. QR codes accessed through mobile devices are just one way this concept can be practiced by students and deployed for the audience, and such composing for (and with) mobile devices in this vein helps students and teachers navigate existing turns and adapt to those yet to come.

Works Cited

Ally, Mohamed, and Avgoustos Tsinakos, eds. *Increasing Access through Mobile Learning.* Vancouver: Commonwealth of Learning; Athabasca: Athabasca U, 2014. 217–29. Print.

Chen, Baiyun, and Aimee deNoyelles. "Exploring Students' Mobile Learning Practices in Higher Education." *EDUCAUSE Review* 7 Oct. 2013. Web. 12 March 2015.

Cochrane, Thomas D. "Critical Success Factors for Transforming Pedagogy with Mobile Web 2.0." *British Journal of Educational Technology* 45.1 (2014): 65–82. Print.

Comstock, Michelle, and Mary E. Hocks. "Voice in the Cultural Sound-scape: Sonic Literacy in Composition Studies." *Computers and Composition Online* Fall 2006: n.p. Web. 11 Mar. 2015.

Cope, Bill, and Mary Kalantzis. "Introduction: Multiliteracies: The Beginnings of an Idea." *Multiliteracies: Literacy Learning and the Design of Social Futures*. Eds. Bill Cope and Mary Kalantzis. London: Routledge, 2000. 3–8. Print.

Lutkewitte, Claire, and Pradeep Vanguri. "Assessing iPad Use by Arts and Sciences Faculty." *Academic Exchange Quarterly* 19.2 (2015): 39–44. Print.

Mac Callum, Kathryn, Lynn Jeffrey, and Kinshuk. "Comparing the Role of ICT Literacy and Anxiety in the Adoption of Mobile Learning." *Computers in Human Behavior* 39 (2014): 8–19. Print.

Martin, Florence, and Jeffrey Ertzberger. "Here and Now Mobile Learning: An Experimental Study on the Use of Mobile Technology." *Computers and Education* 68 (2013): 76–85. Print.

McKee, Heidi. "Sound Matters: Notes toward the Analysis and Design of Sound in Multimodal Webtexts." *Computers and Composition* 23.3 (2006): 335–54. Print.

Parsons, David. "The Future of Mobile Learning and Implications for Education and Training." Ally and Tsinakos 217–29.

Scanlon, Eileen. "Mobile Learning: Location, Collaboration, and Scaffolding Inquiry." Ally and Tsinakos 85–95.

Selfe, Cynthia L. "The Movement of Air, the Breath of Meaning: Aurality and Multimodal Composing." *College Composition and Communication* 60.4 (2009): 616–63. Print.

CHAPTER FOUR

Teaching Rhetorical Analysis
through the Examination of Apps

MELISSA TOOMEY
University of Cincinnati at Blue Ash

Most composition programs require their undergraduate students to complete a rhetorical analysis writing assignment, typically in at least one sequence of first-year composition. Students are asked to analyze everything from political speeches to advertisements to more recently, technologically based spaces such as websites and apps. I have found that having students analyze apps is one of the best means for allowing them to explore topics and arenas they are already invested in, as they readily use handheld mobile devices throughout their daily lives in personal and real ways to mediate their experiences. As Anuraj Gambhir reiterates in his piece "Mobile Innovation Trends," "One of the thriving innovations witnessed in the mobile industry over the past couple years is the increasing penetration of mobile apps" (509). There are now more than 650,000 apps provided by Apple; the app explosion began when Apple opened its "App Store for the iPod, iPhone, and iPad family of devices" (Gambhir 509). Further, we now have additional application stores such as Android Market, which has become Google Play, with at least 400,000 apps and growing (Gambhir 509). Thus, there is a vast array of applications available for students to examine and provide a textual analysis of these mobile spaces.

As composition studies works to expand its notions of literacy alongside the influx of mobile technologies, instructors of composition and rhetoric must too begin to embrace the complex ways and means our students engage in learning, specifically through their use of such devices. In this chapter, I examine how instructors can use mobile technology to teach rhetorical analysis in non-static ways so that we might bring user, interface, and text(s) together without using reductionist methods. Particularly, I argue that through the analysis of applications, students may begin to grasp how rhetoric can be understood and examined through the use of technology.

Theoretical Grounding

In 1964, the National Council of Teachers of English published workshop reports through *College Composition and Communication* (*CCC*) in which they clearly defined what a "rhetorical analysis" from students in the field of composition and rhetoric should look like. Such a definition has come to be what we typically rely on when thinking through how to teach textual analysis in the classroom. They found that

> rhetorical analysis should explore pieces of well-written prose in order to reveal techniques of composition; that it should be preceded by a general, theoretical discussion of the technique being studied—the use of restatement, say, or of qualification in paragraph development—; and that it should be followed by an assignment asking the student to apply what he had learned. (Kane 183)

However, we must continue to expand our notions of what may be viewed for analysis and how so as we begin to examine how knowledge-making and consumption is shifting in today's world. For example, in his text *Lingua Fracta: Towards a Rhetoric of New Media*, Collin Gifford Brooke maintains that "in rhetoric and composition, that step begins with a single revaluation, the move from text to interface (or from page to screen, as the collection edited by Michael Joyce and Ilana Snyder would have it)" (23). As Matthew Kirschenbaum illustrates in his essay "'So the Colors Cover the Wires': Interface, Aesthetics, and Usability," "Interface" has come to include "the image of a 'surface' or a 'boundary' where two or more 'systems,' 'devices,' or 'entities' come into 'contact' or 'interact'" (523). Brooke argues that we can adapt the five classical rhetorical canons (invention, arrangement, style, memory, and delivery) to these digital rhetorical spaces "to construct a rhetoric that will allow us to both understand and produce interfaces" (27). In order to frame his theory, Brooke employs the term *ecology*, which is traditionally connected to the study of the environment, "as a metaphor for human activity . . ." (37). As such, Marilyn Cooper, in her *College English* essay "The Ecology of Writing," proposes:

> . . . an ecology of writing encompasses much more than the individual writer and her immediate context. An ecologist explores how writers interact to form systems: all the characteristics of any individual writer or piece of writing both determine and are determined by the characteristics of all the other writers and writings in the systems. An important characteristic of ecological systems is that they are inherently dynamic; though their structures are contents that can be specified at a given moment, in real time they are constantly changing, limited only by parameters that are themselves subject to change over longer spans of time. (368)

Cooper's focus on this consistent movement is particularly important, especially when analyzing the rhetoric of digital pieces as in the instance of apps on mobile devices, as it allows students the opportunity to understand the changing nature of space and time as writing can help highlight the complexities of the social, cultural, and political that can influence our connectedness to language.

Furthermore, Brooke suggests the following:

> The appeal of ecology as a conceptual metaphor is its ability to focus our attention on a temporarily finite set of practices, ideas, and interactions without fixing them in place. . . .The challenge, however, is to introduce categories that are somehow not static or limited, delineations that preserve the dynamic flexibility of an ecological model while providing us with some ability to distinguish one practice from another. Obviously, I believe that the canons provide us with one such set of categories. . . . (42)

Brooke focuses on the importance of all five canons versus the highlighting of one or two while neglecting the others as composition and rhetoric scholars have often done in more recent rhetorical scholarship (29–30). When examining invention, Brooke maintains that an ecology of invention should in part include traditional features like "freewriting, outlining, [and] mapping . . ." but the "emphasis on conscious, visible activity is necessarily a reduction of the canon" (44). "An ecological model of invention would treat it as the level of generalized activity" (Brooke 44). Brooke adds that it is useful to consider "the canons as relations rather than categories . . . similar to what Kenneth Burke does. . . . For instance, the canon of invention frames the relationship between given and new information, arranging the relationship between discourse and space . . . and so on" (44). Providing an example using Amazon.com, Brooke illustrates Amazon's section ("People who bought this book also bought . . .") as a feature that "is both social in that it aggregates individual purchases and inventional in that it explicitly marks the relation between the *given* of an individual purchase and the *new* of other volumes tracked by their databases" (45). Further, this type of invention is assembled within the interface, thus not particularly needing the customer's input (Brooke 45). Not only do websites provide these interesting means for considering invention but so too do apps, as I highlight later in my classroom assignment on rhetorical analysis through the examination of applications. They provide particularly interesting spaces for the exploration of invention because their mobility and thus adaptability are often based on spatial and temporal considerations.

In addition to invention, Brooke discusses methods for examining arrangement within new media. He describes the work of David Kolb from his essay "Socrates in the Labyrinth," stating that "Kolb calls here for us to attend to the spaces that we build through the creation of place, forms that lie somewhere in between the containers that print has encouraged and the paralyzing freedom of an infinitely open space" (96). Finding that arrangement does not need to be "painstakingly ordered," Brooke posits that it can be more "productively conceptualized as *arrangement as pattern*" (91–92).

When thinking through the third canon of rhetoric, style, Brooke notes that "one of the things that new media interfaces do stylistically is to help us move from the abstracted, single perspective of the reader of a static text . . . to the multiple and partial perspectives necessary for many forms of new media" (114). Using the example of the online game *World of Warcraft*, Brooke highlights this point by noting that there are particular actions one can quickly access in the game by using the numbers on the top row of the keyboard and yet various other actions must be done with the mouse. "Changing the interface does not simply change the 'look' of the game, although it does do that as well; it also affects the physical actions (keyboard and mouse manipulation) used to trigger game actions" (Brooke 138). Thus, Brooke finds that such dynamic combinations "change over the course of gameplay and cannot be taken as static" (138). I find such stylistic variations also can be found in the examination of apps, and by students rhetorically analyzing such elements in mobile spaces, they can begin to see the continued and often changing and multiple interactions between the individual, the interface, and the dimensions of activity within such spaces.

The fourth canon, memory, is explored by Brooke as he shows how persistence is "a memory practice" and "is the ability to build and maintain patterns, although those patterns may be tentative and ultimately fade into the background" (157). He adds that there is still value in memory as "figured simply as storage" (157). Yet he writes that there are key differences between memory practices as "certain media offer us tools for building persistence of cognition, the inductive perception of connections, and patterns across multiple sources" (157).

Finally, Brooke explores delivery, the fifth canon, finding that "delivery in everyday parlance, is a transitive process; it is rare to speak of delivering without an object that is being delivered" (170). Yet it is more than this. It is also intransitive. Discourse can be performed. Brooke states that "on the one hand, it is a small change in attitude . . . —seeing discourse as circulating rather than some*thing* that we circulate—but on the other hand, it is a change that has far-reaching implications for the practice of new media" (192). We see that "new media . . . draws us away from the 'instance of reality,' the one true rendering of reality in discourse, and closer to the 'instance of discourse,' where it is a particular performance, one that constitutes reality, that is taking place" (192). It is through Brooke's theory of the adaptation of the five canons that I wish to show how we might put such ideas into practice by examining how we might teach using the digital space of apps as one way to examine rhetoric.

Description of Assignments and Activities

In my semester-long first-year composition class, students complete the rhetorical analysis assignment over the course of three weeks. I have taught the assignment under two different possible time frames, either as the first inquiry of the semester or as the second. When used as the second, I have students begin the semester with a rhetorical narrative essay where they speak of a time when they have convinced someone of something using rhetorical elements. The rhetorical analysis essay then connects closely since they move from analyzing their own rhetoric to the rhetoric of others. Either scenario works well. I will describe teaching the rhetorical analysis as the first major inquiry since I have found it a pretty common practice for FYC courses to begin with this assignment.

Activity 1: Defining Key Rhetorical Concepts

Before doing anything else, I find that students must understand what rhetoric is and learn what many of the rhetorical concepts are so they might begin to understand their complexities and variations. We explore the terms I have listed in Figure 4.1, though students are free to examine additional rhetorical appeals, and we have a lengthy discussion about how such terms might be used in differing ways with an app versus in a print document. We discuss how in an app like Match.com, for example, we can see stylistic variations in how the interface changes as more and more individuals respond to one's page. It not only changes the way the page appears but also what can be done with the actual data (e.g., profile pictures can be reorganized).

Rhetorical Key Terms

Audience: An audience includes spectators, listeners and/or readers of a performance, a speech, a reading, or printed material.

> Audience assembled: The real life people reading a text at any given time.

> Audience addressed: The particular audience a text is directed toward; the audience an author had in mind when writing a text.

Context: The setting, circumstance, or discourse in which an action, utterance, or expression occurs.

Ethos: *Ethos* can refer to any of the following: the actual character of the speaker/writer, the character of the writer as it is presented in a text, or as a series of ground rules/customs, which are negotiated upon between speaker, audience, and specific traditions or locations. *Martin Luther King Jr. establishes his ethos through both personal experience and academic credentials.*

Pathos: Emotional appeal used by a speaker or writer to bring about a feeling in the audience (such as anger, happiness, sadness, excitement).

Logos: In classical rhetoric, *logos* is the means of persuasion by demonstration of the truth, real or apparent. The reasons or supporting information used to support a claim. Types of *logos* include: using an expert source, fact, statistic, example, and history.

Style: The strategies used by a writer to present voice in their writing. A writer's style involves more than his or her attention to issues of grammar, spelling, etc. Style deals with how a writer approaches writing, how the writer presents ideas, and the choices a writer makes to clearly and eloquently present an argument. Examples of common stylistic devices include: metaphor, diction, dialogue, ALL CAPS, using a list, and parallelism.

Kairos (KY-ross): *Kairos* can be defined as the right time to speak/write; advantageous, exact, or critical time; a window of time during which action is most effective. Good rhetors seize kairotic moments; they know when the time is "ripe" to speak or write. *Stephen "took the floor" once his opponent stopped speaking.*

Rhetorical exigence: A sense of urgency, a problem that requires attention right now, a need that must be met, a concept that must be understood before the audience can move to a next step.

Rhetorical situation: A rhetorical situation is the context of a rhetorical act; that is the social environment, the time period, the political environment, etc.

Tone: A manner of expression in speech or writing.

FIGURE **4.1.** *Rhetorical key terms explored in class.*

Assignment 1: Rhetorical Analysis of an App

To help students understand that rhetoric is everywhere and particularly in their daily lives through their mobile devices, I assign the rhetorical analysis of an app (see Figure 4.2). My purpose is for students to apply the rhetorical concepts learned to a given app and to build on these concepts by exploring the complex and dynamic interactions between users, what's on the screen, and the object (cell phone or other mobile device) that "holds" these apps. Moreover, I provide them with the grading rubric for the assignment, also placing all documents on our Blackboard site, so they are able to revisit such handouts when completing the writing process. Having such handouts continues to prove invaluable as students can use them to understand expectations while drafting and if/when attending the writing center.

Assignment Sheet:

Requirements:
- 3–5 pages in length
- Use MLA Format
- Include a colon title (something interesting on the left and name the rhetorical elements you've analyzed and name the app selected on the right)
- Includes a Works Cited page with 1 entry—the app.

Purpose:
For this essay, we will begin to explore the rhetorical appeals and modes that authors use to communicate information to their audiences. Being able to identify authors' strategies will help you to more carefully analyze the effectiveness and validity of their work. In this assignment, you will look closely at all of the rhetorical aspects of a single text—an app (application).

Assignment:
We will be analyzing apps. What is an app you might ask? According to Anita Campbell in her piece "What the Heck is an 'App'?" she maintains that

continued on next page

FIGURE **4.2.** *Assignment for the rhetorical analysis of an app.*

Figure 4.2. *continued*

> The word app is a noun, and it's short for "application." Application in this case refers to a software application—in other words, a software program. But an app is not just any old software program—it's a special type of software program. An app typically refers to software used on a smartphone or mobile device such as the Android, iPhone, BlackBerry, or iPad, as in "mobile app" or "iPhone app." (par. 4–5)

There are more than 650,000 apps available today. Campbell adds that "In January 2011, the American Dialect Society named 'app' the word of the year for 2010. That action alone says a lot. Being named word of the year signifies that a term is trendy and growing in popularity" (par. 3). Thus, we are going to look at various apps and analyze the rhetorical choices used in them to convince the audience to view or engage with their product/information.

Directions:
You will be randomly selecting an app that includes many rhetorical elements within it. Here are a few examples for potential selection:

Once you have selected your app, you will examine who the audience is. Additionally, you will consider its various rhetorical elements and work to locate between 8 and 10 of these. You may only analyze a single element twice for the entire paper. This means for example, you may look at logos only two times.

Your analysis must include the following:
- a brief summary of the app (what it is and does)
- an analysis of who the audience is
- a discussion of the rhetorical appeals and elements used and their purpose for/in the app
- a Works Cited page with the app as your only entry (see page 161 #58 in your class text *A Pocket Style Manual*)

continued on next page

Figure 4.2. *continued*

Grading Rubric for Inquiry I—Rhetorical Analysis

	Scant	Somewhat Developed	Substantially Developed
1. Follows Directions (e.g., page setup in MLA, length 3–5 pgs, creative title)			
2. Summary 1–4 sentence summary of the main ideas from the text. Includes the apps title (italicized) within the summary.			
Rhetorical Analysis: **1. Quotes (or summarizes) an example from the text to showcase the rhetorical concept you plan to/are discussing** Introduces the quote as needed and cites the par. #(s) or sec. #(s) from which it comes			
2. Names the rhetorical element being used (you should only analyze one idea at a time) Not only names the element as ethos, pathos, logos, or style BUT ALSO is specific in one's naming—it builds ethos . . . what 1 emotion is it exactly? . . . what *kind* of logos? What emotion? What stylistic device?			
3. Explanation of rhetorical element Fully explains/illustrates how/why the rhetorical appeal is what you say it is (if applicable—with "style" you typically won't need to do this after you name your focus—although this is NOT always the case—e.g., metaphor). Thus, if you say it's "logos" through the use of an "expert source," explain how you know this—how/why, in other words, is this individual an "expert source" and how do you know?			

continued on next page

Figure 4.2. continued

4. Discussion Analyzes the possible "Whys." Why do you think the author *may* have used this rhetorical appeal in this way with this quote? Names 2–3 *possible* reasons. Be careful to consider possible groups and how those individuals may react and why.			
5. Works cited *In text*: Introduces (e.g., with an author's last name or first word(s) of the Works Cited if no author available and verb for "says/said") and integrates the quote or summary to be used well. *End text:* Provides a Works Cited page that is accurate; that is, in MLA format (uses *The Everyday Writer*).			
6. Qualifies statements Effectively uses language like: can, could, may, might, some, several, perhaps, often (especially qualifies in the discussions).			
7. Grammar Mechanics, spelling, usage (commas, run-on sentences, etc.)			
8. Well-organized Uses transitions effectively. Essay is clear and logical.			

Activity 2: Practicing App Analysis through Mobile Technology

Before writing the rhetorical analysis essay, we practice analyzing an app together as a class. Before the start of the semester, I email and place on Blackboard information for the students regarding the downloading of two free apps that we will be using in class. One of these is the QVC app (the other CNET), which we use to practice rhetorical analysis. QVC is a television network that also has a website and app you can use to buy products—electronics, clothes, home goods, etc. Because of our focus on mobile technology, I ask that students download the app and bring a charged mobile device to class with the app on it. For students without access to a device, I have extras and/or ask students to bring in two devices if they are willing to share with other students. Once in class, I also pull up the app on my cell phone and show it on the projector with the help of an Apple TV. (Many universities now have Apple TVs in various rooms on campus, and many IT departments will provide a brief handout next to the device on how to use it. Even if you have never tried an Apple TV before, it is quite simple—just remember to bring your own charged mobile device to use for projection.)

To practice their recognition of key rhetorical concepts, I have students gather into teams of three. This way, if one person does not have a device, they can still share and view the app. I also have students download an app called "buzzer button" to use as a means for making the activity fun (not for analysis—though it could be a possible topic for the final paper). I allow students approximately eight to ten minutes to locate and discuss with their group as many rhetorical elements as they can find on the QVC app. Then I set up the activity as a trivia game where I ask students questions such as "If a customer gave a product rating five out of five stars, what rhetorical element could this be and in what ways does the patterning or arrangement of such data influence its purpose?" and "Name one instance of *logos*, through the use of a fact that you found on the app, and explain how the interface affects such data?" In the case of the latter, students have often talked about how the site has "Today's Special Values" and how as time progresses, those products and the factual information surrounding what the product can do for the customer is often moved around on the app, typically moving up the ranks of products shown in a given hour. Such features affect the interface and stylistically the positioning by which someone can view the information and/or the product next to other similar products that they "might need" too. Further, students will highlight how the facts about how long a product will be on air or available shift repeatedly by the flashing of a time clock back and forth with a variety of coloring used to highlight the product and the time remaining.

For every five questions they buzz in and answer, students receive one extra credit point for the semester. Such an activity allows students to locate and examine the rhetoric in the app and its interesting features as shown through a mobile device as well as collaborate in flexible ways where they are able to identify and discuss the rhetorical elements. As they explore the various and often changing and/or interactive videos, images, and quotes from the site, they are able to name and produce effective rhetorical analysis about the material viewed by the app's users. Students also discuss in their groups the valuable point that there are many rhetorical choices available to analyze, and even the same material examined by two different teams can be used for different purposes and in diverse contexts.

Examples of Student Work

Students often find it interesting to examine the TED app. One student analyzed how the mobility of the app allows users to listen anywhere, stressing the kairotic moment as an intriguing element for analysis. She found that in such listening, a user might be able to briefly and quickly view speeches or show another individual something particular from a text despite say, being in a car or perhaps at a restaurant having a discussion about a speaker. Thus, one may skim the information more readily and then stop and listen at a variety of undetermined points versus listening to the beginning, middle, and end of a speech as they might otherwise do. In this case, she found that the user may still ultimately acquire the same data regarding the content of the speech but do so in a more patterned way—skim to a certain moment and listen and then continue to skim to a different moment and then listen and so forth. In this way, the mobility of the app allows one the efficiency of time and the ability to view such information in any number of spatial arenas.

Another student analyzed Shazam, an app that allows users to identify a song that is playing in any location (store, office, car) by touching a round "S" button and letting the app listen to the song for approximately ten seconds. The app then provides the name of the song, which one may then listen to or purchase if desired. There are additional features too, including information about artists as well as a variety of interactive activities for users. In analyzing this app, one student found it interesting that stylistically the interface is updated frequently to get one to check out the newest popular song or what they refer to as their "Trending Shazams." Ultimately, the student argued that such changes in interface can have monetary effects, making money for the app designer and companies whose products are advertised within the app, as well as helping users discover what they might wish to listen to next. They show a small square photo of the album (or single's) cover and underneath the name its title and artist. This information is then moved left or right or out of sight throughout a given day or week based on the number of times it is "Shazamed" and/or the national popularity of the song as specified by entities such as the Billboard hits charts.

Conclusion

Because technologies offer students the chance to mediate their environment and experiences, instructors must begin to understand more fully the complexities of mobile technologies and recognize their students can learn to meaningfully engage with such technologies in a more rhetorically savvy manner through assignments such as the analysis of apps. It is necessary that our students see these digital arenas as dynamic and ever-changing and understand that they and other users are a part of this construction and such systems. It is through the study and examination of rhetorical analysis of apps in mobile, digital spaces that students can begin to visualize how rhetoric is performative and to see how it is not only everywhere in the world around them, but also how it plays an ever-present role in their everyday lives.

Works Cited

Brooke, Collin Gifford. *Lingua Fracta: Towards a Rhetoric of New Media*. Cresskill: Hampton, 2009. Print.

Campbell, Anita. "What the Heck Is an 'App?'" *Small Business Trends*. Small Business Trends, 7 Mar. 2011. Web. 14 Feb. 2016.

Cooper, Marilyn M. "The Ecology of Writing." *College English* 48.4 (1986): 364–75. *JSTOR*. Web. 1 Feb. 2016.

Gambhir, Anuraj. "Mobile Innovation Trends: Beyond the Hype Cycles." *Global Mobile: Applications and Innovations for the Worldwide Mobile Ecosystem*. Ed. Peter A. Bruck and Madanmohan Rao. Medford: Information Today, 2013. 505–19. Print.

Kane, Thomas. "Workshop Reports: Teaching Composition through Rhetorical Analysis." *College Composition and Communication* 15.3 (1964): 183–84. *JSTOR*. Web. 16 Jul. 2015.

Kirschenbaum, Matthew. "'So the Colors Cover the Wires': Interface, Aesthetics, and Usability." *A Companion to Digital Humanities*. Ed. Susan Schreibman, Ray Siemens, and John Unsworth. Oxford: Blackwell, 2004. 523–42. Print.

Kolb, David. "Socrates in the Labyrinth." *Hyper/Text/Theory*. Ed. George P. Landow. Baltimore: John Hopkins UP, 1994. 323–44.

CHAPTER FIVE

Designing Apps in the Writing Classroom

CLAIRE LUTKEWITTE
Nova Southeastern University

During the Winter 2013 semester, I conducted a case study in an upper-level writing course called Writing for Technologies. The course was composed of mostly juniors and seniors majoring in a variety of disciplines such as English and Computer Science. Over the course of the study, I examined students' work on one assignment and two activities that focused on writing for mobile devices. The activities and assignment included:

1. Redesigning a Guide for a Mobile Device Activity

2. Defining App Characteristics Activity

3. App Assignment and Display

While the activities and assignment were designed for an upper-level writing course, they could be adapted for other writing courses, including FYC courses. In fact, I used a modified version of the Redesigning a Guide for a Mobile Device Activity in my own FYC. In this chapter, I describe the assignment and activities as well as showcase the work of one of the students in my study to show how students can develop rhetorical skills when they consider the affordances of mobile devices.

Theoretical Grounding for the Assignment and Activities

Before detailing the assignment and activities, I want to talk more about the *why*. After all, why should students consider writing for mobile devices? At the time of this study, I had been investigating mobile technologies for several years and had been researching uses of mobile technologies in learning environments. In fact, at the same time as I was studying my students, I was also working with a colleague, conducting a college-wide study on faculty's uses of iPads. I became well aware of the scholarship that revealed how powerful mobile technologies could be in the college classroom and why teachers of writing should care about these. Several studies, for example, show a link between learning and mobile technologies as mentioned in the introduction and other chapters in this book. Inspired by these studies, I developed two activities and one assignment to align with my course's three objectives:

1. Demonstrate an understanding of technological theories in professional writing.

2. Identify current trends in technology affecting composing practices.

3. Write and revise compositions using technologically appropriate conventions.

Because I wanted students to approach the assignment and activities from a rhetorical perspective, to think about themselves as writers with a purpose who must take into consideration their audience and their context as they construct texts accordingly, we spent time in class talking about what it means to use mobile technologies while on location. Students brought their mobile devices to class, and we compared their affordances in relationship to how we use the devices on location. In his article about developing an iPhone app for a particular location, Anders Fagerjord, for instance, contended that "location-aware texts require location-aware authors to be effective" (262). In other words, writers must be attuned to the users' needs when those users are using a text in a specific location to mediate their experience.

Much research in the writing field has concentrated on the locations of writing. In fact, *College Composition and Communication* devoted a special 2014 edition to discussing the locations of writing. Though we have the freedom to move with mobile technologies, the learning that takes place because of mobile technologies isn't just learning anywhere; rather, it is learning that takes place somewhere. What this means is that the learning is situated. Martin Owen contends there is a powerfulness "about learning from where you are, either because of the place itself, what is in the place, or the people who are sharing the place with you" (104). As I mentioned in the introduction to the book, my campus's library is a four-story building that houses books, computer labs, a coffee shop, meeting rooms, and artwork. To help visitors navigate the artwork in the library, the library created a paper brochure highlighting the significance of each piece of artwork. For the first activity described below, I ask students to imagine what this brochure would look like as an app and how users would learn about the artwork by using it. In doing so, students had to think about the library itself, what is in the library, and the people who share the library. Thinking about these is important because, as de Souza e Silva and Frith posit, mobile devices do not disconnect people from public spaces but rather act as "an intrinsic *part of* people's experience of space" (45). Mobile technologies offer users a way to build relationships with the places they move to, from, and within.

In his discussion of map-as-interface, Christopher Schmidt argues that instructors need to develop a rhetoric of place if they are going to be successful in working with students in the future. He reasoned that:

> In the next ten years, as writing and reading become more mobile and untethered, it is crucial for the teachers of rhetoric to remind students that the place of writing—what in classical rhetoric Aristotle described as "that in which a plurality of oratorical reasonings coincide" (as cited in Ulmer, 1994, p. 33)—is still a crucial aspect for the crafting of rhetorical arguments. (313)

Essentially, Schmidt argues that like learning, writing is situated and that students need to see the place(s) where writing occurs both on the device and on location as integral to the learner's experience, not minor parts of it. Furthermore, Stacey Pigg writes that by "analyzing how virtual and physical places intersect for mobile composers" we are better able to see "how embodied memory and resulting literacy habits are constructed through place-based interactions" (255). Developing an awareness of a place positions students to make better choices for writing, especially if their writing is meant for a mobile device.

However, understanding a location and how it shapes writing activity is not the only rhetorical strategy needed to understand how an audience might use a text on a mobile device. Students must also strategize about how other affordances play into users' experience. For example, mobile devices allow users the ability to interact with not just written text but also moving images and sounds. They can use a camera to take their own images and record their own sounds. These affordances require different sets of skills, and students have to consider how these sets of skills shape writers' choices. So, from a rhetorical investigation of affordances, students begin to see how such mobile devices mold literacy practices. It is this rhetorical investigation that will be most helpful to students in the future as they work with a variety of evolving mobile technologies.

Description of Activities and Assignment

Over the course of six weeks, students worked on the assignment and activities in and out of class. Because these were assigned in the middle of the semester, students had a working foundation of technological theories in professional writing from which to draw. At the start of the semester, for example, we discussed how to define and read a technology, comparing competing definitions and readings. Leading up to the assignments and activities, we had also looked at several technologies, talking about the different ways in which composers write for those technologies. We looked, for instance, at social media and how writers write for social media outlets.

To create the activities and assignment and to help students, I relied on Apple's "iOS Human Interface Guidelines" published online. In fact, as part of their weekly reading assignments, students read several of these guidelines and they helped me to create the activities and assignment described below. I chose these guidelines because I wanted to make this experience as real as possible, so that students could meet the learning objective of identifying current trends in technology affecting composing practices and think carefully about the rhetorical choices app composers must make.

Activity 1: Redesigning a Guide for a Mobile Device

As mentioned, the Alvin Sherman Library on the main campus of Nova Southeastern University (NSU) created a printed brochure of the library's artwork called the *Art Collection Guide.* To get students thinking about what it means to write for mobile technologies, I had students reimagine this guide (see Figure 5.1) as an app for a mobile device.

As a class, we traveled to the library so that students could experience the artwork in relationship to their locations within the library. They saw how and where visitors might view the

---

Instructions for Redesigning a Guide for a Mobile Device

For this activity, you will need to consider the decisions that a mobile app composer makes when creating an app for a mobile device. Take a few minutes and read through the *Art Collection Guide.* Pay attention to how the information is organized and presented to you, the reader. Now, imagine if this guide was transformed into an app that was designed for readers to access on a mobile device while in the library. After spending some time in the library and looking at the artwork, answer the following questions:

1. If you could redesign this guide so that it was accessed on a mobile device, what changes would you make and why? In other words, what should be included in the mobile version? And, what should not be included in the mobile version?

2. What would the interface (or the point where users interact with the material) look like?

3. How will users interact with the guide as they move from one exhibit to the next in the library?

4. How does the location where you access the material and information influence the design of the material and information?

FIGURE **5.1.** *Instructions for redesigning a guide for a mobile device.*

artwork. They could then account for what was happening: Was it quiet? Was it noisy? Would viewers need headphones? Were there a lot of people sharing the space? How will a handheld connected device mediate the user's environment?

Students had to make a number of rhetorical decisions when answering the activity's questions. For example, students had to think about the audience for their guide and how that audience would use the mobile app guide to learn about the artwork. Students realized that a smartphone and an iPad had many affordances that would provide users with a more interactive experience. And they were keenly aware of the needs of the user as they were redesigning the guide. For example, several students thought an interactive map that locates the artwork in the library would be beneficial to users as they move from one place to the next within the library. Because mobile technologies have GPS capabilities, they thought that the ability to see the user on the interactive map in relationship to the locations of the artwork would help a user to navigate the library. Students in the class also thought that the use of hyperlinks would be appropriate because they would help simplify the guide for a mobile device. The mobile guide would need to be easy to navigate, not cluttered with information, and organized in such a way that made using it less time consuming. Students suggested that the hyperlinks could provide additional information about the artwork and artists for those users who wished to learn more. Finally, they wanted to be able to share their experiences with others, so they suggested having share functions for social media readily available. For instance, they wanted to be able to take pictures and share them with their network of friends and family.

After the students spent time in the library and wrote a reflection in response to the activity's questions, we gathered in the classroom to discuss. In the discussion, students explained their decisions for their redesigns, backing their ideas with rhetorical strategies that took into consideration audience, purpose, text, context, and author. The discussion in class allowed for students to think about all the affordances that mobile devices have to offer and prepared them for the next activity.

Activity 2: Defining App Characteristics

The next activity got students thinking more specifically about different types of apps. Not all apps have the same features, so I wanted students to examine similarities and differences among apps with the goal of figuring out which features were most useful. This activity accompanied one of their major assignments for the semester, the App Assignment and Display (see Figure 5.2), and served as a way to help students brainstorm ideas for this major assignment.

In class, students first chose a category of apps that was similar to the app idea they had for the assignment described in the following section and then created a table that organized their findings about the different apps' commonalities. Students worked

---

For this activity, your goal is to find out what apps have in common to figure out what features are best for your own app. To do so, you will spend time comparing a variety of apps' design features and their functions. You will also examine the language the composers use to sell their apps and help users use the features. If you want to have a successful app of your own, you need to do what other successful apps do. To begin with, you need to access an app store whether through your own smartphone or tablet, using iTunes or via the web at https://play.google.com/store/apps/category/APPLICATION.

Choose one category of apps to which you feel your idea for an app would most likely belong, whether that is business, education, entertainment, food and drink, health and fitness, etc. Then, do the following:

1. Write down the names of five apps in the category.

2. Describe common features of the five apps' designs. What color schemes do they use? What kinds of images or videos do they use? What kinds of animations and sounds do they use? How would you describe the look of the apps?

3. Describe the common functions of the five apps. What do they do? How do they do it? What actions do the users do? How does the user do these actions?

4. Describe the language the composers use. What do the apps say? How do they say it? In what ways do the composers sell their app to the user? How do they explain how to use the app?

5. Describe how your app will be similar to these apps in terms of design, function, and language. Describe how your app will be different.

FIGURE 5.2. *Instructions for defining app characteristics activity.*

on this assignment for an hour in class, investigating each app's features carefully. While it was not a requirement, some of the students even took the time to download the apps and test them out so that they could get a better sense of the functions.

When the students were finished, we made one giant table on the classroom's whiteboard, showcasing the design features, functions, and language of the apps they analyzed. That way students could see what apps from their category had in common with apps in other categories and what made them different. For example, students realized that many of the apps they looked at had similar functions, such as the ability to use GPS, connect with social media, or access a dropdown menu of the app's contents. But they also saw differences between different types of apps. Educational apps were different from food and drink apps because their purposes were different, their audiences were different, and they required different design features and language because of those differences. By discussing the commonalities and differences, students were able to understand what was necessary for their own app designs based on how composers use rhetoric to develop apps.

Assignment 1: App Assignment and Display

To further help students understand what writers must consider when writing for mobile devices, I asked them to create their own idea for an app (see Figure 5.3). My goal was for students to apply the rhetorical strategies they recognized in the previous two activities when they reimagined the brochure and when they analyzed different apps.

In class, students brainstormed ideas, workshopped their ideas, and discussed the readings from Apple's "iOS Human Interface Guidelines." Students rhetorically thought through each of their design decisions, taking into account their audience, the places where the app would be used, the purpose of the app, and so forth. They considered the process that app composers use to create apps from a business standpoint too. Discussions were not divorced from the fact that mobile technology is a big business and decisions can be based on economics and politics.

For this assignment, you will design your own app (without physically making the app or writing the code). Instead, what you will do is come up with a concept; create an app definition statement; develop an app store description; sketch or draw the logo, intro/interface screen, and other screens users will encounter; and write a rationale for how it will work. In the process of creating this app, you will need to consider what writing conventions and rhetorical strategies are appropriate for mobile devices, how users will interact with the app, and what benefits the apps have to offer the user. Your project will consist of the following:

a. App Definition Statement (20 points) and App Store Description (20 points): Before apps are purchased and downloaded from an app store, users often read a description of the app. For the definition and description of your app, you need to create a concrete declaration of an app's main purpose and its intended audience. The definition and description should sell your app to your user. To help you create these, we will be reading Apple's "iOS Human Interface Guidelines."

b. Display for presenting your app to the class (100 points): On the display, you should include drawings of the logo, interface, and screens users will encounter (think of these drawings as screenshots of the app) and descriptions and rationale of how the app and its functions work. Your rationale should explain how your app is better/different than similar apps on the market. Your display could be on poster board or you can do this digitally as long as your display is professional and readable.

FIGURE 5.3. *Instructions for app assignment and display.*

Finally, students also took into account the grading criteria for the project listed in Figure 5.4.

Example of a Student's Work: NSU Study Place App

To show how students rhetorically created their apps, I would like to share one student's project. Kamila, a junior majoring in English at the time, created an app specifically for NSU students called the NSU Study Place App. As Kamila explained in her presentation to the class, the purpose of the app was to make finding a place to study easier for students on or near campus. The following screenshots demonstrate how the user is supposed to interact with the app. Once users get started on the app, they

Grading Criteria	Excellent	Fair	Needs Some Work
The app definition statement was clear, focused, and concise. It was a concrete declaration of the app's main purpose and its intended audience.			
The app store description was professional and persuasive. The language clearly highlighted the app's features and targeted a specific audience.			
The display included appropriate and professional drawings of the app's logo, interface, and the screens users will encounter. The drawings clearly showed the app's features.			
The display contained well-developed descriptions and a rationale for how the app and its functions work. Your rationale should explain how your app is better/different than similar apps on the market.			
The presentation of the app display in class communicated a focus that was clearly developed throughout and adequately explained your project.			

FIGURE 5.4. *Grading criteria for the app assignment.*

can choose a type of study place from the app's list (Figure 5.5). Lists are a common feature of Kamila's app and provide users with a simple interface, one Kamila later explained made the app easy to navigate and beneficial to those who would rather spend more time studying and less time trying to figure out how to use her app.

Once the user chooses a type of study place and whether or not the place is on campus or off campus, the app presents the user with a list of results matching that type of space (Figure 5.6). For instance, if a user is interested in studying in a cafe, the app locates cafes near the user using its GPS capabilities. The

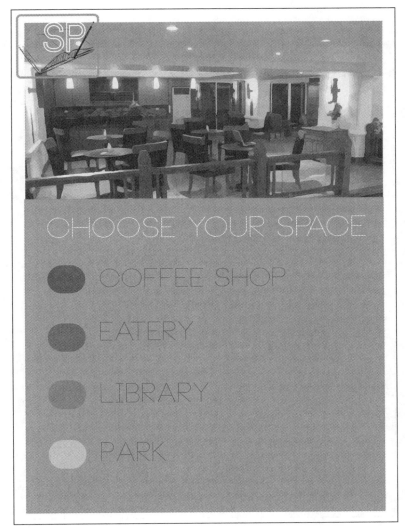

FIGURE 5.5. *Kamila's NSU Study Place app.*

list of results includes not only the names of cafes but also other information about the cafes (such as addresses and hyperlinks to the cafes' websites), information that Kamila thought would be helpful to the app's audience.

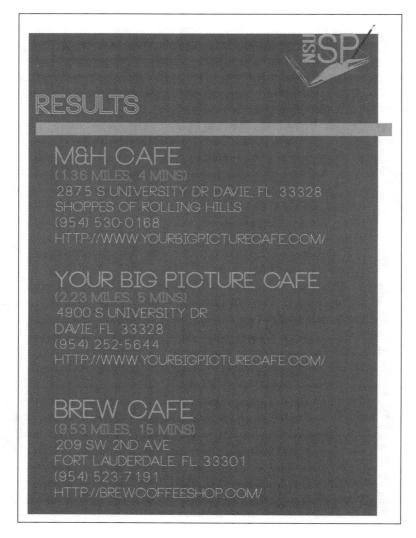

FIGURE 5.6. *The results page of Kamila's NSU Study Place app.*

Next, if the user would like to know more about one of the cafes listed, the user can select it. At that point, the app brings the user to another screen that rates the cafe in terms of noise level, menu, and seating/outlets as well as provides the user with a list of reviews and a link to a map so that the user can locate it

(Figure 5.7). Because we had discussed apps' common features (like GPS) in class while we were completing the two activities described earlier in this chapter, Kamila thought a "Map It!" feature would be helpful to her own users and something they would expect to find on an app such as hers.

FIGURE 5.7. *The "Map It!" feature of Kamila's NSU Study Place app.*

After she presented her app to the class, Kamila reflected on her project. Specifically, she wrote about the importance of knowing her audience as she created her app: "I considered what college students would want to see, where they would want to go, what factors they would consider when choosing a location. For instance, some of the factors included distance from campus, outlet availability, noise level, and food options." NSU happens to be located in an area of South Florida where several other colleges and universities have campuses. So she needed to think about the types of study places on and around campus that would be good for her specific audience and their ability to reach these places. She thought about specific places like libraries, where students could find a nice quiet spot to study.

Further, because apps should have a quick navigation, Kamila thought a lot about the user's attention span. She didn't want to lose her audience with too many options on each screen. She wanted an app that would be easy to navigate, but she also wanted an app whose results gave users the information they needed and that would benefit them. Therefore, she was purposeful in her design choices for each of her app's screens, making sure they didn't overwhelm users but at the same time provided useful information.

Conclusion

As instructors of writing, we have an obligation to understand the connections writers make with texts, people, environments, and technologies, and how those connections help writers to understand and create knowledge. Essentially, helping students critically analyze a wide variety of connections is a large part of our job as instructors of writing. Kamila clearly demonstrated her rhetorical skills in paying attention to her audience and their locations of study. The assignment and activities described above offer students a chance to rhetorically reflect on the decisions they make as writers who live in a society that is saturated with mobile devices and on the connections that arise because of those decisions. As mentioned in the introduction to the book, technologies are texts that can be read and analyzed. In the process of doing such a reading and analysis, students develop the ability to transfer their skills from one text to the next.

Works Cited

de Souza e Silva, Adriana, and Jordan Frith. *Mobile Interfaces in Public Spaces: Locational Privacy, Control, and Urban Sociability*. New York: Routledge, 2012. Print.

Fagerjord, Anders. "Between Place and Interface: Designing Situated Sound for the iPhone." *Computers and Composition* 28.3 (2011): 255–63. Print.

"iOS Human Interface Guidelines." *Apple iOS Developer Library*. Apple, 5 Nov. 2015. Web. 9 Jan. 2013.

Owen, Martin. "From Individual Learning to Collaborative Learn-ing—Location, Fun, and Games: Place, Context, and Identity in Mobile Learning." *Innovative Mobile Learning: Techniques and Technologies*. Ed. Hokyoung Ryu and David Parsons. Hershey: Information Science Reference-IGI Global, 2009. 102–21. Print.

Pigg, Stacey. "Emplacing Mobile Composing Habits: A Study of Aca-demic Writing in Networked Social Spaces." *College Composition and Communication* 66.2 (2014): 250–75. Print.

Schmidt, Christopher. "The New Media Writer as Cartographer." *Computers and Composition* 28.4 (2011): 303–14. Print.

CHAPTER SIX

Critical Literacies in Mobile Social Games: Terms of Service, Privacy Policies, and Games Analysis

STEPHANIE VIE

University of Central Florida

Introduction and Theoretical Grounding

Candy Crush Saga. Hay Day. Hearthstone: Heroes of Warcraft. Worldwide, greater numbers of people are playing these mobile and socially networked games than ever before. *Candy Crush Saga*, for example, features 356 million unique individual players monthly and had revenues of $546 million USD in just the fourth quarter of 2015 alone (Grubb). *Hay Day* sees 6.02 million daily active users ("Most Popular Facebook Games") and *Hearthstone: Heroes of Warcraft* featured 25 million monthly players in February 2015, up from 10 million in March 2014 ("Number of *Hearthstone*"). These numbers are not unique to these three games, however. The global market for mobile games hit a new high of $24.5 billion USD in 2014, with mobile and socially networked games being played on both smartphones and tablet devices (Global Mobile Game Confederation). Global market research firm Newzoo estimates that mobile games will make up 38 percent of the global games market in 2017 (Global Mobile Game Confederation).

While these and other mobile games are immensely popular worldwide, educators don't always consider their potential pedagogical benefits. Scholars have written about the possibilities of teaching with other kinds of games—massively multiplayer online role-playing games like *World of Warcraft* (see Colby and Colby), edutainment or serious games like Valve's "Teach with Portals" program, and others (see the *Syllabus* journal 2015 special issue on teaching with and about games, for example [de Winter and Kocurek]). However, few scholars have examined the possibilities of bringing mobile games into the classroom. Perhaps this is because many people frequently dismiss mobile games as merely addictive, mindless puzzle games: in 2013, *Time* featured an article, "*Candy Crush Saga*: The Science Behind Our Addiction" while *The Guardian* in 2014 told us "this is what *Candy Crush Saga* does to your brain." These dismissals belie the fact that mobile games, like any other genre of video games, are sometimes:

- artistic, such as *Monument Valley*'s beautiful M. C. Escher–like landscapes
- major-award winners, like BAFTA winner *Thomas Was Alone*
- nsmedia interpretations of classic literature: *80 Days* take on s Verne's *Around the World in Eighty Days*
- ed on social justice, like *Papers, Please*, a game that places the role of an immigration officer and "reduce[s] people hers" (McElroy)

mobile games rely most heavily on permutations gameplay (like *Candy Crush Saga* or *Bejeweled*), ese games have much to offer instructors interested in ning students' critical literacies. That is, mobile social games allow educators to hone students' critical literacies through reading and understanding terms of service and privacy policies in mobile games as well as understanding data mining and transmission in mobile social games. Mobile social games, unlike most traditional console or PC games, are particularly well suited for these kinds of examinations because they feature extensive terms of service and privacy policies. Because they are frequently embedded within social networks, these games are important to examine as "rhetorically purposeful actants within a network" (Vie, "'You Are'," 173). This chapter presents an assignment that asks students to analyze rhetorical elements in terms of service and privacy policies as well as embedded sociality in popular mobile social games.

Descriptions of Assignments and/or Activities

This assignment was introduced in a graduate-level writing and rhetoric course (ENC 5930: Special Topics in Professional Writing) that was themed around the topic of social media. Students in this course read a variety of texts all focused on the central theme of social media in professional writing. Our goal was to survey the research and writing on social media that makes up ongoing conversations within the field of professional writing. After spending some time orienting themselves with ongoing scholarly conversations about social media broadly and within professional writing specifically, students composed their own research projects that helped them place their own intellectual work within the field.

This class was offered as a fully online course; as such, throughout the semester, students were asked to participate in weekly discussion board prompts in our course management system, Canvas. Later in the semester, with a firm theoretical grounding in place, students began to explore various subtopics in social media each week: virality and Internet memes, Twitter and microblogging, etc. During each week, students were prompted to engage with their classmates through their discussion prompts and create a discussion question that could encourage classmates to respond further. They were reminded weekly that an excellent discussion post would contribute to an ongoing conversation, would show audience awareness, would provide substantive examples, and would carefully respond to the week's readings using selected quotes, paraphrases, and/or summaries (with brief indications of author's name and page numbers for quotes/paraphrases). This was meant to encourage students in this fully online class to develop the kind of classroom camaraderie that often emerges in face-to-face courses but that is sometimes more difficult to encounter in an online class where students meet only virtually.

One week focused on mobile social games. Before getting started with their discussion prompt, students were asked to read the following three papers from conference proceedings:

◆ Richard van Meurs, "And Then You Wait: The Issue of Dead Time in Social Network Games." *Proceedings of the 2011 DiGRA [Digital Games Research Association] Conference: Think Design Play.* 14–17 Sept. 2011, Hilversum, Netherlands. N.p. Web. 2 May 2016.

◆ Elizabeth Losh, "In Polite Company: Rules of Play in Five Facebook Games." *ACE '08 Proceedings of the 2008 International Conference on Advances in Computer Entertainment Technology.* 3–5 Dec. 2008, Yokohama, Japan. New York: Association for Computing Machinery, 2008. 345–51. Web.

◆ Donghee Yvette Wohn, Cliff Lampe, Rick Wash, Nicole Ellison, and Jessica Vitak, "The 'S' in Social Network Games: Initiating, Maintaining, and Enhancing Relationships." *Proceedings of the 44th Hawaii International Conference on System Sciences.* 4–7 Jan. 2011, Kauai, HI. IEEE Computer Society: 2894–2903. Web. 2 May 2016.

They were also asked to watch a 2010 TED Talk by Jane McGonigal, author of *Reality Is Broken: Why Games Make Us Better and How They Can Change the World* (2011). These sources were chosen because they covered a variety of topics related to mobile gaming, such as dead time (what people do when they wait for lives to refill in *Candy Crush Saga* or plants to grow in *Hay Day*), rudeness and reciprocity (whether or not it's appropriate to ask one's Facebook friends for extra lives or to friend a mere acquaintance to get further in a game), and relationship management (deciding whether or not to block friends who post excessive game-related activity on one's Facebook News Feed). As conference proceedings, they were timely and relatively brief (seven to twelve pages); similarly, the twenty-minute McGonigal TED Talk offered multiple engaging ideas in a short amount of time.

After reading the three conference proceedings and watching the video, students were asked to respond to the discussion prompt and apply their knowledge by playing a mobile, socially networked game and reflecting on the gaming interface, particularly the privacy options offered to them. The week's discussion prompt was as follows:

Important: Before beginning this week's discussion, please log in to Facebook, navigate to the App Center, and play at least one social networking game for a while. When you first access the game, pay attention to the different options that are presented to you as far as terms of service documents, privacy policies, options for how the app will access your Facebook profile, and so on. The App Center is located on the left-hand side of the Facebook screen, below your profile, favorites, pages, and groups.

After playing your chosen social networking game(s) and reading van Meurs, Losh, and Wohn et al., discuss some of your experiences as you first accessed your game and played for a while.

◆ What did you notice about how the game discussed or presented the terms of service options to you?

◆ How about the privacy policies—were they presented to you and how?

◆ How did the game describe how it would access your Facebook profile or post on your behalf?

Relate your gameplay experience back to any of our earlier discussions/readings from class. For example, how can you relate your experience back to our discussions and readings about privacy and surveillance? About memes and virality? Do you see any space for social networking games in the professional writing sphere—for example, in marketing, public relations, and so on?

How did your gameplay relate to any of this week's readings—for example, van Meurs on dead time, Losh on politeness and reciprocity, or Wohn et al. on relationships and networks related to games? After experiencing your game and reading van Meurs, Losh, and Wohn et al., do you agree or disagree with Jane McGonigal that "to do real-world work, games are a powerful platform for change"? Why or why not?

Be sure to tell us what game(s) you played in your post! You may want to tweet about your game experience, too! If you tweet this week, don't forget to use the hashtag #enc5930.

Student Examples

Examining Terms of Service and Privacy Policy Documents

The following student examples illustrate how players of mobile and socially networked games can be prompted to pay attention to elements of games that we often dismiss or ignore—elements such as the terms of service, the privacy policies, and the impact on our networked relationships with friends in social networking sites. For example, Heather quickly made connections between the terms of service and privacy policy documents presented to her and the work she did as a consultant for Disney, writing safety-related documents and procedures that she figured few people wanted to read:

> When I signed in to play, I was immediately shown pictures of two of my Facebook friends and informed that 19 other friends play the game. In terms of what the game accesses from Facebook, the listing was "name, profile picture, gender, User ID, list of friends, and *any other information you made public*" (emphasis added). The Terms of Service was interesting to me because King, Inc., the maker of Candy Crush, is registered to the country of Malta, so I immediately tagged a Maltese friend in the comment regarding that point. I could already start to see how it's possible that "participants perceived three outcomes of their social game use on their social relationships: maintaining, initiating, and enhancing relationships" (Wohn 1).
>
> However, the other thing that struck me about the Terms of Service and Privacy Policy is that they are similar to the writing I do in that they are, I'm sure, carefully and thoroughly researched, they have to cover every possible scenario, they're vetted probably numerous times through the legal department, and yet they will not be read by 99.9% of the people playing this game.

Other students echoed Heather's response. Sandy, for instance, read through the terms of service and privacy policies for the game *CSI: Crime City* and noted that

> both of these documents are fairly massive in terms of what I imagine a typical user would be willing to read in order to play a social networking game. Both documents are hosted by

Ubisoft Forums, and the Terms of Service weighs in at 5,005 words with 11 major sections, while the Privacy Policy weighs in at 4,086 words with 8 major sections. [...] [T]hey seem to be designed to both provide and obscure information for the user.

Finally, Cory stated that when she chose to play *Bubble Epic*, "installing the game provided very little in terms of specifics regarding how *Bubble Epic* would use the data it collected (any and all publicly available information), and I'm assuming my experience with Facebook's Apps Center was typical." These students' responses resonated with the overall pulse of the class: Students were aware that terms of service and privacy policies for these kinds of games existed, but until actually logging in, looking for them, and critiquing them, they hadn't really thought critically about the rhetorical elements at play in the creation of these documents. That is, when students began breaking down the length and organization of these documents, as Sandy did, or considered their country of origin, as Heather did—or even thought about the lack of specifics provided, as Cory did—they began thinking of these documents not as monolithic, static genres but instead as rhetorical documents that reflect the values and ideals of their creators.

Considering Networked Relationships

Along with critiquing the rhetorical elements that go into the creation and dissemination of documents like privacy policies and terms of service, it is important to consider the impact of mobile gameplay on networked relationships. After all, many of these games feature elements of embedded sociality. Jesper Juul notes that this sociality means that in these games, "much of the interesting experience is not explicitly *in* the game, but is something that the players add to the game. . . . [T]he game takes on meaning from the existing relation between the players" (20, emphasis in original). Similarly, Elizabeth Losh illustrates that Facebook games often ask players to engage their Facebook friends in gameplay, but in doing so they risk "violating social norms about aggression, obligation, proximity, and privacy in ways that sacrifice real-world friendships" (350). Students were asked in this discussion board post to consider if sociality was embedded into their chosen game, and if so, describe some of the potential impacts on relationships in social networks as a result.

While Maia began her response by arguing that her chosen game, *Bubble Land*, "didn't have any social aspects within the gameplay itself," she moved on to describe aspects of the game that relied heavily on the friends networks (and personal information) available in Facebook:

> My Facebook profile picture was used to represent me within the game. In addition, at the completion of each level, my score was listed on a screen with the scores of other friends for that level accompanied by their Facebook profile images. Empty slots in the high-score screen were filled by my Facebook friends with the option to send them an invite to play the game. I could also click on a name and ask them to send me an extra life. In addition, in moving level to level, I was presented with all my friends in a customized *Bubble Land* screen that asked me to invite friends to play. This screen warned that there would be obstacles later in the game which could only be overcome with power-ups only available to me once I had invited a certain number of friends. Should I wish to win the game, I was counselled to "start early" in the invite process.
>
> It is clear that the game makers, through the invite process, were attempting to somewhat force contagion across my friends network. Of course, since I had consented to give them access to my friends network, they knew exactly who my friends were and lowered the barriers to inviting them to play by including invites at multiple junctures in the game. I also consented to allow them to post on my behalf in my News Feed, which I imagine they use to advertise the game.

The "forced contagion" Maia described relied on game players consenting to provide personal information (one's personal profile picture and list of networked friends) as well as consenting to the game posting on their behalf (such as through invitations or on the Facebook News Feed).

These automated responses are often described by other players as annoying, irritating, or otherwise impolite, and many players attempt to avoid posting such invitations or notifications if possible. Indeed, the responses can be overwhelming not only for the audience but also for the player herself; Karen described how she didn't even play one of her chosen games, *Rummy Rush*, because it became so overwhelming so quickly:

> *Rummy Rush* offered me a short tutorial and did warn me about that they would be collecting personal information and specifically indicated that they wanted my birthday. I wonder if they were seeking to match me with someone of similar age because this game actually matched me with a real life opponent. However, once the game actually started, I was bombarded with multiple boxes offering me hints, sounds, text messages reminding me what to do and so much input that I found it impossible to actually play so I left the game very quickly. I felt badly that a stranger somewhere in the world was sitting there waiting for me to play.

As students found, though, the games are often programmed to encourage as much sharing as possible—including sending invitations to play, posting on behalf of the player, and asking friends for help at critical junctures in the game. While Sandy began her discussion post about *CSI: Miami Heat Wave* by describing these elements of embedded sociality as "not intrusive," the rest of her response seems to indicate the opposite:

> At the top of the game screen there is a button labeled "Invite Friends," and at the bottom of the screen, I have the option of becoming "Neighbors" with other Facebook Friends who are currently playing the game. Additionally, as a new case loads, the following message appears on the screen: "Need more supplies? Visit your friends' labs and grab some." Later, after solving my first case, was prompted to invite more friends to join the game with the following message: "It's time to invite more friends to join—game on!" As I indicated earlier, this is not something that I am willing to do when playing games on Facebook. I find it annoying when I receive requests to play games, and I am unwilling to perform the same behavior that I find bothersome.

Other students stopped playing their games after the embedded sociality began to intrude too much (either intruding on their own lives or, they perceived, on their friends'). After she reached level 14 in *Candy Crush Saga*, Heather got stuck: "[I] had to either ask friends for a life or pay for more lives with a debit or credit card.

Since I didn't want to be entangled forever with the game, I did not ask friends for lives and also kept my game status private, which was an option." She continued by noting that the game continued to send her requests even though she hadn't actively engaged with friends during the game: "I am receiving requests for lives a week later from various friends who actively play the game. I haven't decided if I'll continue playing the game casually and connect with these friends, or if I'll delete the game in order to halt the updates and requests." However, not all students responded negatively toward the embedded sociality in their games; Derrick saw "inviting and challenging friends, sending and receiving gifts, [and] reading notifications and leader boards" as elements central to playing his chosen game, *Yu-Gi-Oh BAM!*, effectively. These social elements, he said, were there to "encourage you to learn and communicate with friends to help understand the game, learn new techniques, and build better decks."

Conclusion and Further Discussion

While mobile social games currently are poised to continue their massive growth and become an even-larger portion of the global market share, the assignment outlined here will still be relevant even if mobile social games someday experience a downturn. Privacy policies and terms of service documents govern much of our lives online, yet many of us fail to pay much attention to these important papers. When we click yes without reading the privacy policy on the portal to our health care provider, or we scroll rapidly past the terms of service so we can just install the newest copy of that software to our computer, we neglect to attend to the potential collection, dissemination, and use of our personal and private data. Even if we do attend to these documents, it is often difficult for us to understand their implications because they are couched in legalese, written at high reading levels, deliberately obfuscated, and generally uninviting (see Markel for a discussion of corporate misdirection in privacy policies and Vie, "Policies," for a discussion of Flesch-Kincaid readability scores in mobile social games). Furthermore, mobile social games are not just ubiquitous; they are changing how networks are formed and maintained.

Examining the rhetorical elements at play in the technological interfaces that permeate our lives—from mobile social games to websites, computer programs to navigational systems—is a crucial aspect of twenty-first-century digital literacies. Asking students to hone their skills in critical literacy vis-à-vis mobile social games is an important extension of the powerful work that scholars such as Cynthia L. Selfe and Richard J. Selfe Jr., Stuart Selber, and Anne Wysocki and Julia I. Jasken have begun in critical assessment of interfaces. As Wysocki and Jasken posit, "What do interfaces—and our teachings about how we and people in our classes should both shape and read them—encourage or allow us to see, and then, just as often, to forget to see?" (31). In our analyses of the interfaces of mobile social games, through looking at their privacy policies, terms of service, and networked relationships, we can focus on what we see, what we forget to see, and what we are encouraged to not see at all.

Acknowledgments

Thank you to Karen Arlington, Sandy Branham, Cory Bullinger, Maia Monet, Derrick Jicha, Heather Paquette, and Lissa Pompos Mansfield for generously allowing me to quote from their work in ENC 5930 (Spring 2014) at the University of Central Florida. Also, many thanks to Michael De Anda, Jennifer deWinter, Chris Hanson, and Carly Kocurek for comments on an early draft of this chapter.

Works Cited

Colby, Rebekah Schultz, and Richard Colby. "A Pedagogy of Play: Integrating Computer Games into the Writing Classroom." *Computers and Composition*, 25 (2008): 300–12. Print.

deWinter, Jennifer, and Carly A. Kocurek, eds. *Teaching with and about Games*. Spec. Issue of *Syllabus* 4.1 (2015): n. p. Web. 2 May 2015.

Global Mobile Game Confederation. "2015 Global Mobile Game Industry White Book." *GMGC*. Global Mobile Game Confederation, 2015. Web. 27 June 2015.

Grubb, Jeff. "King Is Sweet: *Candy Crush Saga* Giant Beats Earnings Estimates." *Games Beat*. Venture Beat, 12 Feb. 2015. Web. 27 June 2015.

Juul, Jesper. *A Casual Revolution: Reinventing Video Games and Their Players*. Cambridge: MIT P, 2010. Print.

Losh, Elizabeth. "In Polite Company: Rules of Play in Five Facebook Games." *ACE '08 Proceedings of the 2008 International Conference on Advances in Computer Entertainment Technology*. 3–5 Dec. 2008, Yokohama, Japan. New York: Association for Computing Machinery, 2008. 345–51. Web.

Markel, Mike. "The Rhetoric of Misdirection in Corporate Privacy Policy Statements." *Technical Communication Quarterly* 14.2 (2005): 197–214. Print.

McElroy, Justin. "Papers, Please Review: Mundane Tyranny." *Polygon* 9 Aug. 2013. Web. 27 June 2015.

McGonigal, Jane. "Gaming Can Make a Better World." *www.ted.com*. TED. Feb. 2010. Web. 2 May 2016.

———. *Reality Is Broken: Why Games Make Us Better and How They Can Change the World*. New York: Penguin, 2011. Print.

"Most Popular Facebook Games in May 2015, Based on Number of Daily Active Users (in Millions)." *Statista: The Statistics Portal*. Statistia, n.d. Web. 27 June 2015.

"Number of *Hearthstone: Heroes of Warcraft* Players Worldwide as of February 2015 (in Millions)." Statista: *The Statistics Portal*. Statistia, n.d. Web. 27 June 2015.

Selber, Stuart A. *Multiliteracies for a Digital Age*. Carbondale: Southern Illinois UP, 2004. Print.

Selfe, Cynthia L., and Richard J. Selfe, Jr. "The Politics of the Interface: Power and Its Exercise in Electronic Contact Zones." *College Composition and Communication* 45.4 (1994): 480–504. Print.

van Meurs, Richard. "And Then You Wait: The Issue of Dead Time in Social Network Games." *Proceedings of the 2011 DiGRA [Digital Games Research Association] Conference: Think Design Play*. 14–17 Sept. 2011, Hilversum, Netherlands. N.p. Web. 2 May 2016.

Vie, Stephanie. "Policies, Terms of Service, and Social Networking Games." *Video Game Policy: Production, Distribution, and Consumption*. Ed. Steven Conway and Jennifer deWinter. New York: Routledge, 2016. 54–67. Print.

————. "'You Are How You Play': Privacy Policies and Data Mining in Social Networking Games." *Computer Games and Technical Communication: Critical Methods and Applications at the Intersection.* Ed. Jennifer deWinter and Ryan M. Moeller. Burlington: Ashgate, 2014. 171–87. Print.

Wohn, Donghee Yvette, Cliff Lampe, Rick Wash, Nicole Ellison, and Jessica Vitak. "The 'S' in Social Network Games: Initiating, Maintaining, and Enhancing Relationships." *Proceedings of the 44th Hawaii International Conference on System Sciences.* 4–7 Jan. 2011, Kauai, HI. IEEE Computer Society: 2894–2903. Web. 2 May 2016.

Wysocki, Anne Frances, and Julia I. Jasken. "What Should Be an Unforgettable Face . . ." *Computers and Composition* 21.1 (2004): 29–48. Print.

II

WRITING *WITH* MOBILE TECHNOLOGIES

While Vie's chapter ends Part I, it serves as a good segue into Part II, especially since it explains an assignment that has students examining public documents. In the introduction to this book, I mentioned Jessie L. Moore and colleagues' 2010 study on first-year writers and their use of composing technologies. They concluded in their study that there was a disconnect between the types of writing students do in public life and the types of writing they do in the classroom (Moore et al. 10). They argued that students used a range of technologies, including mobile technologies, in order to participate in public life, but at the same time, did not use these same technologies in the classroom. As instructors of writing, Moore et al. contended that we have an obligation to bridge what students do in public life and what they do in the classroom. And for good reason: Mobile technologies offer many possibilities to writing students and instructors that should not be ignored in our classrooms.

For one, mobile technologies allow users to write on location more readily, and writing on location has proven to help students develop a deeper understanding of what it means to write rhetorically. In Chapter 5, I mentioned Christopher Schmidt's argument that writing is situated and that students need to see the place(s) where writing occurs both on the device and on location as integral to their learning experiences. In "Writing in the Wild: A Paradigm for Mobile Composition," Olin Bjork and John Pedro Schwartz contend that "students can better perceive—and learn to challenge—their social, cultural, and historical locations when they research, write, and even publish *on location*" (225). Assignments and activities that allow for authentic learning experiences on location have shown to have a lasting effect on learners and the communities in which these learners learn. For example, students can maintain and build connections with communities as well as make commitments within those communities. Nicole Brown contends that developing assignments based on mobile and location-aware technologies "can invite students to construct place-based, public discourse; to foster rhetorical and critical inquiry; to write as a social act; and to view writing as a means to participate in new media literacies" (241). More recently, Adam Stranz's study on wayfinding that "focuses on the movement of users in physical spaces and their goals in understanding and using those spaces" (165) argues that when students map their work via mobile technologies they can begin to connect daily practices to empirical research (175). In other words, they have the opportunity to be engaged in learning more about the places and spaces they visit.

In Chapter 12 of Part II, Ashley Holmes shows readers the kind of learning students can do when asked to use mobile technologies to compose on location. Holmes writes about a place-based mapping assignment in which students venture off campus to study public places, where they compose texts that help them (re)connect with their surroundings. Her chapter represents a pedagogy that the field of writing should embrace. That is, we need to find ways in which we get our students writing on location.

I realize that is easier said than done as many colleges and universities do not have the necessary resources, policies, and support in place to do so. Yet, even if colleges and universities do not have the infrastructure in place to support learners in communities off campus, there are ways in which mobile technologies can be utilized on campus in order to help students understand writing on location. Jessica Schreyer and Casey McArdle's chapters begin Part II because they both feature students using mobile technologies on their campuses. Similar to Jordan Frith's assignment in "Writing Space: Examining the Potential of Location-Based Composition," which has students using Foursquare on campus to develop texts that "become part of the social layer comprising the hybrid space of Foursquare users," the assignments in Chapters 7 and 8 also "provide students with a deeper understanding of the potentials of location-based composition" (52). These two chapters serve as examples of what we can do as one of the steps

we can take between not using mobile technologies and fully using them off campus.

Other chapters in Part II consider the use of mobile technologies as they relate to writing portfolios (Chapter 9), online writing classrooms (Chapter 10), and developing writing pedagogy
that makes understanding a course easier (Chapter 11). These
chapters feature the voices of faculty members who are new to
mobile technologies as well as those who are quite familiar and
comfortable in their tech abilities. Chapter 11, in particular,
highlights ways in which instructors can effectively respond to
students using mobile videocapturing. And, in Chapter 13, Randy
Nichols and Josephine Walwema tackle digital aggregation and
curation that calls into question many of the traditional print-
centric practices that our field and institutions have relied on to
the expense of our students.

Finally, the book ends with Mike Tardiff and Minh-Tam
Nguyen's chapter on assigning literacy narratives that treat mobile
technologies, such as a smartphone, like identity texts. Such a
chapter reflects on the power of storytelling and how our mobile
devices are containers of artifacts as unique as fingerprints. This
is a fitting way to end a book that tells the pedagogical stories
of many in our field who have come to realize the value of using
mobile technologies in our writing classrooms.

Works Cited

Bjork, Olin, and John Pedro Schwartz. "Writing in the Wild: A Paradigm
for Mobile Composition." Kimme Hea 223–37.

Brown, Nicole R. "Metaphors of Mobility: Emerging Spaces for Rhetorical Reflection and Communication." Kimme Hea 239–52.

Frith, Jordan. "Writing Space: Examining the Potential of Location-
Based Composition." *Computers and Composition* 37 (2015):
44–54. Print.

Kimme Hea, Amy C., ed. *Going Wireless: A Critical Exploration of
Wireless and Mobile Technologies for Composition Teachers and
Researchers*. Cresskill: Hampton, 2009. Print.

Moore, Jessie L., et al. "Revisualizing Composition: How First-Year Writers Use Composing Technologies." *Computers and Composition* 39 (2016): 1–13. Print.

Strantz, Adam. "Wayfinding in Global Contexts—Mapping Localized Research Practices with Mobile Devices." *Computers and Composition* 38 (2015): 164–76. Print.

CHAPTER SEVEN

Composing and Researching on the Move

JESSICA SCHREYER
University of Dubuque

When I began writing with online technologies, I was using dial-up Internet on a desktop computer. My friends and I would write back and forth to each other late in the night in instant messenger or chat rooms, sharing the events of our day and developing elaborate collaboratively written stories. At the time, I never gave much thought to the space I was writing from, probably because it was always from the desk located in the corner of the living room. I also didn't give much consideration to the digital context of our writing. But the lessons I learned from those experiences have resonated often as I've incorporated a variety of technologies into my classes and assignments. The digital writing environment changed my composing process and encouraged me to write collaboratively for the first time. Years later, I realized that despite my efforts to incorporate digital environments into my FYC assignments, I was ignoring the technology students used most and knew best: their mobile devices. I wondered if meeting students where they were might encourage more engagement and interactivity in the writing and research process, or at the very least, encourage them to write more often, since more of them had access to a phone than a pencil at any given class session. As I developed the mobile assignment described in this chapter, I wanted to explore the potential of mobile devices and mobile environments to engage students in composing processes and organizing their research. I also wanted to understand more about how learning while they were on the move, using their devices, was influencing their perspective on writing.

The mobile assignment was assigned in a first-year composition course (FYC) at a small, liberal arts university. Many of the students take developmental courses; about one-third of the students take basic writing prior to FYC. The students generally have widely varying writing and technology experiences. My expectation, based on my informal student surveys and teaching experience at the university, was that all of the students would have a basic knowledge of the functionality of mobile devices, and that some would be active users of their devices in a variety of ways beyond calls, texts, or social networking. The assignment addresses several of the course's learning outcomes, which are aligned with the Council of Writing Program Administrators' Outcomes for First-Year Composition. In particular, this assignment addresses these outcomes:

- ◆ Use writing and reading for inquiry, learning, thinking, and communicating [Critical Thinking, Reading, and Writing]

- ◆ Develop flexible strategies for generating, revising, editing, and proof-reading [Processes]

- ◆ Understand the collaborative and social aspects of writing processes [Processes]

- ◆ Understand and exploit the differences in the rhetorical strategies and in the affordances available for both print and electronic composing processes and texts [Composing in Electronic Environments] (Council of Writing Program Administrators)

While this assignment was created with FYC in mind, it could be modified in countless ways to engage students at more advanced levels in the curriculum.

Theoretical Grounding for the Assignment and Activities

Mobile devices enhance the capability to compose new media texts in digital environments while on the move: "The mobile landscape affords the teacher and student the opportunity to create, view, compose, construct, and participate in learning environments that are portable, interactive, and individually created" (Martin and Meloncon Posner 295). The emphasis on mobile technology having flexibility between devices and platforms, networking ability, and portability was key to the development of the project described in this chapter.

This project grew out of my desire to more fully utilize opportunities presented through mobile learning. Access to computer labs during class times are few and far between at my university, yet almost all of my students had technology of their own that was sitting in their backpacks or that they were attempting to hide from my view during class. Each semester, I noticed more students using tablets in addition to their smartphones, and virtually all of the emails sent by students were now tagged as coming from their smartphones. I knew it was time to get serious about researching and experimenting to see if mobile writing processes could benefit writers in my classes. Years prior to the proliferation of mobile devices, Selfe emphasized how technology was mediating our experiences and opportunities, and encouraged literacy professionals to consider equitable ways to incorporate technological literacy into educational environments (*Technology and Literacy in the 21st Century*). This call was made even more manageable with the introduction of low-cost mobile devices.

Learning with mobile devices is happening in other areas of our students' lives; I needed to find out how my students were using their devices. After some initial discussions in class, it was obvious that my students were using the technology primarily as an informal tool, but some were completing assignments or doing research with them. Woodcock, Middleton, and Nortcliffe explain:

> Increasingly students own smartphones and, as with other aspects of their lives, they will turn to them as a matter of course to enhance their experience of learning . . . once students begin using their smartphones for learning they begin to appreciate the benefits and the further possibilities that exist within their current frame of reference. (13)

Some students already realize the benefits of using mobile devices to improve their learning. Plus, and perhaps most important, they are already composing using mobile devices; initial findings from a Writing in Digital Environments Research Center study noted that "cell phones have become a prominent writing technology for students for self-sponsored writing" (4). By encouraging students to use their mobile devices' full capabilities as pocket computers, professors can help students take advantage of the device's camera, storage space, search capabilities, and collaborative functions to tell a story about the world around them. Teachers can take advantage of this interest and encourage students to brainstorm, collect information, and even write while they are on the move in their daily lives. This can challenge them to consider their composing practices and improve their previous understandings of authorship, collaboration, purpose, voice, and audience, among other things. The most compelling aspect of the research that motivated me to add opportunities for mobile learning to my class was that students were already composing in these mobile environments. In fact, they were composing almost nonstop on their smartphones. However, much of this writing was not valued in the academic sphere and most students did not consider what they were doing to be writing at all. I decided that understanding mobile composing was not just something I should consider as a way to enhance my teaching or excite my students, but rather that teaching students to be more aware of how digital composing environments influence their composing processes may be necessary. McHaney explained:

> Educators should be looking for opportunities to incorporate new media into their classes and promote its use. After all, students will be using these tools and other ones like them in both their careers and their personal lives. Most students, in fact, already embrace new media and use it in their daily lives, and they expect to use it in their educational experiences. It is important to create course pedagogy that ensures our students will not be left behind. (201)

McHaney suggested that many students expect to have opportunities to write using new media technologies, as well as to improve their understanding of digital literacies, but they are often unaware of the complicated contexts of these types of literacies. By encouraging students to explore how new media shapes their lives or their viewpoints in a way that would be difficult for many to examine on their own, school can prove invaluable. Students may be able to teach themselves how to use an app effectively as they research, but they may be less able to understand the complexities of how their use of the app during the composing process has influenced the development of their text and thoughts.

The assignment that will be explained in the next section was crafted with four key pedagogical ideas in mind about the nature of mobile devices in education: they are ubiquitous and can be useful to student learning, they pair well with collaborative writing activities, they allow for experiences that create new understandings of literacy, and they allow students to consider place in unique ways.

First, I wanted to treat mobile devices as ubiquitous and assist students to use them for educational purposes. Almost all students at the university have a mobile device, and these devices influence how students engage in the environment around them and how they engage with other people in that environment. The assignment asked students to actively participate in and consider the communities they write to and about using these ubiquitous devices. While students were already using the devices for varied personal and academic reasons, the assignment asked them to be very intentional and organized in their use of the mobile device for collecting ideas and data, brainstorming, drafting, and even peer review.

Second, I wanted to emphasize that the collaborative aspect of writing could be created within the mobile environment, just as we created it within our classroom. Students engaged in collaboration through face-to-face discussions with peers while also working on their mobile devices within the apps. By collaborating in these diverse environments, students can better understand how there are varied methods available for composing and collecting information. It also takes some of the frustration out of group work, because they no longer have to be in the same place at the same time; while they are researching and collecting information together, they are still composing more individually. This aspect is one that could be adapted as desired depending on the teacher's goals for the class or assignment.

Third, I wanted to engage students who have varied literacies and reinforce that digital literacies can be valuable. Students can use apps on their devices to annotate, draw, or comment on diverse types of texts electronically, and they can also use a range of types of information, like photographs and video more seamlessly with mobile technology. Allowing students to integrate their own audio recordings, photographs, and text within mobile apps can help encourage them to use their various literacies for new purposes in the classroom.

Finally, mobile devices offer a unique way for students to consider place. Place is both figuratively and literally important to the compositions that students create. Students often need assistance to help them better understand how they must position themselves as writers within a place and how to more deeply consider the place when they write. Dobrin (2001) noted, "Writing does not begin in the self; rather, writers begin writing by situating themselves, by putting themselves in a place, by locating within a space" (18). There is a wealth of research about the value of studying place in composition; writing studies scholars, particularly Weisser and Dobrin, have examined this through the lens of ecocomposition. In Chapter 12, Ashley Holmes provides a detailed look at the ecocomposition scholarship and describes how studying place can be connected to students' learning with mobile devices. Following her review of the literature, she noted:

> Part of what I think leads to these moments of potential learning and growth through spatial shock is for students to physically engage with places in their local communities: locations that are new to them or approaching familiar places with an unfamiliar or critical perspective.

This idea of developing a new perspective about and within a familiar place was foregrounded in the project described in this chapter.

Description of Assignment and Activities

My mobile composing assignment invited students to use their devices to do research and writing about varied university spaces where they study, debate, exercise, compete, date, eat, sleep, and play (see Figure 7.1). These spaces and activities help situ-

For this project, you will be observing and documenting a place on campus that helps you define what it means to be a part of the university community. Your final new media project will combine text and visuals to help complete the statement: "*Being a part of the Spartan community means_____.*"
How you choose to complete this statement is entirely up to you. You may choose to focus on a place itself, or you may choose to focus more on the people who are joining together within that place. For instance, possible answers include: *Being a part of the Spartan community means the Butler Hall stage awaits its next star* or *Being a part of the Spartan community means being one of an elite group of pilots.*

Your project may be completed in a wide variety of ways, such as the construction of a website, development of a Prezi, or creation of a video. You should feel free to propose your own ideas as well since the final product is up to your discretion as long as it is approved in advance. We will discuss in class what types of text, visuals, and citations are needed.
We will go through several steps in our investigation.

1. Learning how to use the apps and touring the Heritage Center to discuss how to conduct the research activities (whole class)
2. Meeting in small groups after determining common places on campus you want to document (collaborative groups)
3. Investigating and documenting places over the course of a week using apps (your investigation will be individual, and your documentation will be collaborative within the shared Evernote notebooks)
4. Discussing findings (whole class and collaborative groups)
5. Creating a new media project (individual) with peer critiques (collaborative)
6. Sharing final project (whole class)

FIGURE 7.1. *Project overview.*

ate people within the community in different ways. With this in mind, the students were asked to describe and define what being a part of the "Spartan" (our university mascot) community means to them. Students spend a lot of time on campus engaged in a wide variety of activities but most of them do not intentionally observe or analyze their environment and the people in it. This assignment called on them to investigate and observe the campus in an active way, rather than as passive participants. By asking them to study this place, they gained a better understanding of what the university community offers to them, and what they might contribute to it. They were able to consider the spaces they write in, as well as how being within those spaces influences their writing. Students captured and shared moments in their day using text, audio, and photographs. Then they used this documentation to consider how to describe what it means to be a member of the university community.

When assigning a project like this, it is essential that all students have access to devices and Internet. We have free campus-wide Wi-Fi. To avoid making whether they own a device public information, I did a survey at the beginning of the semester to determine what technology students own and also what technology they have access to in other ways. Since we do not require students to have a device, I have several additional devices should any student not have access to one; notably, in the past two years, every student had a personal smartphone or tablet. Finally, because our students are not required to own a device, much less any specific device, I chose applications that are available for both Android and Apple products.

To launch the assignment, during a class session I asked students to consider the various places on campus that they visited on a regular basis and to talk about what they do and who they interact with there. Since most of them were first-year students, they are often acutely aware of the ways they are adapting to the college environment. They may not, however, think much about how their presence can change the community. As we began brainstorming this concept, I asked students to reflect on the statement: "*Being a part of the Spartan community means* _____." This open-ended prompt allowed students to research and craft their project in a variety of ways, but it also began a conversation about their place within the environment and their evolving identity within the university landscape. I learned quickly that some students felt little connection with the campus itself while others' lives had already become intricately connected to it. Some knew their way around every corner of campus, while others were only aware of how to get from their residence hall to the cafeteria and classes. After introductory freewriting and discussions in class, I challenged students to use their mobile devices to document unique aspects of the campus community. What this meant varied from person to person, but everyone was able to identify a place on campus they wanted to explore. Documenting these places and events was the catalyst for future conversations about being a member of the campus community both online and in class.

While I wanted to leave the overall approach to the assignment and activities up to the students, I offered some suggestions to help them conceptualize several different ways they might examine the community and their participation within it. One example invited them to consider the campus as a whole and how students form communities within a physical location. This was exemplified within a new performing arts center and student union, The Heritage Center. This center is meant to be a campus hub. It is also a place where students and visitors can learn how students have changed, and stayed the same, throughout the university's history. This history is presented in an assortment of ways throughout the building. For instance, there is a large archival exhibit in the main entrance of the building. In the exhibit, there are lettermen jackets, newspaper clippings about successful Spartans, and historical documents. This exhibit helps connect current students with past students, and makes them understand they are part of a community with a long tradition. There is also an art gallery, which frequently features the work of individuals on campus, including students. This exhibit shows that students are considered active members of the campus community. As a class, we walked through the building and examined the artifacts. Then we talked about how they are representative of what it has meant to be a Spartan over time. We discussed the multimodal features of the displays, types of information they might collect, and ways that they might use visual, audio, and textual features like they see in the exhibits within their projects. This visit created some cohesion to the assignment as students formed an understanding of the varied ways one may identify as part of the university community, and how the campus spaces have evolved over time to bring Spartans together.

After these discussions and the Heritage site visit, students commented that they were eager to begin their own research. During class discussions and in online journals, students talked about their readiness to attempt to use their mobile devices to do some of the work, but some of them stated they were uncertain about the device's capability as an academic tool. I asked them to set aside any concerns and told them we would talk more after they completed their first introductory research. We discussed the basic capabilities of most mobile devices. We found that their devices, as expected, shared similar features, such as a camera with video and photo editing software and a web browser with search capabilities. These devices also have a variety of app possibilities that can be used to enhance the value of mobile learning in composition. Very few of my students, however, had used apps in their academic pursuits beyond the calendar functionality.

Before beginning to do the research, we needed to make a plan for sharing, storing, and organizing their information. After discussing the available technology, I introduced students to the apps they would use to gather information to support their multimodal writing. The technologies used for the assignment were mobile devices with cameras and two applications: Evernote and Skitch. I chose apps that would mirror some of the learning activities we were doing in class, like keeping writing notebooks and commenting directly on others' work. I utilized Evernote and Skitch since they are free, flexible, and robust; available for Android and Apple; and easy to learn. These apps are also particularly useful because not only are they available on mobile, but they are also available for desktop, thereby allowing students to use them in varied ways at different times to increase their flexibility. Evernote, like other database apps, helps users create, manage, and interact with varied types of information—files, webpages, pictures, and more—all in one place. It allows users to easily share notebooks and maintain content in the cloud. Skitch works in tandem with Evernote, and allows users to annotate pictures or documents.

While this assignment focused on Evernote and Skitch, it would be very adaptable to other mobile resources. The main focus is on having students observe the world around them while in those spaces and systematically capture and reflect on that information on their mobile devices. Other potential resources include Dropbox, which allows students to share and store files in the cloud. Twitter could be an interesting way to post ideas or photographs quickly that could spark conversations among the students. They would be able to post content, including photos or thoughts, quickly for a broad audience. Pinterest allows users to "pin" information to a virtual bulletin board and is another quick and easy way for students to gather and share information or ideas. Dropbox, Twitter, and Pinterest would be especially useful for my students because they are available both for mobile and for a desktop computer, allowing students to participate with these digital tools in varied ways. Surely, new and advanced resources will develop to make this collaboration even more seamless between students.

Following our initial conversations, we did an in-class activity so students could find a group that was interested in observing similar locations on campus. The group was then responsible for documenting that place using video, photographs, observation notes, and audio. They did not have to go simultaneously; rather they shared the files within an Evernote notebook. Before the next class period, I asked students to explore the varied items entered in Evernote (see Figures 7.2–7.4). They were to focus particularly on the notebook for their group, and do a quick tour of the other groups' notebooks, and add to those notebooks as desired. During our next class period, we viewed the notebooks together and discussed what the students found out about the places through their investigations. We discussed what their research revealed about the people and their relationship to the environments being studied. For instance, within one notebook, we found that one student focused on the food, one on the artwork, and one on backpacks. It was fascinating to hear students talk about what this varied perspective revealed about the places they observed and about the people of the campus community.

During these discussions, the benefits of Evernote emerged. Evernote allows for a variety of types of electronic notes including text, images, or even drawings. Skitch takes this even further. With Skitch, a student could take a photograph and then annotate it with words, arrows, or other markings. Then, students could upload it into a shared notebook in Evernote, allowing other students to view it. Students could also look at another student's picture and annotate it to provide feedback to the peer. By viewing each other's annotated photographs, students began to consider what others focus on within their environment. Further, students created documents in the same notebook to consider new perspectives on what others had explored. By having a notebook filled with text, audio, video, and even Web clippings, students engaged with a variety of types of information about the same topic. These notes allowed them to brainstorm their definition and explanation about what it means to be a Spartan and how this may be very different depending on the person and the perspective they took within a place. I asked students to continue adding to the various notebooks if they visited other sites on campus, but to remain focused on their group's notebook. This allowed a more robust view of their individual perspectives because it highlighted their places over a weeklong period.

Figure 7.2 shows a view of the notebook list within the Evernote app. A list of all notebooks shared among the class members was available. Sorting can be simplified by asking students to start the notebook name with the course abbreviation. Figure 7.3 shows an example of how the shared notebook was displayed for group members. It can be sorted several different ways. In the sample, all of the notes in the notebook are sorted by title, and the tags created are listed. When photos were available, they were previewed on the right. Figure 7.4 displays a note within the shared notebook. It contains photos and text that describes the photo tour shared within the note. At the top, the viewer can see details including the name of the notebook, the number of people who can view the note, and how many tags the writer has assigned.

I encouraged students to continue generating new content through their observations and continue documentation using their mobile devices, while also continuing conversations with their classmates about their investigations. These ongoing conversations helped them learn how others view what it means to be a member of the Spartan community. Students began to understand how the material conditions of campus changed how they define themselves within the campus environment. Some students—particularly those from large cities or rural backgrounds—began to feel like they could be a part of a type of environment different from what they were accustomed to at home.

After a little over a week of this documentation, we had gathered lots of information, and I asked students to use all of the resources to start constructing a clear vision for themselves through writing. It was then time for students to use their mobile sources in their new media project. They integrated text with other evidence to support their claim. They were free to integrate their own notes or notes of their classmates, which gave us an

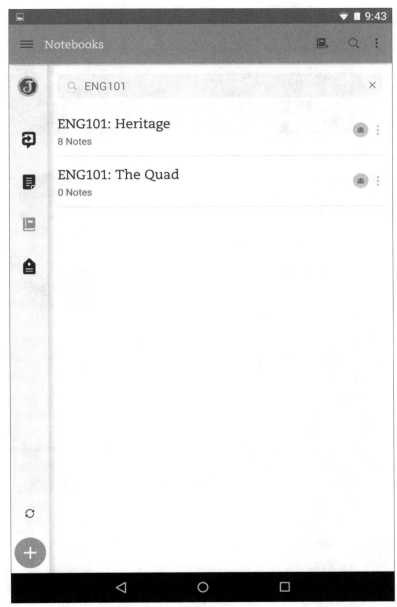

Figure 7.2. *App displaying shared notebook list.*

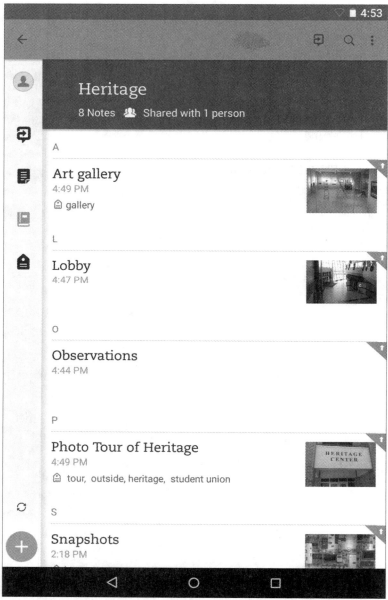

FIGURE 7.3. *App displaying shared notebook notes alphabetically with tags.*

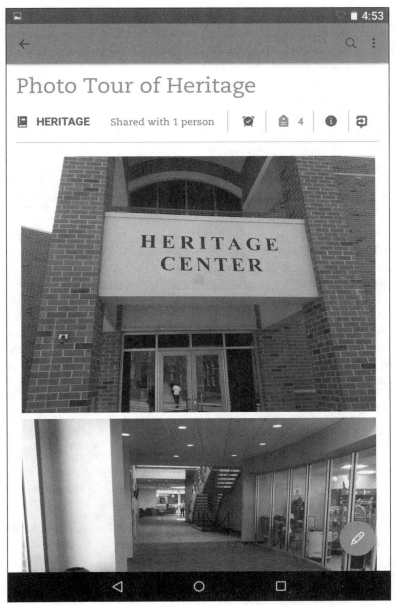

FIGURE 7.4. *App displaying shared note contents.*

opportunity to discuss giving others credit for their ideas and work. Each shared Evernote note and notebook has a unique URL, so students were able to cite these documents easily. With limited time for in-class review, we decided to utilize Evernote in the process. They posted their drafts or links to their projects in the notebooks and their peers reviewed them prior to class. Throughout the course of this assignment, there were various other ways to engage students in the classroom and through mobile devices to continue collaborating with each other and generating ideas for content.

Discussion

By documenting, writing, and discussing the locations and com-munities they participate in, students can appreciate how their writing is influenced by their environment and how they, in turn, influence the environment as well. This mobile assignment was intended to help students reconsider how, when, and why they write, as well as who they are writing with and for. This process reaffirmed Bjork and Schwartz's contention that mobile assign-ments may allow students to understand their writing in a new way:

> Mobile composition helps students understand the interde-pendency of agency and material structures by confronting students with the effects of these structures and by connecting writing assignments to spaces and technologies. When using a tablet computer to document social interactions at an event, for example, a student may begin to see that writing assignments, spaces, and technologies are mutually determining. This insight may lead to further realization that the material conditions shaping what students write and who they become through writing are fluid and changeable. (225)

Students were encouraged to document and write about the spaces they use and to understand how these environments influence their lives; students also began to consider how readily they move between their physical and digital spaces. In fact, these environ-ments may be so blurred that there is often no differentiating between them. Students engage in digital environments when surrounded by others in their physical environment. They also use digital environments to help plan and change things in the physical environments. Therefore, at least in theory, these environments have merged. By inviting online environments into the class, professors can create accessible and collaborative spaces capable of engaging and energizing students with varied literacies in new and exciting ways.

My hope is that online writing environments can help extend my classroom beyond a physical place. My students have explained that they like to be engaged as a part of an interactive group of learners. They are often willing to try new ways of learning, and because they also want to be connected and tethered to their devices, mobile environments are a logical place to begin. The more I can understand how they interact with and create their environment using these devices, the better I can enhance and adapt my pedagogy. I'm optimistic about the value of mobile devices in education and our lives. Ultimately, I hope we can find a balance that reinforces the importance of face-to-face communication while accepting and honoring the desire for online connectivity.

Works Cited

Bjork, Olin and John Pedro Schwartz. "Writing in the Wild: A Paradigm for Mobile Composition." Kimme Hea 223–37.

Council of Writing Program Administrators. "WPA Outcomes Statement for First-Year Composition." *Council of Writing Program Administrators*. CWPA, 2008. Web. 27 Dec. 2013.

Dobrin, Sidney I. "Writing Takes Place." *Ecocomposition: Theoretical and Pedagogical Approaches*. Ed. Christian R. Weisser and Sidney I. Dobrin. Albany: State U of New York P, 2001. 11–25. Print.

Kimme Hea, Amy C., ed. *Going Wireless: A Critical Exploration of Wireless and Mobile Technologies for Composition Teachers and Researchers*. Cresskill: Hampton, 2009. Print.

Martin, Beth, and Lisa Meloncon Posner. "Dancing with the iPod: Exploring the Mobile Landscape of Composition Studies." Kimme Hea 289–307.

McHaney, Roger. *The New Digital Shoreline: How Web 2.0 and Millennials Are Revolutionizing Higher Education.* Sterling: Stylus, 2011. Print.

Selfe, Cynthia L. *Technology and Literacy in the 21st Century: The Importance of Paying Attention.* Carbondale: Southern Illinois UP, 1999. Print.

Woodcock, Ben, Andrew Middleton, and Anne Nortcliffe. "Considering the Smartphone Learner: An Investigation into Student Interest in the Use of Personal Technology to Enhance Their Learning." *Student Engagement and Experience Journal* 1.1 (2012): 1–15. Print.

Writing in Digital Environments Research Center. "The Writing Lives of College Students." *Michigan State U.* WIDE Research Center, 7 Sep. 2010. Web. 4 Jan. 2014.

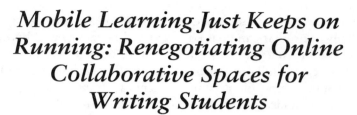

CHAPTER EIGHT

Mobile Learning Just Keeps on Running: Renegotiating Online Collaborative Spaces for Writing Students

CASEY R. MCARDLE
Michigan State University

I am fortunate to teach in what are called REAL Classrooms, which stands for Rooms Engaged for Active Learning. There are tables designed to seat about six students along with adapters in the tables to connect digital technology to the monitors above the table—this also allows me to pull up any student device connected and place it on all of the screens in the room with a push of a button on my podium. There are no desktops or built-in computers for the students, so they must bring in their own devices. I have taught in several learning labs fitted with rows of seats connected to built-in desktops, but this room gives me the chance to see what every student and their group is doing and how they are teaching one another. Consequently, a few semesters ago I noticed over the course of the first few weeks that a quarter of the students were using their smartphones and tablets to access our peer review site Eli Review as well as the class Google Site. It soon became clear that it was not about computing power but about access and mobility. Students were composing research projects, conducting peer review, researching their topics, and collaborating via mobile technologies.

To situate this chapter within the discussion of this book, it is important to note that as classrooms begin to move into the Post-PC era, mobile technologies are affording students the chance to compose, collaborate, and redefine the spaces of the writing classroom. And when "we consider how quickly the move to the Post-PC era is happening, it is imperative that institutions of higher education pay close attention" (Penny et al.). The normal confines of the face-to-face classroom are being reimagined in online spaces that can be used to expand pedagogy and knowledge-making environments managed and guided by instructors as students create and disseminate content. With each new semester of teaching composition classes, students are focusing less on PC-based communication and moving more toward mobile devices.

To capitalize on this idea of mobility, I had students participate in several small activities outside of class to engage with the campus community as well as share their own community with the class. Three of the activities that I created to take advantage of this mobility included:

1. Uploading pictures from various places on campus to their class blog to better understand the rhetorical appeals

2. Utilizing Twitter as a means to research the MSU campus and current events

3. Using mobile technologies to collaborate in groups as a means to create a text that represents what the course is and what it means to students in terms of their education at MSU and its impact on their professional spaces

These activities were part of larger assignments for the class, but they can also be adapted to various writing levels and classes that emphasize culture, digital spaces, digital writing, and multimodal composition. In this chapter, I discuss the larger assignments and the three activities.

Theoretical Grounding for the Assignments and Activities

For this chapter, and for this collected edition, it is important to note that mobile technologies are tied to mobile learning (m-learning) and that such a definition can be malleable. First, *m-learning* can be defined as "the efficient and effective use of wireless and digital devices and technologies to enhance learners' individual outcomes during participation in learning activities" (Rossing et. al. 2). This learning is impacted by the hardware: "computer and communication devices include . . . notebooks that provide [a] relatively small level of mobility . . . [but these] devices are suitable only for transfers. Better mobility is given by [a] smartphone or tablet" (Fojtik 342). Much like some of the authors in this collection, I define mobile technologies as smartphones and tablets that can access Wi-Fi and cell towers to connect to the Internet at any time and are personal—such a definition is tied with the one stated in the introduction of this book.

While my personal smartphone has been more of a way for me to send and receive email, conduct research, check my calendar, and video conference, the thought of using it as an academic device solely for the purpose of classroom engagement had not occurred to me until observing my students using their smartphones and tablets for that very function. While I would normally tell students to put their phones or tablets away at the beginning of class as I saw them as a distraction, it was soon clear that they had become the primary means by which some students were completing tasks for the class. There is no actual paper in my class as all writing and artifacts are completed and stored online, so by keeping everything in the cloud I am doing two things: (1) specifically pushing for students to be able to access all of their writing and research for every assignment at all times; and (2) promoting a greener approach to scholarship that will hopefully transcend their academic space once they graduate from the university (even the US government seeks to reduce costs by encouraging schools to transition from paper-based to digital textbooks within the next five years) (Hefling).

Upon entering our classroom, students set their bags down and immediately begin engaging in their reviews, writing, and collaborating while they are engaged with their smartphones and tablets by pulling up examples to show the members of their group or the nearest classmates. Seeing this unique use of mobile technology gave me the idea of using such technologies for specific activities and to see if students would feel more comfortable down the line using them for larger projects. The goals for these activities were three:

1. Demonstrate an understanding of research and the importance of documenting and analyzing research

2. Demonstrate the ability to conduct research and use it to support your understanding of the rhetorical appeals

3. Collaborate with students to create a text indicative of the class community as well as those involved with the assignment

Through written reflections and meeting with other students, they began to see themselves as writers creating artifacts that went beyond typographical texts and that they can create something with a rhetorical purpose that is not relegated solely to words.

In the book *Writing New Media: Theory and Applications for Expanding the Teaching of Composition*, Anne Wysocki believes that New Media is predicated on the wide range of materiality concerning texts and their rhetorical purposes. She also states that New Media "needs to be informed by what writing teachers know, precisely because writing teachers focus specifically on texts and how situated people (learn how to) use them to make things happen" (Wysocki et al. 5). Such an emphasis on understanding texts, be they typographical or visual or something different altogether, can serve as the basic fulcrum for understanding the importance of technology both in and out of the classroom. This is at the heart of my pedagogy and the activities and assignments I discuss in this chapter. The art of composition is not solely relegated to the written essay; it has expanded beyond such constraints. However, access can still be restricted depending on the hardware employed by instructors as well as financial constraints placed on students: Where books were once too expensive for students to purchase for a class, now the very technology to succeed on or off campus in any class can limit a student's access to information and learning. As more students decide to spend funds on mobile technologies that are less expensive than their laptop and desktop counterparts, the ability to compose and collaborate is becoming ubiquitous. Their phones and tablets are not just for personal use anymore; they can be used for academic and professional purposes as well.

Johndan Johnson-Eilola's book *Datacloud: Toward a New Theory of Online Work* notes that knowledge work is typically concerned with the production of information, as distinct from the production of material goods, and that many of us do not just work with information, we inhabit it (Johnson-Eiola 3–4). We as instructors inhabit the assignments we provide for our students and they in turn inhabit the very texts they create as a result of the assignment. Writing in online spaces has changed not only the way we teach, but also the way we write and think. Modeling the use of technology in and out of the classroom, either purposefully or not, impacts the manner in which students view digital technology as tools and as facilitators of knowledge-making. A recent study examined the behavior and readiness of students and faculty with concern for using mobile technologies for m-learning and found that students were far more open and accepting than the faculty (Cheon et al. 1062).

> It is important for practitioners and researchers to understand what makes end-users accept or resist m-learning and how to improve user acceptance of m-learning. The findings indicated that higher education institutions should implement strategic efforts to build m-learning implementation plans, such as design guidelines, development phases and articulating norms, and considering the current level of students' readiness. (Cheon et al. 1062)

The study also suggests "a new system should be within students' comfort level of using mobile devices in order to ensure their confidence. Since faculty members significantly influence students' use of m-learning, faculty needs to be more familiar with m-learning" (Cheon et al. 1062). Our students mimic what they see modeled by educators, and if I can provide a fertile environment in which students can use mobile technologies to enhance and achieve course goals, I can increase their chances of feeling far more comfortable using such technologies for academic and professional ends.

As real-world communities and online communities are supported by digital technologies, it is important to understand the impact and influence of mobile technologies that allow such communities to also become mobile. For example:

> We learn across space as we take ideas and learning resources gained in one location and apply or develop them in another. We learn across time, by revisiting knowledge that was gained earlier in a different context, and more broadly, through ideas

and strategies gained in early years providing a framework for a lifetime of learning. We move from topic to topic, managing a range of personal learning projects, rather than following a single curriculum. (Sharples, Taylor, and Vavoula 2)

For writing classrooms, the world has become both our textbook and our canvas. Strategic assignments and an emphasis on audience awareness, communication mediums, critical thinking, and even document design are moving writing classrooms towards a better understanding of not just writing, but of understanding where the texts are composed, how they are composed, and where the final texts will reside. A text, then, can be anything and produced by anyone. It can be typographical in nature or include multiple modes of communication—mobile technologies afford students the chance to explore what a text can be and give them the flexibility to be creative with a rhetorical purpose anywhere at any time.

Description of Assignments and Activities

The first major assignment of the semester asks students to contemplate their use of digital technologies over their lives and how such usage has impacted the way they read, write, and learn. It essentially asks them to think about who they were before they used a specific piece of digital technology and who they have become after it. Several reflect on the ability of social media to bring them out of their social shells and feel confident when talking to people they have met online. Others describe their use of video conference technology as a means to circumvent their depression and homesickness as they regularly contact their friends and family back home—calling is one thing, but looking someone in the eye on the screen and seeing their reactions cannot be replaced by just talking (the audio *and* the visual are essential in the development of the student as an individual). This assignment is an introspective examination of their own interactions with digital technologies and serves as an excellent fulcrum for the rest of the semester as we examine the interwoven nature of digital spaces and learning spaces. Getting students to ask why and how they use such technologies can lead to even greater questions about how they currently use them and how their new knowledge will impact them academically and professionally.

Assignment #1: Technology Literacies

Figure 8.1 provides the description of the first assignment that leads to the smaller mobile technology activities I will discuss later. Students have roughly three and a half weeks to complete this assignment, which asks students to rhetorically analyze themselves and their actions. As they begin to deconstruct how and why they interact with digital technologies, many notice that they are unable to complete daily tasks without their smartphones and tablets. As we begin to discuss this dependence, I introduce the first activity, which asks students to post a picture to their personal blog within the Google Site that represents an important connection they have

---

Your task for this assignment is to construct a "tech-literacy autobiography" that gives a **detailed and specific account** of at least one significant way you encounter technology in school, outside of school, or both.

For this essay, you may wish to construct a chronological literacy narrative where you describe your experiences with how your current technology practices reflect technology usage over time (throughout your life, while in high school, etc.). Or, you may wish to provide a non-chronological analysis, selecting non-sequential scenes that tell a story when placed together. Regardless, you might address any of the following questions (but do not answer them as if you are checking them off a list):

- What are the differences between the ways you use technology at home, and how you use it in school?
- What types of technology do you use to read and write in both settings?
- Do you have advantages over some of your friends when it comes to technology use? (or vice versa) How so? With what types of technology in particular?
- Have you taught someone about technology?
- Has someone taught you about technology?

I want you to think about and write about a **specific and detailed example of technology usage** (or a lack thereof). I'm looking for your "stories" about technology and your tech literacies (broadly speaking). Be as specific and detailed as possible. Feel free to write in the first person.

FIGURE **8.1.** *Technology Literacies assignment.*

As you adjust to becoming more comfortable around campus with various buildings and eccentric academic architecture, upload a picture here to your blog via your smartphone or tablet of an artifact of importance that connects you to this community. Examples can be of buildings, rocks, trees, doors, bikes, a person who sits outside on a park bench every morning while they drink their coffee before they go inside to work, and so on. You can only upload a file (image or video), so make sure that you find a way to attach some text to it as you explain what the artifact is, its importance to you, your connection to the campus, and how you would feel if it were to disappear.

FIGURE 8.2. *Activity 1. Week three blog assignment: Mapping Your Personal Campus.*

with the campus (see Figure 8.2). I tell the students that they are required to keep the content Rated PG and to manage their blog and content as if Disney were in control. Their blogs are their own pages that I have created for them within the Google Site, which is password protected. By encasing their blogs within the Google Site I am not only protecting their privacy, I am creating a home base for their writing and interaction with their classmates. Also, as my students tell me, the Google Site translates better to their mobile devices than the larger CMS used by the university.

After introducing the assignment, I show them a photo of a sign on campus that I have taken (Figure 8.3). I tell them that I walk by this sign and hall every morning on my way to my

FIGURE 8.3. *Example of a sign for activity 1.*

office and every time I say to myself that it is the Anthony "Michael" Hall. When none of the students understand this reference, I explain who the actor Anthony Michael Hall is and how during my orientation before teaching at MSU, I made this reference to a few new colleagues and they laughed, but had never thought of the connection to the actor many of us had grown up watching in films. This sign symbolizes my connection with my new community and colleagues as they note they had never thought of the 1980s actor when passing the location.

Many of my students are first-year and international students who have left home for the first time and this assignment gives them a chance to carry on conversations with each other in the class via typographical text and images. Many share images of their dorms, their cars, their friends playing sports on campus, football games, basketball games, various clubs on campus, and student organizations. Several take videos and narrate what they see and upload the video. While the activity begins in week three, it lasts the semester, and by the last week, each individual blog is a visual diary of the student's connections with the campus and community. The ability to pull up their mobile device, take a picture, write a quick caption, take a video and narrate, and submit it online loses its academic feel as students begin to take ownership of their posts. After this activity and throughout the semester, students ask one another before class for better descriptions of pictures, locations, how they can find a more beautiful place on campus to watch a sunset, where the best seat is to watch a basketball game, or what the best Chinese restaurant in East Lansing is. The posts move beyond just observational posts and begin to become significant discussions about location and writing and audience. Experience and writing become an essential theme of the class and this can only be achieved by using mobile technologies to discuss and nurture such ideas. Also, the use of mobile technologies is crucial in the time stamp of the event. Anyone can take a picture and then upload it at a later time, but as the feed of posts becomes active, it also comes alive and this leads to better discussions of rhetoric and writing—of the digital kairotic moment that can be seen via Twitter and other social media. One small activity and the use of mobile technology affords the chance to discuss the rhetorical appeals, audience, medium, communication, learning, culture, writing, and how digital spaces impact our lives. These impacts are immediate and long lasting, and the more students explore them, the more they want to write and learn about them.

The second activity starts at the beginning of week four and also goes on until the end of the semester (see Figure 8.4). Students have already become comfortable discussing mobile technologies and their influence on communication, so this activity affords them the chance to get to know the university and various clubs and organizations associated with their majors. As we discuss the reasons for this activity in a writing class, we talk about Yu-Liang Ting's research on interwoven learning interactions that studied student behaviors:

> The findings reveal that mobile technologies indeed add a new dimension to learning activities, because of both the personal and portable nature of the devices themselves as well as the kinds of learning interactions they can support. More specifically, mobile learning enables learners to interact and capture experiences in both physical and social realms, and makes learning more experiential and multifaceted. Hence, there is a need to better the development and applications of mobile technologies to learning. (Ting 12)

Just by discussing this type of research with the students, professors can lend credibility to the assignment and the students'

I am asking you to search for various search words via Twitter in an attempt to see what is happening in real time. There are several Twitter accounts and hashtags associated with this university via clubs and organizations that tweet information and events hourly and up to the minute updates concerning gatherings. I have posted a number of these accounts in the Google Site and shown you how to follow hashtags for the campus—use these as a way to stay current and see what is happening with the campus. I have also created a class blog in the Google Site where all of you will upload your content. This will keep it separate from your personal blogs.

If you do go to campus events or clubs or anything that you become knowledgeable about via various Twitter feeds and hashtags, document them in the class blog with images and videos. So, if you find that there is a last minute gathering to support student art on campus being held outside the art museum and you decide to attend, explore your experience via images or video and descriptions that put the experience in context so your fellow classmates can understand and even possibly attend. You do not need to have a Twitter account for this activity, but if you want to create one, you are more than welcome to do so.

FIGURE 8.4. *Activity 2. Researching Twitter: Collecting Tweets.*

participation. As I noted before, students will use this credibility to build their confidence to critique certain applications and use the opportunity to create small videos to edit on their phones and tablets, begin using apps to apply special effects, apply geo-tagging, and add animation to their texts they upload. Soon the class blog becomes a multimodal news feed, much like a Twitter feed, of what is happening on campus—it begins to merge all of the various news feeds from different organizations and disciplines into one streamlined feed that resembles a moving and living re-search essay by the end of the semester. This activity asks students to explore what our university is, while in the next activity I ask students to explore what our writing class is.

The third activity (Figure 8.5) forces students to work in groups to build and maintain a collaborative relationship. By week ten, I create an open Google Document that is shared only with the students. I pair them off and give them one week to log into the document via browsers in their smartphones so they can create a multimodal essay of what they feel the class is. They can collect images from campus and after the week ends, we regroup in class and go over the course goals and assignments to see what parts of the document can be arranged into a multimodal text that is an accurate representation of the course. This assignment is crucial in getting students to think about the class as something more than just writing typographical texts and that their mobile devices can be used to compose stories through images. For example, one group of students took a picture of a worn path on campus and

---

For this week I want you to collect images, videos, sounds, and anything you can think of that might be used as a means to explain what this class is about to someone who has never taken it. Think about the readings we have explored, your blogs, and where this class fits within the construct of your education at MSU. What makes this a writing class or not a writing class? Essentially, imagine someone is asking you about what you do in this class and this is your chance to respond beyond a typographical text.

Use Chrome as your browser on your mobile device as it works best with Google Docs. Be sure to open the document in "Desktop" mode so you can add images.

FIGURE 8.5. *Activity 3. Our Writing Class: What Is It?*

wrote a brief note next to it explaining how rhetorical choices made by large groups of people can have visible impacts. This echoes one of the central themes of the class: Everything we do is a rhetorical act. The image they uploaded is indicative of how words can shape actions and actions can shape landscapes. The main question about how this class is a writing class is answered differently by each student, but the central theme comes with the understanding that they write every day in ways they never thought were valuable. They begin to realize that any text, be it social or academic, is one they have written and composed for a specific audience and that their mobile device has aided in their development as thinkers and writers.

By the end of the week, and in preparation for the next large assignment, students have edited and completed the document by turning it into a collaborative Google Slide presentation that they then post to the Google Site. It serves as an excellent introduction for their Remix Project that allows them to turn their first Technology Literacy assignment (noted above) into a multimodal video. Students begin to see their mobile devices as more than just everyday tools for texting and checking status updates; they become something more than they ever imagined. Students are collecting photos to add to a community feed, collecting photos and writing captions to create a multimodal representation of a class, and using the phone to collect videos (and even edit those videos) on their phone for a Remix Project (Figure 8.6) that asks them to combine a previous assignment into a multimodal text that allows them to express themselves beyond standard academic typographical text.

The activities discussed in this chapter serve as excellent paths for supporting larger projects that are more traditional composition assignments. While the fundamentals of rhetoric and writing have not changed for some time (and I do not see them changing any time soon), the technology that we and our students employ to create texts as a means to communicate effectively to targeted audiences for specific goals (rhetoric) evolve. These activities and assignments may also change, but they are built on the foundation of best writing practices that reinforce peer-to-peer learning and rhetoric.

I'm asking you to produce a mixed/multimedia re-presentation of your Technology Literacies (Assignment #1) that develops and advances themes of how you encounter science and technology in your day-to-day life. This assignment is not asking for a history of technology—it is asking you to explore how digital technology has affected *you*, however, for this project you will use a different medium.

The original Technology Literacy assignment was essentially a typographical based piece of writing that asked you to provide a **detailed and specific account** of some technology in your life. Now, with this assignment, I want you to make a **remixed** version of your Technology Literacy paper: take what you wrote for your first project and make it into something entirely new. You do **not** need to add more typographical text, but I **do** want you to expand or develop these projects in any other way you can imagine.

Note that you do **not** have to remix or reconstruct your entire Technology Literacy paper: it is perfectly fine—perhaps even better—to work with only a small "scene" or fragment from the original paper.

Requirements:
- Include some aspect (however small) of your original TechLit project
- Continue exploring and advancing themes of how you personally encounter science and technology in your daily life
- Use no less than three (3) different mediums
- Use no less than seven (7) different artifacts
- Include an MLA-style bibliography citing all artifacts used in the remix
- Include a one (1) page Reflection Memo describing your processes of creating a remix to be posted on the Google Site
- Bring something you can present to the class in about three to four (3–4) minutes
- Upload your video to your Dropbox account and share the link in the Google Site

What are some possible mediums?
By asking you to work with at least three (3) different mediums, I am asking you to struggle with the problems and possibilities of combining radically different types of content, to consider how we make meaning—how we compose, how we write—in non-typographical ways.

You're invited to push this list of mediums in whatever ways you can imagine: what can you come up with? What types of materials would you like to work with?

continued on next page

FIGURE **8.6.** *Assignment 4. Digital Remix.*

Figure 8.6. continued

Deliverables
Essentially, you will be making a video. My hope is that you will surprise me, that you will take this opportunity to make something novel or unexpected, something you *enjoy* and are *proud* to share with the class. Programs like iMovie and MovieMaker, etc. can help you to reimagine your text.

The only caveat here is that you should be able to present your deliverable to the class in about three to four (3–4) minutes. That means your video should be between 3–4 minutes (no shorter).

How does this assignment help me become a better writer?
The Remix project aligns with several key Shared Learning Outcomes of the Tier I writing curriculum at MSU, including the following:

- Work within a repertoire of genres and modes to meet appropriate rhetorical purposes
- Exercise a flexible repertoire of invention, arrangement, and revision strategies
- Demonstrate an understanding of writing as an epistemic and recursive process and effectively apply a variety of knowledge-making strategies in writing
- Read in ways that improve writing, especially by demonstrating an ability to analyze invention, arrangement, and revision strategies at work in a variety of texts
- Demonstrate the ability to locate, critically evaluate, and employ a variety of sources for a range of purposes
- Understand the logics and uses of citation systems and documentation styles and display competence with one citation system/documentation style

Remember: Rhetoric is not just about reading and writing. It is a way of thinking. You are rethinking your first assignment and using a new medium to communicate it to a new audience.

Discussion

As we move much of our content for classes into online spaces, it is important to utilize digital technology to take advantage of students who multitask. Scott Warnock points out:

> Teachers often view technology as a distraction, but that's because our teaching is at odds with the e-environment. I, too,

can be annoyed when students "do screens" [play on Facebook or social sites] while in my onsite classrooms, but think about it: in our writing classes, while we are talking, they are often diligently writing away—and yet we see this as an obstacle (Slager). The text-based e-environment is an increasingly familiar environment for students[;] . . . in short, we can teach them while they are there. (XXIII)

Such "distractions" can be turned into learning moments and bring in various discussions about writing and thinking by the student. The principles of getting students to write and think critically have not changed, but the tools we use to communicate and disseminate such knowledge have changed—essentially, the topics remain the same, but the spaces in which students interact change. Warnock says "we can teach them while they are there," but that "there" is mobile and in constant motion as students take the class with them from the face-to-face REAL classrooms to the bus stop to basketball games to social clubs and to anywhere they want to go. It is not just that a majority of our course content and student interaction is moving toward an online space, the fact is most of it is already there, and we, as educators, need to meet our students there and give them the tools to navigate such spaces and to think critically and rhetorically about them.

Digital technologies will change and the smartphones will become smart watches and then smart holograms and then insert next digital technology revolutionary device here, but what doesn't change are the goals of each assignment and activity that ask students to think critically and rhetorically about who they are, what they are doing, and how and why they are doing it. And as mobile technologies become the norm, the when and the where complete the final equation. The assignments and activities listed above continue the basic questions that have led inquiry since rhetoric's inception. They will not change, but as our students and the tools they use do change, we can explore the spaces with them: For as mobile learning keeps on running, we can renegotiate our pedagogy to keep up.

Works Cited

Cheon, Jongpil, Sangno Lee, Steven M. Crooks, and Jaeki Song. "An Investigation of Mobile Learning Readiness in Higher Education Based on the Theory of Planned Behavior." *Computers and Education* 59.3 (2012): 1054–64. Print.

Fojtik, Rostislav. "Mobile Technologies Education." *Procedia—Social and Behavioral Sciences* 143 (2014): 342–46. Print.

Hefling, Kimberly. "Obama Administration's Challenge to Schools: Embrace Digital Textbooks within 5 Years." *Huffington Post.* 1 Feb. 2012. Web. 2 Apr. 2015.

Johnson-Eilola, Johndan. *Datacloud: Toward a New Theory of Online Work.* Cresskill: Hampton, 2005. Print.

Penny, Chris, Jordan Shugar, Douglas McConatha, David Bolton, and Priscilla Taylor. "The Higher Education Classroom in the Post PC Era." *Proceedings of Society for Information Technology and Teacher Education International Conference* 25 Mar. 2013. Ed. Ron McBride and Michael Searson. Chesapeake: AACE, 2013. 3760–62. Print.

Rossing, Jonathan P., Willie M. Miller, Amanda K. Cecil, and Suzan E. Stamper. "iLearning: The Future of Higher Education? Student Perceptions on Learning with Mobile Tablets." *Journal of the Scholarship of Teaching and Learning* 12.2 (2012): 1–26. Print.

Sharples, Mike, Josie Taylor, and Giasemi Vavoula. "A Theory of Learning for the Mobile Age." *The Sage Handbook of E-Learning Research.* Ed. Richard Andrews and Caroline Haythornthwaite. London: SAGE, 2007. 221–47. Print.

Ting, Yu-Liang. "Using Mobile Technologies to Create Interwoven Learning Interactions: An Intuitive Design and its Evaluation." *Computers and Education* 60.1 (2013): 1–13. Print.

Warnock, Scott. *Teaching Writing Online: How and Why.* Urbana: NCTE, 2009. Print.

Wysocki, Anne Frances, Johndan Johnson-Eilola, Cynthia L. Selfe, and Geoffrey Sirc. *Writing New Media: Theory and Applications for Expanding the Teaching of Composition.* Logan: Utah State P, 2004. Print.

CHAPTER NINE

Using Mobile Technology to Revitalize Process Writing Instruction

JOSH HERRON
Anderson University (SC)

As my flight was about to land, it occurred to me that a portion of this chapter's drafting and revision took place on an iPad Mini. As established in this book's introduction, such work on mobile devices—from almost anywhere—has become quite common in the professional realm and deserves attention from those in the academy, especially in composition studies. This chapter examines the impact of tablet devices integrated into first-year composition curriculum, specifically highlighting a mobile electronic portfolio environment and how ubiquitous technology can impact traditionally static, paper-based writing processes. As will be evidenced throughout this chapter, digital tools impact students' written composition processes just as much as they afford new opportunities for multimodal composition.

As part of Anderson University's (SC) thoroughly planned Mobile Learning Initiative, the English Department's First-Year Composition Committee—Assistant Professor Paige Ellisor-Catoe, Lecturer Cari Brooks, and the author—researched and implemented an electronic portfolio environment designed specifically for process writing courses, along with a redesign of classroom activities and assessments based around the new portfolio system and its capabilities on tablets. The committee took on "the challenge . . . of designing courses that speak to students' past, present, and projected interests, needs, and concerns, and that help prepare them to 'work in and understand electronic literacy environments'" (Shipka 7). An important factor in selecting a portfolio system was that it not be designed just for collecting final papers but that it would also serve as a digital interface in which users could compose, revise, peer review, and compile work in the same system, anywhere and anytime. This distinction was an important component in allowing a unified writing experience with mobile capabilities that would offer a different experience than the static, archival approaches inherent in some portfolio systems that are vestiges of paper-based writing processes.

With the help of the director of instructional design (now dean of the Center for Innovation and Digital Learning) who led the Mobile Learning Initiative, the composition committee researched numerous solutions, including the capabilities of the university's LMS, blog platforms, (e.g., Wordpress), document sharing sites (e.g., Google Docs), and paid portfolio options that were generally archive-oriented rather than process-based. The committee ultimately decided on Marca (www.gomarca.com), a writing portfolio system that was built for process writing instruction and originally developed for the English department of the University of Georgia as a tool called Emma. Further rationale for the selection of this system is discussed in the following section.

Theoretical Grounding

There is growing evidence that portfolios are a more accurate assessment of writing instruction than final written essays. As Roemer, Schultz, and Durst assert in a study of the transition from an exit exam to portfolios at the University of Cincinnati, "Portfolios provide a mode of assessment that dovetails neatly with process theories about writing" (455). More thoroughly, Erin Herberg's "Can a Metamorphosis Be Quantified?: Reflecting on Portfolio Assessment" highlights the many theories in the field of composition studies that suggest a portfolio assessment more closely reflects what happens in the actual classroom. Herberg also recognizes that "while there are many claims for portfolios' superiority as an assessment tool, there is little hard evidence that portfolios achieve what they claim to achieve" (73). This chapter will provide evidence in this area and also reflect on students' acquisition of process writing skills using portfolios in a mobile learning environment.

Research concerning composition and computers is not new, but often, mobile devices are lumped into that conversation without differentiation. But as many researchers in mobile learning studies are recognizing, these devices have particular effects of their own, even in composition. In "Writing in the Wild: A Paradigm for Mobile Composition," Olin Bjork and John Pedro Schwartz note, "Mobile composition relocates writing and even publication in the place of the object and embraces process-as-product genres" (235). Thus, while there is evidence of how electronic composition has impacted our field, mobile devices also have a particular role in process writing, especially through the concepts of place and space (including interface). The role of mobile devices should not be overlooked, and they should not be treated merely as a substitute for more stationary computers in this chapter.

This study focuses mainly on the benefit of a dynamic electronic portfolio environment in a process-based writing program, but considering that the revised first-year composition curriculum was also a move away from the final written exam to a portfolio assessment in our department, this chapter does include data comparing the use of no portfolio (using a final written exam instead) to written portfolios and to electronic portfolios during the composition committee's pilot study. Including this data offers a more complete picture of the impact that the move to an electronic portfolio in the first-year writing program had on helping students meet the revised course outcomes most effectively.

Importantly, no part of the charge of the First-Year Composition Committee was to force technology into the curriculum. Rather, the course goals and approaches to teaching and learning writing were the main concerns, with the knowledge that the resources and tools of the university's Mobile Learning Initiative were available to incorporate. The English department had sensed its current-traditional, modes-based approach was no longer the most effective approach for preparing students, so the committee researched peer and aspirant institutions and studied the latest research and statements of first-year writing program outcomes from national organizations.

Most influential in the development of program goals was the Writing Program Administrators (WPA) Outcome Statement for First-Year Composition (originally using the 2.0 version but later the 3.0 version after its release). While the English Department adopted all of the areas covered in the WPA Outcomes Statement, two outcomes were key in the revision of the writing program: Processes and Composing in Electronic Environments (WPA 2.0). These two sections of the Outcomes Statement (2.0) gave the committee clarity and credibility for the larger changes it began to envision for the writing program. WPA Outcomes Statement 3.0 integrates the Composing in Electronic Environments outcome section throughout the other outcomes.

Having identified the goals and outcomes for the first-year writing program, the composition committee performed a thorough search for the electronic portfolio solution that would be most effective. Kathleen Blake Yancey describes three electronic portfolio models in "Postmodernism, Palimpsest, and Portfolios: Theoretical Issues in the Representation of Student Work." The first is "an *online assessment system* . . . where students store pre-selected pieces of work"; the second "we might call 'print uploaded' is a version of portfolio that is identical in form to the print but is distributed electronically"; the third "is what we might call 'Web sensible,' one that . . . not only inhabits the digital space and is distributed electronically but also exploits the medium" (24–26). While many of the portfolio solutions match Yancey's first two models, the option that the committee chose, Marca (www.gomarca.com), met the more elusive third model that she describes. Marca offered a "Web sensible" solution that could make full use of mobile learning to create a unified writing experience for students from which they could work anywhere.

The impact of composing in an electronic environment, particularly the area of electronic portfolio assessment, has received growing attention in composition studies. Pamela Takayoshi suggests, "computers make more visible the ways in which writing processes are recursive rather than discrete stages[. . . .] In a traditional classroom where students deal with hard copy text, it's possible to point to a text and say, 'this is the original draft' or 'this is the second draft.' In an electronic classroom, however, there are no discrete stages marked by distinct drafts" (247).

Another study, which tracked the implementation of electronic portfolios in a writing program at the University of Washington, suggests similar differences exist in the shift from paper to screen (Corbett et al.). Our conjecture was that a mobile device extends the paper-to-screen difference by creating an even more fluid writing process experience.

As intimated by much of the research cited already, the move to embrace the digital in composition courses by way of electronic portfolios is not just a move solely for efficiency reasons or to replicate what occurs in one medium in another. Rather, taking full advantage of a digital interface with mobile devices affords new opportunities for students and instructors in the teaching and learning of composition. Scholars who work at the intersection of new media and composition studies, such as Collin Brooke, continue to make the argument that "rhetoric and composition remains bound by the particular media for which we invent, and for the most part we invent (and ask our students to invent) for the printed page," and as such we theorize to arrive at goals based on the "solidity or sturdiness" that comes with this medium, as the reference to Takayoshi above emphasized, too (68). The move to a dynamic electronic portfolio interface—as opposed to an archival, print-based option—was one step toward beginning to fully realize the digital affordances available to composition courses. Further, joining this move to a digital portfolio interface with a mobile learning initiative allows students to move away from the "solidity or sturdiness" and fixed nature of desktop and laptop computers.

Descriptions of Assignments and Activities

Part of the development of the revised first-year writing curriculum was ensuring effective assignments and activities that aligned with the pedagogical research and program outcomes. The one-stop and anywhere-accessible features of the tablet and portfolio application enabled the teacher and the student to engage continuously and fully at all stages of the writing process. Students were also able to use the iPad's recording features and apps for multimedia content creation and editing. However, while these multimedia affordances were important drivers in the department's integration of the mobile devices and the "Web sensible" portfolio option (as Yancey describes it), the focus of this study and assignment descriptions are written processes.

In some ways, the types of activities and assessments used in the designed courses are not drastically different from a typical process writing classroom, but the emphasis and ability for students to see the writing process as unified in one interface played a role in their attitudes and acquisition of skills, as discussed later in this chapter. Moreover, there were stages of the writing process that were able to receive attention that might have been glossed over in the paper-based approach, which inherently emphasizes separate products rather than steps within processes, thus reducing the instructors' and students' focus on certain stages.

Most process-writing instructors, for example, would defend the importance of the pre- writing or invention stage of a project. A paper-based approach to process writing, however, often plays a role in the "reduction of invention" in composition courses due to efficiencies and a focus on discrete products over continuity (Brooke 62). With the electronic portfolio system and affordance of the tablet devices, students could begin exploring topics and sources in the classroom—with and without peer assistance at times—and have material that they could use to begin drafting their writing projects later in the same interface. Instructors would use built-in forums or journals to have students brainstorm ideas or resources that they could then carry over to the built-in word processor in the portfolio interface when working on projects. More formally, students could create an annotated bibliography or research prospectus that would go into a low-stakes writing project folder in the same interface.

In the revising and editing stage of projects, peer reviews become more effective as students are able to access one another's files with ease. Students would have drafted the project within the portfolio interface, and their original documents duplicate when peers begin to review them, so the student has an original document as well as peers' revisions in the same place. The instructor then has access to all of the reviews to ensure that each student is receiving helpful and sufficient feedback to use later when noting whether a student took the advice of peers in revising a draft.

Students keep a copy of the reviews they wrote as well for use in the portfolio.

The peer review process was often completed on the tablets in class with instructors observing in real time—via their own devices—the feedback being given by students in the portfolio system, allowing the instructor to be physically mobile in the class. Along with taking note of the feedback being offered, instructors could offer direction to students in the moment. Other times, students would perform the peer reviews outside of class and use the tablets to review and discuss feedback during class time. With the same capabilities described earlier, instructors could engage with students individually or as a whole during class time as students conferenced with one another.

The use of the tablets and the electronic portfolio application even impacted office hours and writing conferences with instructors. During such meetings, students and faculty were able to access all stages of a writing project and add real-time notes and revisions on their devices that would be accessible later to both parties. While the tablets may seem to be only a small advantage over a laptop in this situation, their convenience and efficiency increase the likelihood that they will be used for live work on the assignment during these sessions. The tablets also eliminate the barrier between the instructor and student during the visit just a bit more than if both parties were using a laptop. In general, conversations about a writing project between instructor and student become more fluid when using the electronic portfolio on the tablet.

In the final revision and reflecting stages of the writing process, students have all work in one place to prepare for the portfolio and to consult when writing reflective pieces. To further emphasize the holistic, continuous nature of the writing process, one particular portfolio assignment had students trace changes in a paragraph across multiple drafts, and students were able to complete such an activity with more ease than tracking down paper copies or even electronic copies of drafts saved in multiple places.

Having these assignments and activities take place in a single interface and available to use anywhere and anytime via tablets reinforces a holistic and continuous writing process for students, a main goal for the first-year writing program. Since instructors have the same access to all of each student's material, they are able to offer a more holistic assessment of the students' achievement of this goal by being able to monitor how a student arrived at a final version of a project and at what stage a student seems to excel or struggle by having all pieces in one portable interface.

Student Examples

The following images are from actual use of the electronic portfolio system, Marca. The system was incorporated throughout the semester to emphasize all elements of the writing process in one place and to make it a true process-based portfolio system and not just an artifact-based portfolio system used at the end of a term. Using mobile devices with the portfolio reinforced these principles.

In the Projects interface of the portfolio environment (Figure 9.1), students were able to perform all steps for a project—creating the document, revising, peer reviewing, and reviewing feedback from an instructor. The instructor and student could navigate between all of their projects in the class (sidebar of Figure 9.1 shows different project folders). To help distinguish stages within a particular project folder, students mark the stage of the draft during creation—the example in this figure includes "Ready for Peer Review." Students would select private or shared depending on whether the file is for final grading or peer review. Students have access to compose, store, or review the all-in-one interface from anywhere and on any device that has Internet access.

Specifically, Figure 9.1 shows the shared files from students with reviews by peers indicated by indented file links below the original. Instructors would have the ability to select files that are labeled at various stages or view all files. The Projects page is a main component of the portfolio interface, on which students commented that "everything I needed to do was on one site and all around the same place" or that "see[ing] everyone's papers . . . can in turn help your own paper."

The portfolio tab in the application (Figure 9.2) was where students could pull from their assignments (which they would be continuing to revise) and display their final work in the course.

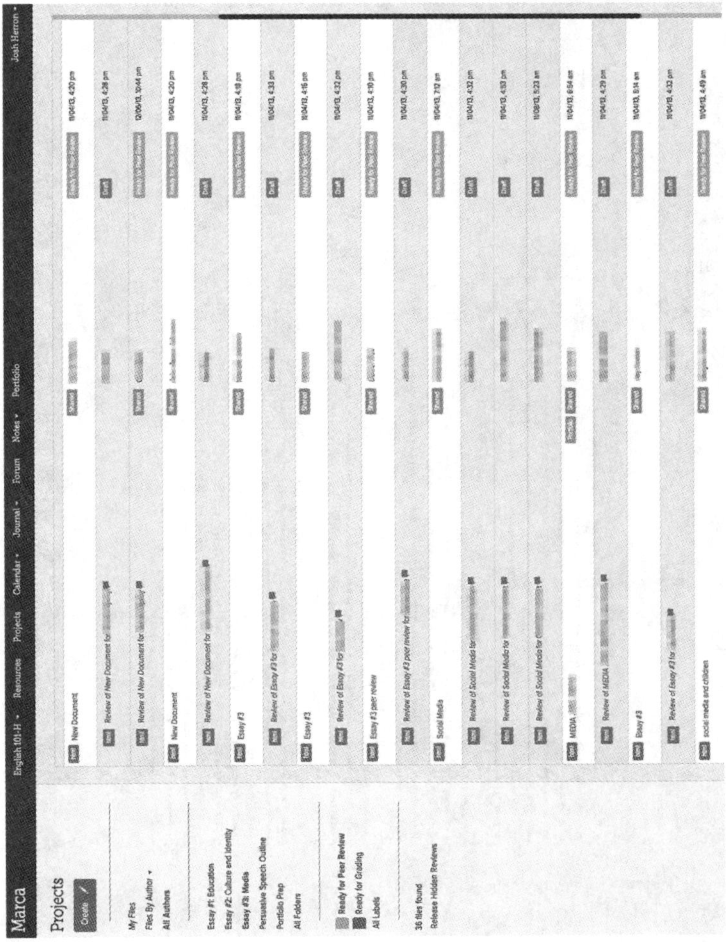

FIGURE 9.1. *Student projects page in Marca.*

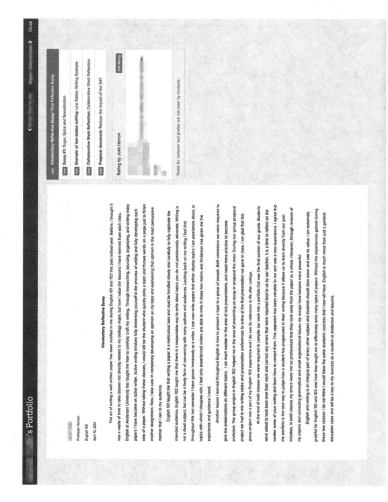

FIGURE 9.2. *Portfolio page.*

Students were able to go into the portfolio tab of Marca and select their revised papers from their project folders as shown in Figure 9.1. Along with revised essays, students would upload a reflective piece, a link to multimedia pieces, and a low-stakes writing piece. Students could also upload a peer review exhibit, which was easier because of the ability to pick from their auto-stored reviews on which they felt they offered helpful and thorough suggestions.

Since first-year composition at Anderson University is part of a two-course sequence, students have access to their documents from the first course to use as part of the second course to emphasize even more of a holistic, unified experience across the sequence. The use of the portfolio feature in the interface and its capabilities on a mobile device doubly encourages students to see writing as an ongoing, constant process throughout both composition courses, in part because the tools are "so accessible and convenient," as one student wrote, which will be further discussed using the student feedback data covered in the next section.

Conclusion and Further Discussion

Feedback received from students as part of a university-approved study comparing experiences with students using a paper-based portfolio to those using a mobile electronic one confirmed the expectations of the composition committee that emphasizing the latest pedagogical approaches, harnessing the university's Mobile Learning Initiative, and incorporating the right electronic portfolio application would improve student outcomes related to process writing. A survey, which included Likert items that were designed to measure students' attitudes toward the broad aspects of the writing process (invention, drafting, reviewing, revising, and reflecting) and qualitative data related to elements of processes, practices, and attitudes toward composition, were the source of the data analyzed during this pilot study.

Of the several Likert statements and open-ended questions posted to students regarding their writing processes without a portfolio, with a paper portfolio, and with an electronic portfolio, the electronic portfolio stood out as having the most impact on instilling a sense of the full writing process. Two hundred and twenty-two first-year composition students were surveyed from one of the courses in the composition sequence in Spring 2013 or Fall 2013. Surveys were administered near the end of the courses. By this point in the pilot, the process writing pedagogical approach had been adopted in all of these classes where students were surveyed, so the use or absence of a final portfolio was the only dependent variable. Twenty-three percent of students used paper portfolios, 28 percent used electronic portfolios, and 48 percent used no portfolio.

One particularly noticeable change in student attitude and skill acquisition is shown in Table 9.1. There was a 25 percent increase in the number of students agreeing with the highest "Breadth of Revision" selection when using an electronic portfolio system rather than a paper-based approach. As the Breadth of Revision question might suggest, the figures from the pilot study demonstrate that the intentional use of ubiquitous technology and the portfolio application led to students revising more in that version of a first-year writing course, a central goal for our first-year composition students. In fact, students using the mobile electronic portfolio gave more positive responses than the paper portfolio participants in all statements related to the importance of various writing stages. As the research suggested, affording students the opportunity to make all of their changes in one interface rather than printing drafts and editing/revising off-screen, as well as the intentional use of mobile technology, significantly impacted student achievement of course goals related to process writing.

Further, despite numerous technical glitches during the pilot (both user and application developer issues), 55 percent of students using the electronic portfolio agreed that it "enhance[d]

TABLE 9.1. Percent of Students Agreeing with Highest "Breadth of Revision" Question Selection

	No Portfolio	Paper Portfolio	Electronic Portfolio
Breadth of Revision: selected "large-scale, continues after submitting essay"	33%	48%	60%

their learning and writing experiences." One student noted the ease of editing and other features of the interface: "[It] made it easy to find older projects with their reviews for future editing." Another noted the unified experience and how it "enhanced . . . learning by having a neat and organized layout and everything in one place." The portfolio application and mobile devices led to more students embracing all stages of the writing process, even those stages that had been reduced or omitted in paper-based approaches.

There were certainly some challenges to overcome during the first year, including procuring the right application to fit specific needs as well as instructor and student training. Based on data from the first year of implementation of the electronic portfolio environment, there is evidence for further intentional incorporation of mobile devices to enhance the first-year composition classroom to not only impact student writing but to explore options outside of just an alphabetic writing environment as well as prepare students to effectively create and analyze in a digital world, only referenced sparingly in this study. This move toward multimodal composition is an important part of the revised first-year composition curriculum at Anderson University and its selection of the current e-portfolio system, but not enough significant data was collected on this aspect. The tablet becomes a one-stop device for creating, editing, and publishing multimedia—an advantage that needs further exploration in the area of composition studies and mobile devices.

As mentioned earlier, the unique characteristics of a mobile device provide a different experience from just using a laptop computer. The mobile devices lend themselves to the type of writing described by Nedra Reynolds: "a writing [that] takes place on the screen in a more fluid, spatial medium that doesn't lend itself to 'frozen' representations" (5). While we can expect the devices to further introduce new composition methods and processes in our classrooms, as Reynolds goes on to discuss, we can see that it is already making a difference in some of the process writing skills that most composition faculty seek to instill in their students.

While much of this chapter highlighted one particular system, the goal is not about praising a particular product but about recognizing the need for a holistic, process-writing based application that can make full use of the tablet device's potential for a fluid, unified writing experience for students. In fact, the university's English department is exploring some of these capabilities within a new learning management system—potentially providing students an even more seamless experience. As evidenced, digital media impacts how we interact with previous modes, and the potential that exists in revitalizing and embracing new forms of creation and analysis in various contexts is important to preparing composition students for the twenty-first century.

Works Cited

Bjork, Olin, and John Pedro Schwartz. "Writing in the Wild: A Paradigm for Mobile Composition." *Going Wireless: A Critical Examination of Wireless and Mobile Technologies for Composition Teachers and Researchers.* Ed. Amy C. Kimme Hea. Cresskill: Hampton, 2009. 223–37. Print.

Brooke, Collin. *Lingua Fracta: Towards a Rhetoric of New Media.* Cresskill, Hampton, 2009. Print.

Corbett, Steven J., Michelle LaFrance, Cara Giacomini, and Janice Fournier. "Mapping, Re-Mediating, and Reflecting on Writing Process Realities: Transitioning from Print to Electronic Portfolios in First-Year Composition." *ePortfolio Performance Support Systems: Constructing, Presenting, and Assessing Portfolios.* Eds. Katherine V. Wills and Rich Rice. Fort Collins: WAC Clearinghouse; Anderson: Parlor, 2013. 183–204. Print.

Council of Writing Program Administrators. "WPA Outcomes Statement for First-Year Composition (2.0)." *Council of Writing Program Administrators.* CWPA, 2008. Web. 28 Mar. 2009.

———. "WPA Outcomes Statement for First-Year Composition (3.0)." *Council of Writing Program Administrators.* CWPA, 17 July 2014. Web. 10 May 2016.

Herberg, Erin. "Can a Metamorphosis Be Quantified? Reflection on Portfolio Assessment." *Composition Studies* 33.2 (2005): 69–87. Web. 3 Feb. 2016.

Reynolds, Nedra. *Geographies of Writing: Inhabiting Places and Encountering Difference.* Carbondale: Southern Illinois UP, 2004. Print.

Roemer, Marjorie, Lucille Schultz, and Russell K. Durst. "Portfolios and the Process of Change." *College Composition and Communication* 42.4 (1991): 455–69. Print.

Shipka, Jody. *Toward a Composition Made Whole.* Pittsburgh: U of Pittsburgh P, 2011. Print.

Takayoshi, Pamela. "The Shape of Electronic Writing: Evaluating and Assessing Computer-Assisted Writing Processes and Products." *Computers and Composition* 13.2 (1996): 245–57. Print.

Wills, Katherine V., and Rich Rice, eds. *ePortfolio Performance Support Systems: Constructing, Presenting, and Assessing Portfolios.* Fort Collins: WAC Clearinghouse; Anderson: Parlor, 2013. Print.

Yancey, Kathleen Blake. "Postmodernism, Palimpsest, and Portfolios: Theoretical Issues in the Representation of Student Work." *ePortfolio Performance Support Systems: Constructing, Presenting, and Assessing Portfolios.* Eds. Katherine V. Wills and Rich Rice. Fort Collins: WAC Clearinghouse; Anderson: Parlor, 2013. 19–39. Print.

CHAPTER TEN

Beyond the Hesitation: Incorporating Mobile Learning into the Online Writing Classroom

JASON DOCKTER
Lincoln Land Community College

JESSIE C. BORGMAN
Western Michigan University

Years of experience teaching writing online has made us realize the unique challenges that mobile learning technologies pose, particularly in the online domain. We understand the hesitation online teachers face when considering how to adjust their teaching to accommodate a mobile student, as both of us have experienced this in regard to using less traditional methods of composing in our online courses (Anderson et al. 3). In this chapter, we define mobile learning as learning accomplished with the assistance of mobile technologies, and we define mobile technologies as devices that deliver and collect information at any location (rather than stationary technologies situated at a fixed location). Here, we share two assignments that are based on the use of mobile technologies and also that vary in their incorporation of such technologies. Jessie provides the perspective of an instructor who is just beginning to incorporate mobile technologies into her online writing courses (OWCs), asking students to critically evaluate their usage of such technologies. Jason, having already incorporated multimodal assignments in his OWCs, brings an experienced perspective, encouraging students to use their mobile technologies to capture material(s) to potentially compose with.

Mobile learning should be a part of the OWC because as Principle 1 of the CCCC *Position Statement of Principles and*

Example Effective Practices for Online Writing Instruction (OWI) states: "Online writing instruction should be universally inclusive and accessible" (CCCC Executive Committee on Best). Mobile technologies are *the* primary composing and researching tools of today—how can they *not be* incorporated into a composition class, particularly one that is based entirely within an online technological space? Therefore, incorporating alternate composing strategies, like the assignments described in this chapter, into the OWC allows students to critically reflect on the use of mobile technologies in our culture and their function as composing tools students will use in their educational journey and beyond. With practice and reflection on how such composing tools can be used for writing, students gain experience with "writing on the go"—collecting information and raw material that can be used to communicate immediately, in the moment.

Some students access their online courses exclusively through mobile technology, a fact that should not be overlooked (Smith). A recent study conducted by the Pew Research Center documents that "younger adults" and "[t]hose with low household incomes and levels of educational attainment" rely on their smartphones for online access (Smith). Students are accessing their online courses via mobile devices, and more students than we probably realize are also composing their written work with this technology. To provide increased access for online students, many of whom could be included within both of the aforementioned groups, mobile technologies have to be considered when developing an online course and the projects to be completed within that course. Our hope is that by providing two different perspectives of online instructors (new and experienced), we can inspire other instructors to integrate mobile learning into their online writing classes.

Theoretical Grounding

Because students have these technologies and use them for communication, research, and even as part of their daily writing processes, it's important to find ways to integrate this technology into our writing courses to expand students' conceptions of what it means to write and also to improve their ability to use their devices as composing tools. John Traxler argues instructors "can ignore desktop technologies but not mobile technologies because desktop technologies operate in their own little world while mobile technologies operate in *the* world" (5). The longer we ignore the composing possibilities these tools provide the more likely writing instruction will seem irrelevant to students.

Beyond the sheer ease of use and the clearly evident reliance that many have on mobile devices, the use of these technologies necessitates an expanded definition of writing done within the writing classroom. These technologies become increasingly important within writing courses because of how they can help instructors reframe what it means to compose (Halbritter 167–69). The NCTE's "Position Statement on Multimodal Literacies" suggests that the "Integration of multiple modes of communication and expression can enhance or transform the meaning of the work beyond illustration or decoration" (CCCC Executive Committee on Multimodal). Using mobile technology in the already technology-driven online classroom allows instructors a better opportunity to draw clear connections for the students between the work they are doing in school and the work they may do in the future, in other courses and beyond. Using mobile technologies in the OWC can help students understand that composing is far more complicated than just writing a traditional school essay and that the mobile devices they use every day are powerful writing tools as well. Claire Lauer explains,

> Over the past two decades, rhetoric and composition has adapted a wide variety of composing technologies and practices that have changed the way we teach and the way our students communicate[. . . .] Changes in composing technologies have not necessarily changed the fundamentals of rhetorical thinking and problem solving, but they have expanded them to include additional modes and media through which to construct meaning. (60–61)

Since mobile technology can capture moments and ideas through multiple media forms, mobile technology-based assignments can help move students beyond a limited perception of writing as something only done with alphanumeric text, which only happens in sentences and paragraphs. The media created with mobile technology can capture information through multiple modalities of meaning: aural, visual, gestural, spatial, and linguistic (see New London Group). Pamela Takayoshi and Cynthia Selfe note "students need to be experienced and skilled not only in reading texts employing multiple modalities, but also in *composing* in multiple modalities" (3). While writing in words, sentences, and paragraphs has been privileged in composition classes, they aren't always the best way to communicate a message (Dunn; Fortune 49). Projects using mobile technology increase opportunities for how students can communicate the messages they wish to get across—providing a wider range of rhetorical contexts for students to consider (see Ball 61; Bezemer and Kress 233; Fortune; Kress, "Gains" 296; Kress *Multimodality*, 5; Rice 384; Sheridan and Rowsell 3–4). Mobile technology promotes rhetorical thinking to consider all the possibilities, both modalities and media, for how material might be created, collected, and best composed and communicated in a message.

Jessie's Assignment: For the Instructor Who Is Beginning to Incorporate Mobile Technologies in the OWC

Overview

While assignment 1 still has students producing an essay, it forces them to incorporate the use of their mobile phones and imbed images into their traditional essay text to create a visual multi-genre essay. The goals of this assignment are:

1. To get students writing a more substantial text (than a brief biography) earlier in the course

2. To assist students in thinking about what defines/shapes their identity; illustrate to students how they can be a writer, thinker, and academic on the go

3. To help students understand the ways that technologies can aid them in their school writing and beyond

4. To connect their everyday activities to their academic work

Instructors should provide students with videos (videos available online or videos the instructor makes) that show how to embed images into a text using Microsoft Word. Instructors might also want to provide students with some early week one readings on identity formation and/or composing with technologies, such as "How Mobile Technologies Are Shaping a New Generation" by Tammy Erickson, "Our Cell Phones, Ourselves" by Christine Rosen, or "Our Creepy Attachment to Cell Phones Could Be an Addiction" by Anna Almendrala. Not all students own a mobile phone or use it regularly, so an alternate assignment accommodates for this challenge.

Assignment Directions for Students

In place of doing a simple introductory/biography discussion in week one, you'll be posting a brief mixed-genre essay in week two. For this first assignment, you're required to use your mobile phone. You may be asking: "Why on earth am I using my mobile phone in a writing course?" Well, our writing skills and writing styles are shaped by our actions and our surroundings; we make sense of our environment through writing. Similarly, most of us make sense of our environment through the use of our mobile phones; we look up things we don't know, we take pictures of things we want to remember, we make lists, communicate with people, and entertain ourselves with games and social media sites.

During week one of the course, you need to capture images with your camera, screenshots of your phone, and a list of your mobile phone activities. At the end of week one spend some time writing a short essay of 2–3 pages that discusses how your mobile phone shapes and defines you as a person (based on your activities in week one) and includes some of the images that you took as evidence to support your discussion of identity. Once you finalize your essay at the end of week one, please post it as an attachment to the week two discussion thread no later than Wednesday by 11:59 p.m. EST of week two. Then make sure that you reply to at least two of your classmates' essays no later than Saturday by 11:59 p.m. EST of week two.

Alternate Assignment: If you don't own a mobile phone, or you don't use it except to make phone calls, then write about why you've chosen to opt out of such a cultural phenomenon and how you think not being tied to your cell phone defines you. Also, consider what other technologies (mobile or other) define you, for example, television, video games, computer/Internet time, etc.

Abbreviated Student Example: Kaitlin Weber

Her Introduction: "In today's world, it is quite uncommon to find someone without a cellphone. People seem to be constantly on their phones. Their entire life is on them and many would be devastated if they did not exist: 'With more than five billion mobile users worldwide and a massive global network, small mobile devices with significant computing power have become a routine part of day-to-day life for people of all ages' (Erickson). Over the course of the past week, I logged much of my phone usage in my planner. I have a smartphone, so I am able to do just about anything on my phone. I mainly used it for taking pictures, looking up directions, posting to social media, such as Instagram and Facebook, listening to music, making use of the stopwatch, and writing 'to do' and 'to buy' lists for my apartment move in this next month. . . . [M]y phone allows me to be creative, keeps me organized, and helps me to keep track of my health."

On Taking and Sharing Pictures: "It has a great camera and sometimes the pictures look just as professional as the pictures taken with my actual camera. It is convenient to have a quality camera that is portable and easy to snap a few pictures with and then be put away in a purse or a pocket. There are also several different apps on my iPhone that assist me with editing pictures. Apps such as Afterlight, which allows me to change my pictures in pretty much every way imaginable. A Beautiful Mess gives me access to unique fonts and patterns to place on my pictures. Pic Stitch lets me put collages together, specifically anywhere from two to ten pictures in a single collage. . . . I enjoy using Instagram to post my pictures because it allows everyone who follows me to see some of my favorite pictures in one account. I have even met new people over Instagram because they found one of my pictures by searching a certain hashtag. If it was not for my cellphone, I probably would not take nearly as many pictures as I do now."

WRITING *WITH* MOBILE TECHNOLOGIES

On Using Her Phone for School: "With the help of my phone, I am able to stay extremely organized with everything from to-do lists, to setting dates in my calendar. . . . Every time I randomly think of something I need to do or buy, I simply take my phone out and type it into my notes app. . . . I separate all of my apps into different categories so they are easy to find when I need them. Categories such as school, utilities, and social media apps are only a few. In my school app I have my e-mail account, which sends me an alert each and every time I receive a message. I also have a Canvas app for Lake Michigan College and the Black-board app for Central Michigan University. These two apps let me check future assignments and current grades in seconds just by logging in. They also send me notifications to remind me that certain homework assignments are due soon. This is much more convenient rather than reminding myself to log into my laptop four or five times a week to check e-mails and school networks."

On Using Her Phone to Exercise: "Being active and healthy are two of my favorite ways to utilize my phone. . . . Everyone knows that working out is not always our top priority or our favorite thing to do. When I am feeling this way, I grab my phone and put together a motivating playlist in my music app. . . . It is truly amazing that so many different apps can be used to get me through the day on one tiny phone."

Her Conclusion: ". . . According to Rosen (2004), with endless amounts of productive tasks that can be completed by just having a cell phone, people state that its convenience is the number one draw to owning one (Our Cell Phones). . . . Owning and using a cell phone in a constructive way is great, but many temptations to use it in inappropriate situations, such as at work or school, can give a cell phone a bad reputation. It is way too easy to sit around on a phone and be entertained all day, but using it to work out and track health, take pictures, and stay organized are three useful ways to use a phone."

Her images:

Jason's Assignment: For the Instructor with Some Experience Using Multimodal Assignments in the OWC

Overview

This assignment was developed as a second major writing project in a first-semester writing course. Throughout the class, students complete work within four genres (Public Service Announcement, Interview, Annotated Bibliography, and Academic Article). Within this unit, focusing on the interview genre, students are acquainted with the genre through general observations of examples that I've located for students to review. Students then locate their own examples and evaluate those examples based upon a rubric of the genre's conventions the class has collectively created. A quick Google search of "Rolling Stone Magazine Interview" or "Radio Interview" or even "Nightly News Interview" can provide examples within different formats, using different media, of the interview genre. These explorations should be guided, helping students to identify conventions that are specific to this genre, but possibly vary depending on the format.

From there, students begin to plan and document their ideas for the development of their own text within this genre. Ultimately, students are tasked with determining an interviewee, developing the interview questions, conducting the interview, and then designing their interview text based on decisions they've made for what media and modalities they believe to best communicate the purpose of their text. Mobile technology plays a critical role in this project, for it helps students to capture material to compose with: images, sounds, recordings of the conversation, video, etc. These raw materials can be captured with the students' mobile technology and then later used within the composing of their interview text. Through our study of the interview genre, we'll collaborate on determining the criteria used in evaluating these assignments and determine how different media and communication modes can enhance the interview itself. These criteria will differ with the various media used to compose each interview.

Summary of Assignment Directions for Students

In any given issue of *Rolling Stone*, *Time*, and *Esquire* (among others), one might find articles related to pop culture, politics, sports, worldly issues, or, really, just about anything. Here, we'll also come across a unique genre within these publications: the interview. However, the interview is not a genre that is exclusive to written texts. Every day on radio programs or TV shows, people conduct interviews to learn from others and to share that information directly from the source with an audience.

No matter the format of the interview, students will work to get useful information from the one being interviewed and determine the best way to communicate and present this information to the audience. In this project, students should consider themselves as interviewers in order to gain the information they wish to use within their text. They should then transition to the role of interview writer/designer, in which they will make the necessary, purposeful rhetorical choices to develop the most engaging piece for the reader.

> **Your Task:** Using a mobile technology, capture moments or elements of your interview (audio, video, images). With these assets, compose an interview using the media that you think best communicates to the audience in your chosen interview format: video, audio, or print-based.

Abbreviated Student Example: Joshua Kuhl

Buzzcuts and Bloodletting: Inside Barbershops

There once was a time when barbers did much more than a buzz cut or the occasional shave. At one point, they served as dentists and surgeons, as well as fulfilling their follicle duties. Although it has been quite some time since emergency appendectomies or impacted molar removals have been performed inside barbershops, one trait of the old days still remains. Behind the shearing and shaving, barbershops serve as an unofficial town hall, not far off from the Greek forums of millennia ago. Barbers serve as officiants each and every day, guiding the discourse like a debate moderator or a talk show host. Donna Williams does not perform surgery or emergency dental work, but she has been a barber for nearly forty years and is the owner of The Avenue Barbershop. I discussed with her the role of barbers and their shops, and the understated role they have in communities nationwide.

Q: What made you want to choose barbering as a career all those years ago?

A: Well when I was in high school, one of the things I wanted to do was that [barbering], nursing, and interior design. I didn't do that [barbering] until my thirties. All of the careers was about taking care of people. It's a service thing.

Q: What were barbershops like years ago?

A: Years and years ago, guys sometimes wouldn't get a haircut. They'd just sit around and talk, it was a hangout. They had old potbelly stoves and played cards. They actually even had little spittoons. There was no such thing [as the chain salons]. Hair was sometimes even done in the home. Women never went into barbershops, they only went to beauty shops. It was around the 70's or 80's when men went into the beauty shops because barbers couldn't do perms. Lots of barbers could take lessons [on perms], but were old and didn't want to. In the 30's and 40's, there was also a barter system. Men wouldn't pay for their cuts in cash, but instead they'd offer a trade or favor or brought something in. All businesses did that then, including grocery stores.

Q: How have barbershops changed since then?

A: The hairstyles have changed. They don't do face shaves anymore. Back then, the razors weren't disposable. The old chairs even had headrests that went back for the full shave. There aren't any new shops anymore, and the old shop owners are retiring and dying off. There used to be a barber school in town, but that closed down. Now, people have to go to Taylorville or Peoria to go to barber school. We don't do the dentist work or surgery anymore. They used to do something called bloodletting, and afterwards they'd leave the bloody bandages outside to dry out. The wind would pick up and cause the bandages to swirl the red and white, which became part of the barber symbol.

Q: You've owned . . .

Conclusion/Further Discussion

As evidenced by the 2013 CCCC *Position Statement of Principles and Example Effective Practices for Online Writing Instruction (OWI)*, accessibility is at the forefront of OWI concerns. Mobile technologies play an increasingly important role in providing access to Internet-based materials, including online courses. Because OWI students will use their mobile devices to access and complete work within their online courses, even if instructors prefer they don't, the online domain is the ideal place to integrate mobile technology into the curriculum. Within online courses, technology drives the class, providing a unique context through which literacy instruction occurs through the very technologies students should be critically exploring. Instructors can maximize the opportunity for technology use offered by assigning projects that promote both the investigation of and the use of these technologies. Even small assignments that allow students to think about their mobile phone as a composing tool will bridge the gap between the technology-driven online course and use of technology within students' daily lives. In fact, starting simple and providing structured opportunities for students to compose with these tools can ease an instructor into integrating these technologies into their OWI courses. As we have demonstrated here, including mobile technologies into OWCs can help students to become more critical users of such technologies and more aware of the rhetorical possibilities that these tools provide. This is increasingly important with the variety of composing tools available to students and how these tools are changing literate activity, including how students write with these devices.

In his *Kairos* webtext, "Cell Phones, Networks, and Power: Documenting Cell Phone Literacies," Ehren Helmut Pflugfelder argues that just because mobile technologies are accessible (available) doesn't mean that students are rhetorically aware of the potentials for how to use these technologies. Subtly making students aware of the possibilities of using mobile devices to become "writers on the go" can powerfully affect their rhetorical development. As indicated earlier, mobile technologies are present and are a part of any experience a writer wishes to communicate to an audience, whereas the desktop computer is waiting elsewhere (home, work, campus, library) for the writer to get through with the experience to return home to write about it. Our students are contemplating their technologies and how such technologies are composing tools, perfect for enhancing many formats of written communication. Through the guided practice of assignments such as the two we have outlined here, a writing instructor can provide richer rhetorical opportunities for students composing with the tools they interact with every day, literally teaching students to view their mobile phones as composing tools. Including mobile technologies in OWCs can help students to become more critical users of such technologies and more aware of the rhetorical possibilities that these tools provide. This is increasingly important with the variety of composing tools available to students and the way these tools are changing literate activity, including *how* students write with these devices. In the 2009 *Position Statement of the International Reading Association*, the authors elaborate on the expanded definition of literacy, positing that "because of rapid changes in technology, it is likely that students who begin school this year will experience even more profound changes in their literacy journeys. . . . Thus, the new literacies of today will be replaced by even newer literacies tomorrow as new ICTs [information and communication technologies} continuously emerge among a more globalized community of learners."

Both of the assignments described in this chapter accommodate for the fact that technologies change; mobile phones will not become obsolete, but most likely continue to morph into smaller-sized personal computers, having more advanced features and capabilities. Further, both of these assignments address the challenges that might arise for instructors and students when working for/attending colleges that provide little or no institutional support to do mobile learning activities: no computer labs, no discounts on software, no tech support, or no resource labs where students can learn how to use technologies. Yet these assignments force students to think about how they are using mobile devices to create meaning to expand their literacies. As writing instructors, we should be concerned about literacy development, and as online writing instructors, we are in the ideal context to help students interrogate their use of technology. As Cynthia Selfe argues, "literacy instruction is now inextricably linked with technology" (5). The rhetorical strategies that they practice with these assignments will facilitate connection between "real-life" and "school" (Yancey) and students will be able to adapt to changing technologies and continually expand their literacies to include writing, thinking, being an academic or worker on the go, and to use these skills in future situations to assist them in creating meaning.

We know that the thought of incorporating mobile technologies can be daunting to many online writing instructors, but the payoff of utilizing these devices is rewarding. When incorporating mobile learning or any type of multimodal assignment into the online writing classroom it is best to start small and know what resources are available, so in addition to the texts listed on our Works Cited page, here are some great resources:

- *A Position Statement of Principles and Example Effective Practices for Online Writing Instruction (OWI)*: http://www.ncte.org/cccc/resources/positions/owiprinciples

- The Open Resource Journal: http://www.ncte.org/cccc/owi-open-resource, an online journal where instructors share classroom techniques and assignments centered around the OWI Principles.

- Blair, Kristine L. "Teaching Multimodal Assignments in OWI Contexts." *Foundational Practices of Online Writing Instruction.* Eds. Beth Hewett and Kevin Eric Depew. Fort Collins: WAC Clearinghouse, 2015. 471–91. Print.

- Gos, Michael W. "Nontraditional Student Access to OWI." *Foundational Practices of Online Writing Instruction.* Eds. Beth Hewett and Kevin Eric Depew. Fort Collins: WAC Clearinghouse, 2015. 309–46. Print.

Works Cited

Almendrala, Anna. "Our Creepy Attachment to Cell Phones Could Be an Addiction." *HuffPost.* TheHuffingtonPost.com, Inc. 5 Sept. 2014. Web. 2 May 2016.

Anderson, Terry, Liam Rourke, D. Randy Garrison, and Walter Archer. "Assessing Teaching Presence in a Computer Conferencing Context." *Journal of Asynchronous Learning Networks* 5.2 (2001): 1–17. Print.

Ball, Cheryl E. "Assessing Scholarly Multimedia: A Rhetorical Genre Studies Approach." *Technical Communication Quarterly* 21.1 (2012): 61–77. Print.

Bezemer, Jeff, and Gunther Kress. "Writing in Multimodal Texts: A Social Semiotic Account of Designs for Learning." Lutkewitte 233–57.

CCCC Executive Committee on Best Practices for OWI. *A Position Statement of Principles and Example Effective Practices for Online Writing Instruction (OWI)*. Mar. 2013. Web. 22 Apr. 2013.

CCCC Executive Committee on Multimodal Literacies Issue Management. "Position Statement on Multimodal Literacies." 2005. Web. 22 Aug. 2014.

Dunn, Patricia A. *Talking, Sketching, Moving: Multiple Literacies in the Teaching of Writing*. Portsmouth: Boynton/Cook-Heinemann, 2001. Print.

Erickson, Tammy. "How Mobile Technologies Are Shaping a New Generation." *Harvard Business Review*. Harvard Business, 18 Apr. 2012. Web. 14 Feb. 2016.

Fortune, Ron. "'You're Not in Kansas Anymore': Interactions among Semiotic Modes in Multimodal Texts." *Computers and Composition* 22.1 (2005): 49–54. Print.

Halbritter, Bump. *Mics, Cameras, Symbolic Action: Audio-Visual Rhetoric for Writing Teachers*. Anderson: Parlor, 2012. Print.

International Reading Association. *New Literacies and 21st Century Technologies: A Position Statement of the International Reading Association*. Newark: IRA, 2009. Web. 2 May 2016.

Kress, Gunther. "Gains and Losses: New Forms of Texts, Knowledge, and Learning." Lutkewitte 283–301.

———. *Multimodality: A Social Semiotic Approach to Contemporary Communication*. New York: Routledge, 2010. Print.

Lauer, Claire. "Expertise with New/Multi/Modal/Visual/Digital/Media Technologies Desired: Tracing Composition's Evolving Relationship with Technology through the MLA *JIL*." *Computers and Composition* 34 (2014): 60–75. Print.

Lutkewitte, Claire, ed. *Multimodal Composition: A Critical Sourcebook.* Boston: Bedford/St. Martin's, 2013. Print.

New London Group. "A Pedagogy of Multiliteracies: Designing Social Futures." *Harvard Educational Review* 66.1 (1996): 60–92. Print.

Pflugfelder, Ehren Helmut. "Cell Phones, Networks, and Power: Documenting Cell Phone Literacies." *Kairos: A Journal of Rhetoric, Technology, and Pedagogy.* 19.2 (2015): n. pag. Web. 21 June 2015.

Rice, Jenny Edbauer. "Rhetoric's Mechanics: Retooling the Equipment of Writing Production." *College Composition and Communication* 60.2 (2008): 366–87. Print.

Rosen, Christine. "Our Cell Phones, Ourselves." *The New Atlantis* 6 (2004): 26–45. Print.

Selfe, Cynthia L. *Technology and Literacy in the 21st Century: The Importance of Paying Attention.* Carbondale: Southern Illinois UP, 1999. Print.

Sheridan, Mary. P., and Jennifer Rowsell. *Design Literacies: Learning and Innovating in the Digital Age.* New York: Routledge, 2010. Print.

Smith, Aaron, and Dana Page. "U.S. Smartphone Use in 2015." *Pew Research Center.* Pew Research Center, 1 Apr. 2015. Web. 15 June 2015.

Takayoshi, Pamela, and Cynthia L. Selfe. "Thinking about Multimodality." *Multimodal Composition: Resources for Teachers.* Ed. Cynthia L. Selfe. Cresskill: Hampton, 2007. 1–12. Print.

Traxler, John. "Will Student Devices Deliver Innovation, Inclusion, and Transformation?" *Journal of the Research Center for Educational Technology* 6.1 (2010): 3–15. Print.

Yancey, Kathleen Blake. "Made Not Only in Words: Composition in a New Key." Lutkewitte 62–88.

Chapter Eleven

Using Mobile Videocapture to Facilitate Student Writing and Learning

Ghanashyam Sharma
Stony Brook University

Soni Adhikari
Stony Brook University

It was in 1994, at a "computer training center" in Nepal, when one of us (Shyam) first encountered the "print screen" function on a computer keyboard. When asked what it was, the instructor pressed that "PrtScr" key, entered some commands, and printed out exactly the same image of the typing tutor application that was running on the desktop computer. The instructor, who was the owner of the only two PCs in town, then wrote with a pen on the printout to describe the functions of the said button and some other less common ones on the keyboard. That handout was quite a treasure to take home.

By 2016, even students and teachers in Nepal are able to capture still images of the computer screen and also moving visuals in them. Today's computers are further able to capture sound/voice from outside (and inside), integrate the visual image of users (and other objects shown in front of an integrated camera) within the same frame, and allow users to edit, publish, and instantaneously share audiovisual recordings of all the inputs in a single product. In fact, the introduction and advancements of mobile computing devices, alongside developments in Internet technologies, have added and enhanced features such as mobility and ease of use, multimodality of composition, multidimensionality of the product, accessibility to the material for anyone from anywhere, and synchronicity and collaboration among users.

Here in the United States, while we were drafting this chapter, Shyam created teaching materials for an online course with the help of a smartphone, achieving most of the above goals with the functions and applications available on that phone. Specifically, he used iPhone apps that captured, edited, published, and shared multidimensional audiovisual materials with his students, quite quickly, easily, inexpensively, and with minimal expertise. Similarly, Soni created videocaptures (also with a cell phone) that showed and told students how to use applications required by the course, including the course site, cloud documents, and library databases. Providing students with these materials saved class time, also allowing students with different learning styles and abilities to use the materials as needed. It can help students come to class more prepared and have more productive conversations in class as well as during office-hour meetings. Thus, the advancements in screen and videocapturing technologies in mobile devices allow teachers "to bring the classroom to the student when they need it" (Carlson 156), including for teaching and engaging students in activities that go beyond class.

In this chapter, we define and theorize mobile-based screen and videocapturing practices in the context of teaching writing. Then we describe how we use videocapturing for creating instructional materials, providing feedback, and working with students, further adding how our students also use it for creating/presenting multimedia texts and for interacting with us and one another. After noting some of the challenges and limitations, we conclude by highlighting the benefits afforded by the advancements and convergence of mobility, multidimensionality, multimodality, and mutuality (through synchronicity) in what used to be originally symbolized by the "print screen" button on computer keyboards.

We use the term *mobile videocapturing* to refer to the multidimensional act of creating multimodal texts by using mobile devices, as we will further describe and illustrate. While *screencapturing* could both signify capturing still images and recording moving images in or on a device, we use *videocapturing* to highlight how *mobile* devices converge screencasting and videorecording. And, finally, the phrase "mobile videocapturing" also best accounts for the fact that mobile devices can be used to alternately or simultaneously record audio and visual activities from themselves, from other devices, and from the user and nearby sources.

Theoretical Framework

When cameras and microphones were added to the computer, software was able to add new media and dimensions to screen recording by capturing audio and visual input from both inside and outside the machine. Similarly, when computers became compact and mobile, they could be easily pointed at other devices for recording the latter's screens and sounds, and to other targets including the face and body of the user/speaker. Their mobility also allowed zooming and panning through physical movement and with software. And, finally, the Internet redefined the act of screensharing by introducing synchronous access of texts and interfaces, allowing collaboration and enhancing engagement. In the following subsections, we theorize such multidimensionality, as well as the complexity of mobility (which blurs, for instance, the boundary between handheld and laptop mobile devices), multimodality of output, and the blurring of lines between recorded and synchronously shared/collaborated activities.

Mobility

Because they can freely travel with the user, mobile devices can record any source of sound and visual and also capture their own screens. The increasing processing power and dynamic functions of the applications on them further make videocapturing of screen and world flexible and versatile. And their constant connection to other devices, applications, and users through the Internet and data networks add to and enhance what mobile devices can do in terms of recording and sharing sound and image. In fact, emerging affordances on *mobile* devices can have particularly powerful impacts on student learning because, as Claire Lutkewitte notes in the introduction to this book, the "mobility" of these devices can signify intimacy/attachment and ownership toward them and it can reinforce engagement in learning.

Traditional videocapturing required a separate camera device (which used to be expensive in itself) and a large computer with complex audiovisual editing applications; the process was far more time-consuming and it also required much more technological skill for editing and publishing the material. So when writing teachers wanted to show and tell students how to do things, they required students to use various technologies for completing coursework, or asked them to collaborate with the teacher and with one another; the method of screencapture was not an appealing option. In contrast, because they have introduced a variety of affordances, mobile devices and the applications and functions they offer now greatly alleviate the challenges teachers used to face in the past.

It must be noted here that in practice "mobility" is not an absolute but rather a complex spectrum. So, while a cell phone is mobile for most users in most situations, a smaller/lighter laptop may be as mobile for some users in some situations, whereas even a mid-sized tablet may not be mobile for other users in other situations. In fact, even with the most advanced functions, applications, and processing capacity, the compactness of mobile devices may pose enough challenges to make traditional devices more appealing or appropriate for some users and uses.

For example, at present, mobile phones are capable but rather inconvenient for capturing slides along with a lecture (especially when the user wants to include his or her image within the frame). In our context, while being versatile in their own ways, mobile phones and tablets still do not offer native apps to videocapture their own screens (they need to be mirrored or simulated on desk/lap-tops or recorded with another camera/device). By contrast, integrating one's image while capturing activity on the screen is extremely easy (and free) with independent or browser-based applications such as Media Core Capture on desktop or laptop computers. Learning management systems like Blackboard offer integrated lecture capture through applications like Adobe Connect. Native apps freely included with operating systems of laptops and notebooks (such as Apple's) are capable of recording parts or the entirety of their screens, including sound input from inside or outside, and editing and publishing the material. Thus, compactness and mobility often come with compromises; not all things mobile are convenient to use, and mobility itself is a function of who is using them, when, why, and how.

However, in the context of videocapturing screens and other audiovisual sources in order to create basic instructional resources and engage students in and beyond the classroom, the mobility of mobile devices opens up tremendous possibilities as we further discuss.

Multimodality

Mobile devices can now capture, process, and produce multiple media, including sound and voice, still and moving images, screen-shots and screencapture videos, and even animations. From the act of simply grabbing the still picture of a screen, screencapture technology has moved to integrating many modes from many sources, and the capability of mobile devices to do so makes it possible to compose and share semiotically rich multimodal artifacts.

There is some research showing the benefits of multimodality in the context of videocapture in educational settings, including creating video lectures, providing instructor feedback, and helping students to work on multimodal projects. For instance, Richard Mayer compared different kinds of presentations—ranging from text only, to text with images in the frame, animations with text, and commentary along with animation—and found that students best remembered information from the last combination. Other scholars have also highlighted that combining sound and visual when providing feedback appeals to students with different learning styles (see Stannard; Séror "Show Me"). In a study described by Chientzu Chou, Lanise Block, and Renee Jesness, "Students with disabilities, economically disadvantaged students, and ELL students in the classroom with mobile devices all performed better than students of the same categories in the whole district" (12).

Perhaps the most significant impact of mobile videocapture is that it allows teachers to include their voice and image in the instructional material and when giving feedback to students. As Graham Currell states in his article, "The Use of Screen-Capture Video as a Learning Resource," videocapturing can enhance student-teacher interaction and relationship by adding a "valuable extension" to their meeting in person. Multimedia learning resources created by using mobile devices may lack in quality but as scholars have suggested, less-than-professional products add to teachers' authenticity and relatability.

In short, while multimodality has become a norm with many computing devices, the ease of use of mobile devices enhances multimodality in the composition and production of videocaptures in unique and powerful ways.

Multidimensionality

Compact and therefore mobile devices are also easy to point to other screens and also into other targets, zooming and panning on the object being captured. So the third feature and advantage of mobile videocapturing is this multidimensionality. This ability of mobile devices blurs the boundaries between screen and world and also between the types of input and output. Today's mobile devices can incorporate all of the above inputs (and also existing assets in the device or from connected sources) in the final product, allowing teachers and students to create richer educational materials and experiences.

Furthermore, the many-in-one mobile devices are able to incorporate or substitute other devices and applications for recording (they incorporate microphones and their cameras are able to capture flickering screens); for editing and overlaying the input (so they replace computers with once-expensive video editing software); for publishing and sharing (because they have browsers); and for playing back all the media. These capacities often redefine the meaning and function of videocapturing. Likewise, mobile devices that can connect to data and Wi-Fi networks add other dimensions, such as videoconferencing, that allow users to talk to someone while looking at and working on shared screens or documents/media. Mobile devices are able to access cloud documents and allow users to collaboratively edit them while talking on the phone.

The different dimensions of mobile videocapturing described here greatly benefit not only teachers but also students. In "Disabling Assumptions," Patricia Dunn highlights the benefits of emerging features like writing by voice, text-to-voice reading, and oral and visual feedback for all students. Students can benefit from more focused teacher feedback (due to multidimensional resources), the ability to review material (or use it after being absent in class), and to independently practice using an application at their own pace and convenience.

Mutuality

Users can now use mobile devices to share and even collaboratively work on what they both/all see and hear on their respective devices. This extension of the notion of screencapturing is an emerging and highly intriguing one. By allowing teachers to invite students into interaction and collaboration, screensharing invokes *mutuality*, as described by composition scholars David Wallace and Helen Ewald, "in that knowledge is not a prepackaged commodity to be delivered by the teacher but . . . an 'outcome' constituted in the classroom [and beyond] through the dialogic interaction among teachers and students alike" (4).

Technologies often simply replace an existing tool (such as the printout of the computer given to Shyam by his computer teacher). Technology theorist Ruben Puentedura calls this substitution (cited in Chou, Block, and Jesness). But as Puentedura adds, technologies can take us three more steps beyond substitution: augmentation (such as when the instructor added writing on the printout), modification (his teaching method changed from orally describing the idea to using a visual resource as a primary aid), and redefinition (if he had videocaptured the teaching moment for future review). We propose the idea of mutuality—or the ability to synchronously access and support or collaborate with learners—as a dispersed form of screen- or videocapturing that is best described by the last aspect above, redefinition. That is, videocapturing redefines teaching and learning by allowing teachers and students to create, share, access, and collaborate on educational resources, events, and experiences in more convenient ways than ever before. Interactive feedback and discussion on students' writing can transform teaching/learning because it helps to build rapport between students and teacher, as well as making teaching and learning more effective. Synchronous access through screensharing, especially through mobile devices, promotes mutuality in the form of teacher support and collaboration among students and teacher.

Educational Uses and Implications

In this section, we share some of the practical ways in which we have used mobile videocapturing in our college-level writing courses. The cases of teaching and learning that we present here highlight the different affordances that we theoretically discussed above (albeit with rough correspondence).

To begin with, the most convenient practice of mobile videocapturing in our teaching, one that particularly highlights the affordance of mobility, is the use of an iPhone app named YouTube Capture (created by YouTube and free for download from the App Store) for creating video lectures and illustrations and providing feedback on students' work. As we demonstrate in a brief video published on YouTube (https://youtu.be/MSFlfbFsTBI), this app combines the functions of camera, a convenient video editor, and a web browser for not only uploading but also accessing/managing and sharing videos—all from one simple interface. We typically start by using the front camera to address students and preview what we are about to provide, then we pause the clip to use the back camera for capturing the screen of our laptops. We turn the camera to printed materials (such as syllabus or assignment instruction) when we want to encourage students to print and read such resources, or to other audiovisual sources as needed.

YouTube Capture stores video clips in the cell phone's video folder, while ordering all the clips taken during a session in one "project" so when the "next" button is tapped, the clips are in the order they were taken, ready for editing. The clips can be trimmed, reordered, and removed with the simple act of dragging and dropping. At this stage, the app also allows users to add or overlay other videos and music/audio files stored in the device. A third tap, on the "next" button, takes users to the final screen that allows them to enter video information (description, tags and category, copyright information), set privacy level (private, unlisted, and public), "publish" the video to YouTube, and copy or share the hyperlink to various networks. The app asks users to sign in to their YouTube (or Gmail) account when publishing videos for the first time, saving login information for full access and management of their YouTube account in the future. Using an inexpensive tripod, which came with a Bluetooth remote control, we press the record/pause button to start a session, press it to pause and start new clips, and when we are finished recording, we use the cell phone to complete the three-step process of editing, adding information, and publishing/sharing videos through YouTube as described above.

Second, videocapturing can also be used for teaching students how to compose multimodal assignments, including through the use of videocapturing with their mobile devices. One assignment that we are currently developing for our students, foregrounding multimodality that mobile devices are capable of handling, asks students to use YouTube Capture or similar apps for creating "sixty-second" digital narratives that describe, argue, or reflect on an object, event, or experience. To create this project, students start by recording a scripted narrative (which they can overlay with videos in the editing process), then videorecord people, objects, and events to visualize the narrative (or argument). Students should convey the theme with a telling title, may choose to ad lib their narrative until they get the product close to sixty seconds, and must include a credits page at the end if external sources are used. As we have found from similar assignments in pre-mobile days, assignments like this can "bridge learning in school, after-school, and home environments" (Shuler 5); mobile devices can further enhance this benefit.

Third, to assist students in the preceding assignment, we create video demonstrations of how to use YouTube Capture by using the same app. Since the smartphones and tablets that we own do not yet have the capacity to videocapture their own screens—unless we jailbreak them to download apps that can do so—we connect them to our laptops and capture their screens with QuickTime. As we demonstrate how to use the app on the smartphone, we also capture our voice from the laptop. This can also be done by "mirroring" the smartphone's or tablet's screen on the laptop by using apps like Reflector (in the case of Apple devices).

The fourth practical application of mobile videocapturing foregrounds both the strength and weakness of mobile devices already mentioned, further showing the challenge of determining what is "mobile." For providing feedback on individual students' assignments (especially multimodal ones), we sometimes use a smartphone to videocapture printed assignments as we comment and write on them. However, as we migrate to online submission, require cloud-based collaboration, and teach some of our courses fully online, our laptops increasingly become our preferred mobile devices. While applications like Google Docs for smartphones technically allow us to comment and suggest edits on students' writing, the screen size makes it inconvenient to do so. Also, having to capture the screen on a second device while using both hands to type feedback makes smartphones inefficient for providing feedback.

The free laptop-based app that we use in this case, Media Core Capture, essentially helps us bypass smartphones' affordance of mobility and multidimensionality by incorporating our moving image in one corner of the screen that is being captured as we navigate and work on it.

Our final practical use of mobile videocapturing takes feedback one step further into synchronous collaboration, foregrounding the final affordance of mutuality. When using the traditional, asynchronous method of providing feedback, we insert marginal comments or use track changes on students' drafts on collaborative cloud-based documents such as Google Docs. Doing so "captures" the screen in the sense that the student will see exactly the same screen on the other end, at any point of time. Especially in the online writing course that Shyam teaches, we require students to meet with us over their assignment drafts on Google Docs, using videoconferencing (Skype or Google Hangout) or office phone during appointment times that they pick in advance. By using the same approach, our students also peer review one another's drafts at different stages of the writing process, using rubrics or video guidelines that we provide.

As Jérémie Séror ("Screencapture") has shown in a study of ELL students' composition process, the process of drafting assignments can also be captured for later review both by students and by teachers. In a perfect illustration of the "dispersal" of videocapturing into different users and actions, a student in an online class recently asked Shyam if it was okay to record his voice during a Skype meeting over his assignment on Google Docs. Shyam gave the student permission to record the screen as well, so the student could later review what his teacher said "while" he moved the cursor, typed comments on the margin, and used the "suggesting" mode to insert edits in the draft. The amount of feedback provided, this student told Shyam, was so overwhelming that being able to record the screen and conversation "was a big relief."

As we have indicated, there are significant implications of using mobile videocapturing in the writing classroom. Most significant, using the convenient but powerful apps of mobile devices, teachers can create instructional videos, students can compose multimodal texts, and teachers and students can greatly enhance feedback and collaboration. Traditionally, screencapturing was only done with applications inside the same machine. As described by the Faculty Development and Instructional Design Center at Northern Illinois University, "Screencasts have been applied in a number of innovative ways in higher education including capturing lectures, conducting website tours, software and database training, demonstrating library functions, and providing feedback to students." When the capturing device is "liberated" by using the approach in this chapter, the possibilities dramatically increase, and the other affordances of mobile devices we described above further enhance those possibilities. For instance, in the context of providing feedback on students' work, videocapturing is far more effective than just writing comments on it. With the addition of voice, the act of pointing to the video on the screen (with the cursor or finger) becomes the powerful equivalent of using a pen to write and draw on printed drafts of student work, alongside other affordances of mobile devices.

The process of mobile videocapturing can also be unbundled as made possible or limited by different teaching/learning conditions. For example, teachers can use mobile devices to record audio-only feedback and send it to students, who can listen to the sound file while looking at the same document the teacher has commented on. Even though they lack the visual dimension of videocapturing, approaches like this may be necessary when disk or Web space is limited or students don't have access to video-capable devices but want to retain the human touch of our voice when providing feedback on students' work.

With traditional devices and applications, videocapturing lessons, assignments, and feedback used to involve a great deal of planning, resources, and expertise—as evidenced by the details included in the 129-page long *The Screencasting Handbook*, written by Ian Ozsvald. Those challenges become more significant when teachers start teaching and supporting students in how to complete assignments involving videocapture. Adding new dimensions to the screen as we discussed above would seem to make that process even more daunting to teachers and discouraging to students. Fortunately, the processing power and emerging affordances of mobile devices, including the power of their interfaces, applications, and connectivity, have made it incredibly easy to do all of the above.

Conclusion

Due to all the features and affordances that today's mobile devices are capable of, and also due to the convergence of screencapturing and videorecording (which we describe as "videocapturing"), what we describe in this chapter is now within the reach of most teachers and increasingly more students. The mobility of devices and affordability and availability of user-friendly applications in them allow us to create multimodal teaching/learning resources and teach multimodal assignments with minimal time and expertise. These features can motivate faculty to adopt emerging technological tools and affordances (Kozma), leading to instructional improvement and then to more effective learning.

Mobile devices are becoming increasingly popular, and so are the instructional materials and learning experiences they can create; the diversification of student bodies also makes multimodal learning resources necessary for more students. Similarly, as increasing numbers of writing courses are offered online, creating quick, easy, and affordable video resources by using mobile apps has become an effective method to provide students with class lectures, assignment prompts and guidelines, and feedback. Because online writing courses require a larger number of technologies, may involve more advanced functions, and depend more heavily on technological affordances, videocapturing resources can help teachers more effectively teach how to use particular tools in particular contexts and to provide focused and multidimensional feedback.

As we mentioned earlier, there are certainly limitations of mobile videocapturing. Not all students or even teachers may have devices that are capable of these functions, applications, and processing power. We have the experience of running out of space on our smartphones, audio input mysteriously disappearing after publishing the video, having to direct students with questions about non-Apple devices to the university Helpdesk because we can check how things work only on our Apple devices, and wishing that we had a third hand to zoom and pan the phone camera on the screen while we type on the screen! Often we have tried to refine our use of technology and/or adapt our pedagogy to it—until we felt like putting our smartphones back in our pocket or purse and going to class with printed handouts instead!

The continued evolution of technology will make today's applications and even affordances irrelevant sooner or later. For instance, while revising this chapter, the two of us used a Google Docs file to track changes, showing where we have modified the text (a feature that was added one year ago) and thereby enhancing the dimension of mutuality we discussed above; this powerful function of both capturing and manipulating a shared text may be obsolete sooner than we feel comfortable. On the other hand, teachers and students will overcome or bypass most limitations posed by today's form factors, operating systems, and available applications on mobile devices today. But we hope that the broader discussions and illustrations of current technology here will provide some food for thought for educators in schools and colleges, even when the specific applications we used for illustration become outdated.

Regardless of how the technology evolves, the fundamentals of teaching and learning will remain relevant, even as new technologies and new methods serve us better. After all, it is what our teachers did to help us learn, using whatever tools were available to them at the time, however primitive and simple, that we ultimately value and remember.

Works Cited

Carlson, Kathleen. "Delivering Information to Students 24/7 with Camtasia." *Information Technology and Libraries* 28.3 (2009): 154–56. Print.

Chou, Chientzu Candace, Lanise Block, and Renee Jesness. "A Case Study of Mobile Learning Pilot Project in K–12 Schools." *Journal of Educational Technology Development and Exchange* 5.2 (2012): 11–26. Print.

Currell, Graham. "The Use of Screen-Capture Video as a Learning Resource." *New Directions* 1.3 (2007): 37–40. Print.

Dunn, Patricia A. "Disabling Assumptions: Challenging Stereotypes about Disability for a More Democratic Society." *English Journal* 103.2 (2013): 94–96. Print.

Kozma, Robert B. "Communication, Rewards, and the Use of Classroom Innovations." *Journal of Higher Education* 50.6 (1979): 761–71. Print.

Mayer, Richard E. *Multimedia Learning*. Cambridge: Cambridge UP, 2001. Print.

Northern Illinois University. Faculty Development and Instructional Design Center. "Screencasts as a Pedagogical Tool." *Spectrum Newsletter* Spring 2010. Web. 2 Feb. 2016.

Ozsvald, Ian. *The Screencasting Handbook*. Open source digital book. 2013. *TheScreencastingHandbook.com*. Web. 3 May 2016.

Séror, Jérémie. "Screen Capture Technology: A Digital Window into Students' Writing Processes." *Canadian Journal of Learning and Technology* 39.3 (2013): 1–16. Print.

———. "Show Me! Enhanced Feedback through Screencasting Technology." *TESL Canada Journal* 30.1 (2012): 104–16. Print.

Shuler, Carly. "Pockets of Potential: Using Mobile Technologies to Promote Children's Learning." New York: Joan Ganz Cooney Center, 2009. Web. 3 May 2016.

Stannard, Russell. "Using Screen Capture Software in Student Feedback." *English Subject Centre of the Higher Education Academy.* HEA English Subject Centre, 2007. Web. 3 May 2016.

Wallace, David L., and Helen R. Ewald. *Mutuality in the Rhetoric and Composition Classroom.* Carbondale: Southern Illinois UP, 2000. Print.

CHAPTER TWELVE

Write on Location: A Place-Based Approach to Mobile Composition

ASHLEY J. HOLMES
Georgia State University

As a teacher who values community engagement, place-based composition, and digital rhetorics, I am interested in the intersection between digital, online spaces and physical, material (typically local) places. My course assignments often prompt students to engage their surrounding community, beyond the boundaries of the classroom or campus, through service learning, client-based professional writing projects, or other community-based activities. In agreement with theorists in curriculum studies advocating for a public pedagogy, I believe that "schools are not the sole sites of teaching, learning, and curricula, and that perhaps they are not even the most influential" (Sandlin, Schultz, and Burdick 2). Because many of my course projects involve students venturing off campus for their educational experiences, mobile composition has become a central way for me to transfer course-based writing and research skills to more public venues for student learning.

Mobile technologies make it increasingly possible for us and our students to write, revise, and publish from public places outside of the office or computer lab, changing not only *how* we write but also *where* we write. As smartphones, tablets, and Wi-Fi hotspots proliferate, though, we become ever more telepresent, collapsing our sense of time and space; as Nedra Reynolds contends in *Geographies of Writing*, this time-space compression results in "the sense of loss of public space" (27). While digital technologies have a tendency to distract us from our physical surroundings, I argue that a place-based approach to mobile composition offers the potential to ground student experience and writing in material places, reclaiming local public space. In the following pages, I describe a multimodal mapping project and a Write on Location freewriting assignment that I argue encourage the mobile writer to (re)connect with local places, using one's material surroundings as a site for invention. Similar to how Benjamin's flâneur came to represent a new kind of public person—one that Reynolds presents as "mobile and detached" (71)—mobile composing and publishing represent new methods for students to engage with and write the publics around them.

Theoretical Grounding

Since the early 2000s, composition specialists have been researching and arguing for the significance of attending to places and spaces as they relate to writing. Some of the earliest place-based scholarship came out of the ecocomposition movement, whose proponents claimed that "relationships between texts and nature are impossible to avoid" (Dobrin and Weisser 2). Sidney I. Dobrin and Christian Weisser's *Natural Discourse*, as well as their edited collection *Ecocomposition*, helped build a foundation for composition teachers and scholars to theorize the impact of place on writers and writing. In the years that followed, works such as Reynolds's *Geographies of Writing*, Christopher Keller and Christian Weisser's *The Locations of Composition*, and Jonathon Mauk's article "Location, Location, Location," drew on spatial theories from cultural geography and helped shift scholarly discussions to consider places other than the natural and ecological to include cities, schools, museums, coffee shops, and more.

To support my own approach to composition teaching, I found this body of scholarship offered theories and pedagogies that provided opportunities for students to meaningfully connect with place, both extending the classroom beyond traditional academic spaces and helping interrogate the "academic/nonacademic dichotomy" (Mauk 362). Shifting students' academic experiences to outside of the classroom has a significant impact on their learning; indeed, this impact is often prompted by students' visceral reactions to new community places. For example, in a recent service-learning partnership with a local middle school, students in my course immediately reacted to the locked school doors, complex buzz-in and sign-in procedures, visible video cameras around the school, and school codes that did not allow students to carry backpacks between classes. Students' reactions to the urban middle school space aligned with how Jenna Vinson defines "spatial shock": "students' feelings of discomfort, uneasiness, or alarm that surface in the moment of crossing a material boundary and visiting an unfamiliar place" (n.p.). Like Vinson, I believe moments of spatial shock—sometimes personal and emotive—can be productive for student learning (see Holmes); spatial shock can bring "both recognition of socially-produced assumptions and, potentially, reflection on one's own subject-position as an outsider to that place" (Vinson). Part of what I think leads to these moments of potential learning and growth through spatial shock is for students to physically engage with places in their local communities: locations that are new to them or approaching familiar places with an unfamiliar or critical perspective. A challenge I have faced, however, is how to continue students' valuable material experiences in local places, while still providing opportunities for students to employ digital tools to engage with and represent places virtually. The compromise I have found that allows me to meet both of these goals is mobile composition.

I see mobile composition as a pedagogical approach that invites students to move into and across various academic and public spaces, employing the tools of writing, research, and publishing via mobile technologies. Because mobile composition in some way implicates location and positionality, it dovetails with scholarship that employs spatial theories and place-based composition pedagogies. In her contribution to Amy Kimme Hea's edited collection *Going Wireless*, for instance, Nicole R. Brown examines metaphors of mobility such as graffiti and public art, which she claims can help composition specialists "build location-aware pedagogies" (242). In her assessment of the metaphor of public art, she argues that the focus on "invention, publication space, the composing process, and reader response/participation fit[s] well with pedagogical objectives related to writing instruction" (246). In the assignments I describe in the following section, local places become the sites for student research and writing; in line with Brown's argument, these public locations prompt invention, publication, composition, and reader response—all important pedagogical goals within the writing classes I teach. Moreover, when these objectives are initiated within a course on *digital* writing and publishing, mobile composition represents an invaluable pedagogical tool for encouraging students to (re)connect with local places while utilizing digital and mobile methods.

Descriptions of Assignments

I began using a place-based approach to mobile composition in the Digital Writing and Publishing course (English 3120) I teach at Georgia State University in downtown Atlanta. This 3000-level course is part of the Rhetoric and Composition undergraduate major course offerings, though students enrolled in the course range from majors in English and journalism to business and art. One of the course projects asks students to choose a local public issue, develop an argument, and represent the issue and argument multimodally using a Google map. Most recently, I have assigned the textbook *Writer/Designer: A Guide to Making Multimodal Projects* by Kristin L. Arola, Jennifer Sheppard, and Cheryl E. Ball; we use terminology from the New London Group, as it is introduced in the textbook, to discuss different modes of communication: auditory, gestural, linguistic, spatial, and visual. Students are required to ground their projects in the spatial mode by producing their own Google maps with approximately three to five sites (or dropped pins) that link to additional multimodal content they create and compile through blogs, websites, online presentations, videos, podcasts, and/or photos. Having worked with the Google Maps platform for a few years, I remind students that they need to find a way to post additional multimodal content to an online space. Google Maps allows for a small amount of linguistic content and a few photos to be posted, but students wanting more space or a different platform must find a method for posting that content online to then link within their Google map. This often means using programs such as Prezi, YouTube, SlideShare, or Flickr to host student-generated videos, PowerPoint presentations, or photos.

A significant component of the assignment is that, whether implicitly or explicitly, students' maps and multimodal projects as a whole must make an argument to an audience of their choosing. In fact, I developed in-class activities that ask students to investigate different maps and discuss whether and how they make an argument. For example, I have used world maps with a south-up orientation—sometimes referred to as "upside down" or reversed world maps—to prompt discussion about Northern Hemisphere bias and the privileging of up versus down. I have also used maps from government or political organizations to discuss rhetorical choices in displaying data spatially. Finally, I have invited students to explore maps on the website http://judgmentalmaps.com, to which users post humorous maps of cities identified by different sections using judgmental, often stereotypical labels. By the end of the discussion, students begin to understand maps as yet another set of texts that are composed by writers and designers who make rhetorical choices in how to represent content.

The multimodal mapping project is a designed series of mini-assignments that walk students through the composing process, including: mobile composition invention activities, in-class drafting and production, peer review, a statement of rhetorical choices submitted with the final draft, and an end-of-project reflection on students' learning and experiences with the project. In this chapter, I focus on the mobile composition activities but also quote from students' final projects, statements of rhetorical choices, and reflections. As an invention activity to help prepare for the digital mapping multimodal project, students complete three Write on Location mobile composition assignments. For each assignment, students are required to visit a location they plan to include on their map, take a picture of the location (with a mobile device, such as a cell phone or tablet computer), and compose a 250-word freewrite while on location. I should note that the class is designed as a hybrid, meaning we meet face-to-face for seventy-five minutes on one day each week and students complete out-of-class or online assignments (asynchronously) for the second seventy-five minutes of class time for the week; I provide this as a rationale to students when I ask them to visit and write at different locations off-campus.

I developed the Write on Location assignment as a combination of what Olin Bjork and John Pedro Schwartz call "writing in the wild" and what Marissa Juarez calls "spontaneous composing." Bjork and Schwartz suggest a paradigm for mobile composition that involves students writing in the wild; they describe assignments that invite students to visit "places of rhetorical activity," such as "city parks, waiting rooms, shopping malls," in order to "research, write, and (ideally) publish on location" (224). In their choice to situate student writing in the "wild," we can see connections back to early ecocomposition scholarship, even though Bjork and Schwartz advocate for a range of public, commercial, and natural places for student writing experiences. Making similar arguments, though drawing on the spontaneous prose-writing style of Jack Kerouac, Juarez contends that spontaneous composing can help students "step outside of essayist literacy practices" and compose in "whatever media they choose: tape recorder, sketchbook, journal, blog, Blackberry" (n.p.). Juarez explains her assignment in this way: "Using the medium of their choice, students write freely about their observations and experiences in different spaces and places and move in and through different spaces and places; they do not concentrate on form, style, or correctness, but instead try to capture their own reflections and insights regarding these experiences" (n.p.). While Juarez's assignment does not require mobile technologies, the emphasis on personal reflections and insights while in different spaces and places encourages students to use writing to document their place-based experiences on location.

The Write on Location assignment invites students to both spontaneously compose in the way Juarez writes about while also engaging with the kind of mobile composition that Bjork and Schwartz advocate for because I encourage students to use mobile technologies to take pictures and write on location. This assignment strongly urges students to use mobile technologies, such as a cell phone, tablet, or laptop, to freewrite on location; thus the assignment is not suited for a traditional on-campus, classroom computer lab. However, students who prefer to write on pen and paper first are allowed to do so, but I require that they write at the actual location and publish their writing digitally while on location (or as soon as possible after). Because I want to be mindful of issues around digital access, both in terms of mobile devices and wireless connections, I offer the option for students to complete the assignment with pen and paper. I also provide students with information about how to check out mobile equipment on-campus to support their writing and photography while visiting public locations. Students are required to take digital photographs while on location, which typically results in the use of a mobile device or, at the least, a digital camera. Offering students flexibility in terms of how they complete their mobile compositions also makes this assignment translate effectively over the years, even when specific programs, applications, or devices change. The Write on Location assignments students submit become an important invention activity to help students narrow the focus of their issue and develop an argument; moreover, as a process-based activity students use photos they took and excerpts from their freewrites in their final projects.

Student Examples

The Write on Location assignments function as invention activities to initiate students' ideas for the larger digital mapping multimodal project. However, in reviewing students' work for this project, I found that the Write on Location assignments also help ground students' digital work in their physical experiences in local, material places. Moreover, I believe students' mobile composition experiences, through freewriting and taking pictures on location, added a significant component—visceral and sensory—to their digital projects that would have been absent, or at least less intensely communicated, without the requirement that they use mobile composition to write on location. In the following pages, I offer two example student projects that demonstrate the importance of writing on location.

First, Marilyn's project investigates a small creek—Intrenchment Creek—near her home that few local residents know about because it runs through a densely urban area in the middle of Atlanta. Figure 12.1 is a picture Marilyn took for her first Write on Location assignment; it is paired with an excerpt from the corresponding freewrite she submitted from the same day. Marilyn's

"This place is disgusting. I'm not sure how much is the result of the shopping center and how much is people dumping. [. . .] I knew I would find trash here, but did not know I would find this much waste. [. . .] This level of waste makes me uncomfortable. [. . .] How can this be justified? How can anyone think that dumping their trash here is a good idea? How can a store turn a blind eye to the area behind them? [. . .] While it is obvious something needs to be done about this, how do I tell it and to whom? There are certainly some people that will not care, for those are the ones contributing to the problem. How do I reach the ones that will care?"

Figure 12.1. *Marilyn's Write on Location photo of Intrenchment Creek.*

freewrite suggests that she is surprised by the extent of trash on the creek's banks. Her response is at first visceral, "this is disgusting," but then moves into a series of rhetorical questions, as she wonders how and why this could ever happen. At the end of this excerpt, she begins moving toward rhetorical action, or at least considering issues such as audience and purpose, and how she might persuasively motivate an audience to care about Intrenchment Creek.

In her final project, which combines a Google map with links to a WordPress site, Marilyn employs multiple modes—spatial, visual, linguistic—to build her argument for local Atlanta residents to get involved in creek cleanup and restoration efforts. Figure 12.2 is a screen shot of Marilyn's Google map; the icons are the dropped pins Marilyn selected to rhetorically represent significant locations associated with Intrenchment Creek. When users click on each icon, they are provided with a title for that location, a brief description, and a link to the WordPress site Marilyn created with additional content. The WordPress site includes a series of photos Marilyn took while visiting various locations along the creek's path, links to websites for watershed organizations and fact sheets for restoring streams, as well as section headings and paragraphs of text composed by Marilyn (see Figure 12.3).

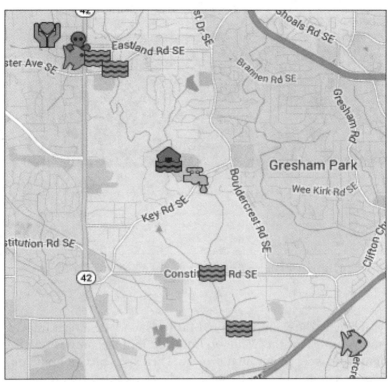

FIGURE 12.2. *Marilyn's Google Map of Intrenchment Creek.*

Marilyn's linguistic content on the WordPress site is a mix of excerpts from her freewrites—impressions from her Write on Location site visits—and calls to action for her readers. In the final paragraphs on her site, Marilyn builds to her claim that "We are destroying our homes by ruining our environment." Speaking directly to Atlanta residents, her selected audience, she implores readers to stop dumping in the creek and calls for better enforcement of dumping laws; she argues that "we can restore the land around the creek" and provides links to a current restoration project.

FIGURE **12.3.** *Screenshot featuring a portion of Marilyn's WordPress site.*

I believe the examples from Marilyn's work demonstrate how vitally important the Write on Location mobile composition assignments were to her final project. The experience of going out into the community—into local public spaces to write, research, and reflect—imbued her digital representation of Intrenchment Creek in her mapping project with a more vivid sense of physical and material place. Marilyn reflected that the Write on Location assignments "encouraged me to place more emotion and experience into the assignment that could have been dry or too removed from personal experience without it." Looking back at her freewrite from the first Write on Location assignment, we can see some of her emotion coming through; I believe her disgust, bewilderment, and frustration at seeing all of the trash along the creek helped fuel the rhetorical arguments in her digital project. Had Marilyn not been required to visit locations and encouraged to use mobile devices to freewrite and take pictures for her project, she likely would have found online images and read secondary sources (if they were even available for such a little-known creek) that would have led to a very different, likely more removed and less compelling, digital project.

Similar to Marilyn's reflection, another student, Ayesha, reflected that "Writing on location made my assignments more personal." Ayesha's project, called "Remembering and Restoring Our History: Auburn Avenue" focuses on four historic sites in downtown Atlanta—areas very close to Georgia State University's campus—that she argues are in need of restoration. Meeting the requirement of the assignment, Ayesha plots her locations on a Google map, selecting a satellite-style street view to rhetorically represent this urban area (see Figure 12.4). From each dropped pin, Ayesha provides a title and brief description for the location, as well as a link to a separate Prezi for each site. When users click the link for the Prezi, a song begins playing immediately and continues as readers move through the linguistic and visual modes Ayesha used to offer historical information, to highlight the photographs she took on location, and to forward her argument for historical preservation (see Figure 12.5).

What struck me in reading, viewing, and listening to Ayesha's multimodal project was the way she was able to set a mood and rhetorical tone with the music. For one site, The Royal Peacock, she selected "Little Girl Blue" by Ella Fitzgerald; for the Original Atlanta Life Insurance Building, John Coltrane's "In a Sentimental Mood" plays in the background. In reading Ayesha's reflection, I came to understand how purposeful her music choices were and how they were tied to her experiences with the Write on Location assignment. Ayesha explained that "writing on location definitely made me appreciate the experience of physically being in a place versus seeing a place digitally. Realizing this made me

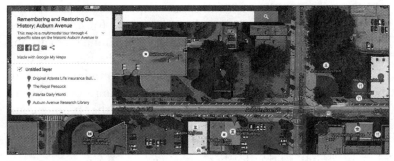

FIGURE **12.4.** *Ayesha's Google Map of Auburn Avenue.*

Atlanta Life Insurance Company

For decades, the Atlanta Life Insurance Company was a symbol of black prosperity, entrepreneurship, and self-sufficiency. It was the flagship company for the Sweet Auburn Business District. Even though the company still is around today, the building from whence it started is slowly becoming an eye sore that if not cared for will suffer the fate of many other buildings of its same caliber and location.

FIGURE **12.5.** *Screenshot from Ayesha's Prezi for the Atlanta Life Insurance Company.*

want to add more to the project to try and capture the feeling of physically being there, which is why I made the decision to add music to the [P]rezis." Indeed, my experience with Ayesha's project left me with the feeling that I was there (or *wanted* to be there)—standing in front of the buildings, imagining them among the bustling streets of downtown Atlanta at the height of their historic importance. Her rhetorical and multimodal choices to include music successfully communicated the aura of the places she visited, and, as in Marilyn's case, I believe that mobile composing at the actual locations helped Ayesha develop a sense of material place that translated into a captivating and persuasive piece of digital writing for her audience.

The digital maps produced by Marilyn and Ayesha highlight how students can connect with local communities, people, and places and, in turn, relay that sense of place within their digital compositions. However, several student reflections noted the challenges they faced in representing meaningful experiences they had in physical places within a digital format. For example, Wendell described how he felt like he had to "flatten the three-dimensional spaces to make them work on a [digital] map." I would argue that, with perhaps more time, peer review, and instructor feedback during the composing process, Wendell might have come to see that some options in multimodal composing can bring a seemingly flat space to life, as in the case of Ayesha's use of music. However, I understand and appreciate Wendell's struggles with digital representation of physical places, and I plan to build in more class discussions and process-based assignments to help students think through these important issues when I next teach this project. As in the case of another student, Richard, who conducted research on Atlanta's public bus system, I hope that the Write on Location assignments would "challenge [students] to think critically in the physical space," but students also must be challenged to think critically in digital spaces—to creatively imagine digital possibilities for initiating in readers the same sense of place they felt when engaging in mobile composition.

Conclusion

A place-based approach to mobile composition has allowed me to continue incorporating my passion for students to engage with people and places in their local community while also inviting students to compose and publish using digital technologies. The Write on Location mobile composition assignment disrupts dichotomies—between material and digital, physical and virtual, academic and nonacademic, public and private—in ways that invite students to critically examine how and where they use mobile technologies for writing and how to best represent places using those technologies. Christopher Schmidt, in writing about GPS and digital mapping, notes that "mobile writing technologies [and] . . . GPS-enabled devices have, on the one hand led to a hyperawareness of real-world location. . . . But at the same time, smart phones and writing tablets refract and multiply the actual place of writing into virtual *dis*location" (304). However, I believe that a place-based approach to mobile composition allows students to engage with physical places in a way that *re*locates rather than *dis*locates them within their communities. When we develop place-based mobile composition assignments, we reclaim student experience in local spaces, while still supporting critical engagement with digital media, multimodality, and mobile composition.

Works Cited

Arola, Kristin L., Jennifer Sheppard, and Cheryl E. Ball, eds. *Writer/ Designer: A Guide to Making Multimodal Projects*. New York: Bedford/St. Martin's, 2014. Print.

Bjork, Olin, and John Pedro Schwartz. "Writing in the Wild: A Paradigm for Mobile Composition." Print. Kimme Hea 223–37.

Brown, Nicole R. "Metaphors of Mobility: Emerging Spaces for Rhetorical Reflection and Communication." Kimme Hea 239–52.

Dobrin, Sidney I., and Christian R. Weisser. *Natural Discourse: Toward Ecocomposition*. Albany: State U of New York P, 2002. Print.

Holmes, Ashley J. "Transformative Learning, Affect, and Reciprocal Care in Community Engagement." *Community Literacy Journal* 9.2 (2015): 48–67. Print.

Juarez, Marissa M. "A Visual-Spatial Approach to Spontaneous Composing in First-Year Composition." *Kairos: A Journal of Rhetoric, Technology, and Pedagogy* 16.3 (2012): n.p. Web. 14 July 2015.

Keller, Christopher J., and Christian R. Weisser, eds. *The Locations of Composition*. Albany: State U of New York P, 2007. Print.

Kimme Hea, Amy C., ed. *Going Wireless: A Critical Exploration of Wireless and Mobile Technologies for Composition Teachers and Researchers*. Cresskill: Hampton, 2009. Print.

Mauk, Jonathon. "Location, Location, Location: The 'Real' (E)states of Being, Writing, and Thinking in Composition." *College English* 65.4 (2003): 368–88. *JSTOR*. Web. 27 Nov. 2009.

Reynolds, Nedra. *Geographies of Writing: Inhabiting Places and Encountering Difference.* Carbondale: Southern Illinois UP, 2004. Print.

Sandlin, Jennifer A., Brian D. Schultz, and Jake Burdick, eds. *Handbook of Public Pedagogy: Education and Learning Beyond Schooling.* New York: Routledge, 2010. Print.

Schmidt, Christopher. "The New Media Writer as Cartographer." *Computers and Composition* 28 (2011): 303–14. Print.

Vinson, Jenna. "Spatial Shock: Place, Space, and the Politics of Representation." *Kairos: A Journal of Rhetoric, Technology, and Pedagogy* 16.3 (2012): n.p. Web. 14 July 2015.

Weisser, Christian R., and Sidney I. Dobrin, eds. *Ecocomposition: Theoretical and Pedagogical Approaches.* Albany: State U of New York P, 2001. Print.

CHAPTER THIRTEEN

Untangling the Web through Digital Aggregation and Curation

RANDY D. NICHOLS
Limestone College

JOSEPHINE WALWEMA
Oakland University

In a work that is ancient by digital standards, Richard Lanham notes that the great problem we (will) face in our Digital Age is not paucity of information, but rather the lack of ability to situate the information epistemologically. As he puts it, ". . . the most precious resource in our new information economy? Certainly not information, for we are drowning in it. No, what we are short of is the attention to make sense of that information" (Lanham 6). At the outset, let us recognize one of the significant challenges that face scholars in the (increasingly digital) twenty-first century: making sense of our resources.

In 2008, Nicholas Carr posed the question "Is Google Making Us Stupid?" As academics working in the emerging areas of digital literacies, our immediate response was a loud and clear "No!" Surely Google (which stands for the Internet and Web and the new digital environs) was making our students smarter! But when we incorporated the article into our course reading so our students could reflect and respond in an intelligent and scholarly critical fashion, we discovered that they struggled. These digital natives (who were immersed in new media) struggled to read an article about how digital natives (who are immersed in new media) can't read an article. Many find resonance with Carr's own admission in the article:

My concentration often starts to drift after two or three pages. I get fidgety, lose the thread, begin looking for something else to do. I feel as if I'm always dragging my wayward brain back to the text. The deep reading that used to come naturally has become a struggle. (Carr)

The Tempting Option: Going Back

Naturally, this challenge causes us to wonder if our students will ever regain the level of concentration Carr laments. And so, we rush to fix the problem by including some of this language on our syllabi and/or assignment prompts: *No Wikipedia; No blogs accepted as sources; Only peer-reviewed articles from approved databases.*

This fix (nudging student writers away from the video screen and back toward printed books and journals) seems natural and right, and completely in harmony with our academic experiences and scholarly practices in the print-centric universe in which we practice. However, this fix will be found, at length, to be unsatisfactory for a few reasons outlined below.

First, it presupposes that we should only consider valid digital resources that arise from, or have been tamed into, a mode of print-centricity. We intimate that only library databases lead to valid research materials.

Second, this fix accepts only knowledge that is commensurate with fields in which the speed of the machinery of print does no harm, e.g., new media.

Third, this fix removes, almost entirely, the students' agency as researchers to critically evaluate sources. Limiting research to peer-reviewed articles relieves the student of responsibility for evaluation and relegates this rhetorical power to the unseen experts who edit the journals and to the teacher who sanctions the practice. Moreover, the idea that the student has met the requirements of academic authorities (Horowitz; Dewald) by doing so is especially troubling.

Fourth, this fix depends on a system that is not fully available to all learners at all times because of inequality of access (Van Dusen). If the peer reviewers comprise one gatekeeper, there is yet another gatekeeper—that of subscription and access. Consider Sarah Kendzior's recent *Vitae* article "Lip-syncing the Academic Conversation," where she asks, "What happens when that conversation takes place behind a paywall through which you cannot afford to pass?"

Finally, the fix ignores the need for handling work in emerging areas such as digital literacies where the lion's share of the work about new media is done in and through new media (Hockly; Bittman). Next year's journal publication is, for many issues in digital culture and communication, simply too late. As Kevin Kelly observes, we are already well into a "second Gutenberg shift" from the page to the screen, but the larger the bureaucracy, the longer the resistance to accept the writing on the wall. Moreover, some shunned resources such as blogs, tweets, and other micro-blogging content constitute rich sources for research (Bruns and Liang; Puschmann and Burgess).

The Promising Option: Going Forward

If returning to the traditional practices of the past fails to address the contingencies of an increasingly digital landscape, how might we proceed? Engaging this landscape requires, among other elements, what Bill Cope and Mary Kalantzis in "The Things You Do to Know" have called "situated practice" (7), the "immersion in meaningful practices within a community of learners who are capable of playing multiple and different roles based on their backgrounds and experiences" (20). Situated practice recognizes that learning is activated across many areas with no separation of social and school, which James Paul Gee identifies as one roadblock to digital literacy. Gee challenges educators to bridge this gap by inviting the digital-social into the print-classroom ("New People" 41).

Situated learning leverages familiar areas to "overtly instruct" and "critically frame" writing practices with the goal of developing students as communicators of meaning (7). In situated learning, students become more than consumers of received knowledge; they become composers of texts via a network of varied new media practices, include authoring, remixing, and distributing content in multimedia.

In the era of the "internet of things" and "ubiquitous computing" (Weiser), students are constantly connected through mobile apps and handheld devices and appear to be at ease with technology. Situated learning projects, such as a digital curation project, help students move beyond the digital literacy "partitions," as exemplified by a now familiar meme: *Question*: "What would be the most difficult thing to explain to someone from the 1950s?" *Answer*: "In my pocket I have a device capable of accessing all of mankind's knowledge. I use it to look at pictures of kittens and start arguments with strangers." (See Figure 1 at http://bit.ly/rhetsoupimages for one version of this meme.)

One Step Forward: Digital Aggregation and Curation

One useful approach to directing students' attention to the rhetorical potential of digital resources is a digital aggregation and curation project. Students need to learn about existing digital resources and how best to use them, first by managing them so they are not overwhelming, and preserving them from the inevitable ephemeral fate that many digital resources suffer (Kwastek). Curation gives digital content some fixity, allows the curator to revisit the content, and prompts new discoveries. Students will not uncritically consume available content, nor will they simply reproduce sanctioned content, but rather, they will engage in epistemological activities that interrogate, shape, repurpose, remake, and transform content.

In this proposed digital curation project, students learn to design meaning in, and through, digital media. This project is well-suited for upper-level undergraduate classes that focus on multimodal composition or digital literacies, in that the goal of the digital curation project is to help students develop, not a specific grammar or a taxonomy, but rather a workable approach for forming grammars, methodologies, heuristics, etc., where none exist as standards. And, indeed, to interrogate what Cope and Kalantzis have named "catalogues of convention" ("'Multiliteracies': New Literacies" 176), the standards that experts have put in place, and the philosophical/pedagogical prejudices of the "catalogues."

Curation and Digital Curation

The impulse to preserve predates the technology of writing. For example, the cave paintings at Lascaux in France tell a story through a succession of images or via "associative assemblage" (Staley). Written curation as preservation has become invaluable in fields such as science and engineering where data are gathered at great expense so as to be made readily accessible as "raw ingredients for discovery and dissemination of knowledge" (National Science Foundation 44). And now we face the challenge of approaching curation in the digital era.

For our purposes, let us consider digital curation to be the process that intentionally aggregates, critically sorts, and produces a repository of resources to which a researcher may constantly return. (Scholars may gain perspective from considering definitional approaches from various fields of study, many of which are listed at http://bit.ly/rhetsoupimages.)

Sue Ann Sharma and Mark Deschaine, who offer that digital curation supports teaching, learning, and assessment, i.e., the work of teachers, recommend what they call "the five Cs of curation," namely:

+ **Collect**—to discover, organize, share through tools like Delicious

+ **Categorize**—to compare and generalize through visual book-marking (Pinterest)

+ **Critique**—to help discriminate and evaluate, using tools like Diigo for highlighting, sticky note annotations

+ **Conceptualize**—to help reorganize and repurpose through tools like Protopage

+ **Circulate**—make assets available through Scoop.it (Sharma)

Execution in the Proposed Assignment: Play Exemplars and Worked Examples

Though the contemporary digital landscape is like the Wild West—with few enforceable rules, often away from the eyes and reach of authorities—this digital world has power to "engage in powerful, deep, and complex thinking and learning" (Gee, *New Digital Media and Learning* 12). In this world, students author or repurpose games, videos, websites, and social media in a new participatory culture. And so the following is an intentional, active compositional assignment that will serve as a "worked example" or "play exemplar" developed by James Paul Gee in *New Digital Media and Learning* (41–53). Gee develops "play exemplars" as a pedagogical tool for emerging fields to work much as "worked examples" do in established fields (Atkinson et al.). Worked examples have been effectively used to teach difficult concepts in subjects such as math and science, and can be similarly useful in new fields.

In traditional worked examples, teachers publicly walk learners through the well-articulated problem as a way of modeling strategies, steps, and techniques to arrive at a solution; play exemplars are designed for new and emerging fields where expertise has not been established. Gee states that play exemplars are "in some ways, a polar opposite of the sorts of exemplars that have historically formed new areas, namely worked examples" (*New Digital Media and Learning* 47). Whereas worked examples (in the classic sense) serve to pass along established conventions, grammars, rules, and principles from the experts to the novices, play exemplars (or worked examples in this new sense) encourage the novices to pretend to be experts, and the experts to embrace novice status as they work together to propose new practices from collaborative experience.

In providing exemplars, such as the digital curation project that follows, we are not so much claiming certitude as we are working our way through an emerging field alongside our students, encouraging exploration informed by theoretical and critical grounding, and demonstrating, via play exemplars, how these concepts unfold in an emerging area.

A Play Exemplar: Digital Aggregation and Curation Project on Oculus Rift

Project Situation: Since students' interaction with research materials takes place in a world that is increasingly digital, where grammars, conventions, and rules from older media no longer serve the contingent realities of the new media, students and faculty should work together to propose new practices by interactive collaboration within those new media.

Project Goals: Student researchers will develop a workable approach for forming grammars, methodologies, heuristics, and conventions in the emerging area of contemporary digital research. Students will propose, analyze, theorize, debate and discuss these proposals among your immediate (and extended) community of scholars. In short, students will be involved in creating new literacies for new media. "New media are new languages, their grammar and syntax yet unknown" (McLuhan and McLuhan).

Project Summary: Students will gather and collect research on an assigned topic using free, popular, universally available, and easily accessible apps, namely Flipboard and Pinterest. Students will employ these apps as tools of critically reflective "meaning-making" through rhetorically intentional aggregating and curating, and will reflect on how the medium and the tools shape their approaches to research.

Assignment Description

Project Introduction: Digital Aggregation and Curation

1. Students will complete a digital curation project using free apps on mobile devices and situate the project in light of classroom lectures, readings, and discussions (see Project Situation in the play exemplar).
2. Students will set up their own Flipboard and Pinterest accounts (if they do not already have such) and familiarize themselves with the apps using Flipboard Tutorials (https://about.flipboard.com/tutorials/) and Pinterest Tutorials (https://help.pinterest.com/en/guide/all-about-pinterest).
3. The instructor will demonstrate how these apps are useful for more than crafts, recipes, and wedding planning with examples of the instructor's use of the apps for academic purposes. The instructor will show how Flipboard can be used to aggregate research (see Figure 2 at http://bit.ly/rhetsoupimages) and how

Pinterest can be used to curate research (see Figure 3 at http://bit.ly/rhetsoupimages).

Project Activities: Research with Mobile Technology

1. **Topic:** Students will research **Oculus Rift** as the topic for this project.
   Rationale: Oculus Rift is one of the most-discussed new virtual reality (VR) technologies. Technologies like Oculus Rift have significant implications for entertainment, education, marketing, medicine, and other areas. Because VR technology is new and is changing so quickly, researchers who wish to be relevant must leverage contemporary resources such as magazines and blogs.
2. **Aggregation:** Students will use the Flipboard app to gather current resources on Oculus Rift by adding "Oculus Rift" as a topic (see Figure 4 at http://bit.ly/rhetsoupimages) and by following related magazines, topics, people, or sources. Students will review, analyze, and reflect upon their aggregation work via related blog prompts. (See the following Student Writing section.)
3. **Curation:** Students will use the Pinterest app to curate the materials gathered via Flipboard (and other research means). Students will create Pinterest "boards" to serve as their archive for research on Oculus Rift. (See Figure 5 at http://bit.ly/rhetsoupimages.) Students will build their research archives using Sharma and Deschaine's "5 Cs" approach: **Collect** (This step was completed in the Flipboard aggregation.) **Categorize** (Students will read and summarize the material collected, remarking on whether the material described Oculus Rift, reported on current uses of the technology, told of proposed future developments, or speculated on implications of the technology.) **Critique** (Students will determine whether each source is relevant, credible, and useful for their research by interrogating the source's authorship and publication *ethos*. Sources deemed useful will be "pinned.") **Conceptualize** (Students will form a visualized archive by "pinning" each accepted source to their "Oculus Rift" board [See Figure 5 at http://bit.ly/rhetsoupimages].) **Circulate** (Students will share their research archives by way of class blogs as project presentations, as well as through social media in future research.)

Student Writing: Reflections on Research and Process

Research Process Blog Responses: Students will respond to the blog prompts below at designated times throughout the project. These blog posts will be linked to the class blog for collaboration, peer review, and inspiration. Blog posts must be posted by due dates, but may be updated, improved, and revised before the Research Summary Post is due.

1. **Mobile Apps as Research Tools**—Describe your experience approaching research on a mobile device. In what ways is your experience better or worse, similar or different from working with print books and journals, or in the library database?
2. **Aggregating and Discovery**—Compare and contrast the available sources in Flipboard to other research environments, such as library databases. What tricks, tips, or procedures did you discover that you would recommend to others doing research with a mobile device in Flipboard? (Share your Flipboard Magazine link in your blog.)
3. **Curatorial Decision Making**—Describe your decision-making process on which sources "made the cut" for your Pinterest board. What were your chief concerns as you made your evaluations? Give examples of how resources did, and did not, meet your research standards.
4. **Creating a Digital Archive**—Describe your experience with using Pinterest as a research archive tool. How is the experience similar or different from your experiences in more traditional research settings? Are there advantages or disadvantages to working with this tool? What strategies, tips, or procedures did you discover that you would recommend to others doing research with a mobile device in Pinterest? (Share your Pinterest board link in your blog.)

Project Research Summary

1. **Research Summary Blog Entry**—Students will write a summary blog post based on their research that provides an introduction and overview of Oculus Rift. The blog entry must incorporate and cite the sources used, and must address these questions: *What is Oculus Rift? What can Oculus Rift do at the present time? What is the future of Oculus Rift? How could Oculus Rift change our lives?*

Review and Assessment

1. **Post-Presentation Reflection**—Review and summarize your experience building and using a digital archive via a mobile device.

What aggregation and curation practices or conventions from older media were you able to employ toward your research in this new medium? How did you incorporate these practices? How might your reading, writing, and thinking be shaped differently by using a mobile device to gather information? (Refer to previous readings and discussions such as Nicholas Carr's "Is Google Making Us Stupid?".) Is the future of research digital? Is it mobile? How might research and writing change as your experience becomes more common? Did you discover rules, strategies, or principles that might contribute to a "rhetoric" or "grammar" for working in these new media?

Project Assessment and Grading

Each student will complete the following writing assignments by promptly posting responses that demonstrate engagement with the research tools, thoughtful connections with class readings and lectures, attention to all questions in the prompts, and collaborative gestures with colleagues.

- ◆ **Process Blog Posts—40%**
  (Mobile Apps as Research Tools—10%, Aggregation and Discovery—10%, Curatorial Decision Making—10%, Creating a Digital Archive—10%)
- ◆ **Project Research Summary—30%**
- ◆ **Post-Process Reflection—30%**

The instructor should call attention to how each student-scholar's work will not only receive a summative assessment for the project, represented by rubrics and grades, but will also be part of an ongoing formative assessment conversation among their community of new media scholars as their work serves to encourage continued development of new literacies (Gikandi 2336–37).

Conclusion/Further Discussion

We live in a brave new digital world where the advancements in our technologies often outpace our theoretical apparatus to frame, situate, and critically engage the ever-shifting new media landscape. Our interactions with new technologies take place in diverse and often novel situations where traditional distinctions between experts and non-experts do not apply. Such interactions have reached a point of ubiquity where new grammars, taxonomies, heuristics, and approaches are demanded. We believe assignments such as the digital curation project here can serve to facilitate development of such grammars and heuristics.

We see two major strengths of using such an assignment: It encourages a rhetorical and critical self-awareness of the scholar working through a new field, and it requires scholars to develop theories on new media by working in new media themselves. In his *Gramophone, Film, Typewriter*, Friedrich Kittler recounts how Nietzsche's writing style was changed by his adoption of the typewriter as a mode of composition, and quotes Nietzsche, "Our writing tools are also working on our thoughts" (200). For many student scholars, the writing tools shaping their thoughts are smartphones and tablets. In this project, students use mobile digital technology to research, write, publish, and collaborate in the very media they will study, critique, and construct literacies for.

This chapter will remain relevant in the future as digital technologies evolve because it focuses not on the technology itself but on engaging students to develop literacies in an ever-shifting digital landscape. We offer the assignment as a play exemplar, to be used, augmented, revised, resituated, and repurposed by other educators and scholars. We hope that, in turn, these scholars would share their new work and findings with the broader discourse community of new media explorers.

Works Cited

Atkinson, Robert K., Sharon J. Derry, Alexander Renkl, and Donald Wortham. "Learning from Examples: Instructional Principles from the Worked Examples Research." *Review of Educational Research* 70.2 (2000): 181–214. Print.

Bittman, Michael, Leonie Rutherford, Jude Brown, and Len Unsworth. "Digital Natives? New and Old Media and Children's Outcomes." *Australian Journal of Education* 55.2 (2011): 161–75. Print.

Bruns, Axel, and Yuxian Eugene Liang. "Tools and Methods for Capturing Twitter Data during Natural Disasters." *First Monday* 17.4 (2012): n.p. Web. 30 June 2015.

Carr, Nicholas. "Is Google Making Us Stupid? What the Internet Is Doing to Our Brains." *Atlantic* 302.1 (2008): 56–63. *Academic OneFile*. Web. 1 Apr. 2010.

Cope, Bill, and Mary Kalantzis. "'Multiliteracies': New Literacies, New Learning." *Pedagogies: An International Journal* 4.3 (2009): 164–95. Print.

————. "The Things You Do to Know: An Introduction to the Pedagogy of Multiliteracies." *A Pedagogy of Multiliteracies: Learning by Design*. Ed. Cope and Kalantzis. London: Palgrave, 2015. 1–36. Print.

Dewald, Nancy H. "What Do They Tell Their Students? Business Faculty Acceptance of the Web and Library Databases for Student Research." *Journal of Academic Librarianship* 31.3 (2005): 209–15. Print.

Gee, James Paul. *New Digital Media and Learning as an Emerging Area and "Worked Examples" as One Way Forward*. Cambridge: MIT P, 2010. Print.

————. "New People in New Worlds: Networks, the New Capitalism and Schools." *Multiliteracies: Literacy Learning and the Design of Social Futures*. Ed. Bill Cope and Mary Kalantzis. London: Routledge, 2000. 41–66. Print.

Gikandi, Joyce Wangui, Donna Morrow, and Niki E. Davis. "Online Formative Assessment in Higher Education: A Review of the Literature." *Computers & Education* 57.4 (2011): 2333–51. Print.

Hockly, Nicky. "Digital Literacies." *ELT Journal* 66.1 (2012): 108–12. Print.

Horowitz, Daniel M. "What Professors Actually Require: Academic Tasks for the ESL Classroom." *TESOL Quarterly* 20.3 (1986): 445–62. Print.

Kelly, Kevin. "Becoming Screen Literate." *New York Times*. New York Times, 21 Nov. 2008. Web. 12 Jan. 2010.

Kendzior, Sarah. "Lip-syncing to the Academic Conversation." *Vitae*. Chronicle of Higher Education, 27 Mar. 2015. Web. 10 Apr. 2015.

Kittler, Friedrich A. *Gramophone, Film, Typewriter*. Trans. Geoffrey Withrop-Young and Michael Wutz. Stanford: Stanford UP, 1999. Print.

Kwastek, Katja. *Aesthetics of Interaction in Digital Art.* Cambridge: MIT P, 2013. Print.

Lanham, Richard A. *The Economics of Attention: Style and Substance in the Age of Information.* Chicago: U of Chicago P, 2006. Print.

McLuhan, Marshall, and Eric McLuhan. *Laws of Media: The New Science.* Toronto: U of Toronto P, 1999. Print.

National Science Foundation. "Sustainable Digital Data Preservation and Access Network Partners (DataNet)." Arlington: NSF, 2012. Web. 3 Jan. 2016.

Puschmann, Cornelius, and Jean Burgess. "The Politics of Twitter Data." HIIG Discussion Paper Series No. 2013-01. *Social Science Research Network.* SSRN, 23 Jan. 2013. Web. 2 Feb. 2016.

Sharma, Sue Ann, and Mark E. Deschaine. "CMU Five C's Digital Curation." *Sharma & Deschaine.* WordPress, 2015. Web. 08 Apr. 2015.

Staley, David J. "Digital Historiography: Information." *Journal of the Association for History and Computing* 2.2 (1999): n.p. Web. 14 Dec. 2015.

Van Dusen, Gerald C. *Digital Dilemma: Issues of Access, Cost, and Quality in Media-Enhanced and Distance Education.* ASHE-ERIC Higher Education Report Vol. 27, Number 5. San Francisco: Jossey-Bass, 2000. Web. 14 Dec. 2015.

Weiser, Mark. "The Computer for the 21st Century." *Scientific American* 265.3 (1991): 94–104. Print.

CHAPTER FOURTEEN

The Stories in Our Pockets: Mobile Digital Literacy Narratives

MIKE TARDIFF
Kennebec Valley Community College

MINH-TAM NGUYEN
Michigan State University

Take out your phone or tablet and ask yourself: Could you, using only the contents available on and through your device, tell a story of how you came to this book at this moment? Could you stitch together important moments, characters, and places that led to your interest in teaching, writing, and mobile technologies?

Our bet is that you could. And we think, in addition to reflecting on important "artifacts"—the stuff that helps you tell this story—you'd probably learn something about how you use mobile technology as well as how to tell a compelling story using words, images, sound, voice, and other resources afforded by mobile devices.

You might, for instance, start by collecting images of people who have supported your academic career. Culled from Facebook, your photo roll, and other places, this cast of characters might include family members, friends, mentors, scholars you admire, etc.

You might then move to places important to your development as a teacher and scholar: the schools where you've learned, grown, and shared; the coffee shops where you've written, prepped, and chatted; and on and on. These might be reflected in pins on a map or a short Vine.

Or maybe you start in some different places: a song in your library with lyrics that inspire you, a set of notes or memos you scrawled during a meeting or conference, or a book in your library that piqued your interest in reading. Wherever your story begins, your mobile device contains many artifacts that help tell *your* story.

In this way, each individual's personal mobile device is a bit like a fingerprint in that its contents are unique. Or perhaps an even more appropriate and academic metaphor: the mobile device is an identity text—a unique and incredibly rich set of artifacts that tells an impressive array of stories about one's life and literacies.

This chapter explores innovative uses of mobile devices on two fronts: (1) as rich identity texts perfect for exploring the scenes and sponsors of literacy and (2) as platforms for multimodal composition. In the end, this work connects two areas of thought familiar to writing teachers: the literacy narrative and multimodal composing. To adequately explore the value of this approach, we survey the mobile phone's cultural importance and concomitant literacies, the idea of identity texts, as well as traditional and emerging approaches to the literacy narrative genre. First, we explain the exigency for this approach.

Why Mobile Devices? The "When" and "What" of Digital Literacy Narratives

This assignment is less a stroke of pedagogical genius and, like many assignments, more a result of pedagogical frustration and infrastructural necessity.

On the first front, we were each teaching two separate assignments: the traditional literacy narrative and the remix assignment, both of which seemed prime for reimagining. What we longed for was an experience in which multimodal composing and critical literacy reflection could interact in meaningful and generative ways, where the two tasks weren't seen as necessarily separate learning outcomes but braided ideas that can and should be practiced and examined simultaneously.

As writing teachers who embrace the use of technology, we had used other approaches to teach multimodal composing, usually in the form of a remix assignment, where students take an existing assignment, change modalities and media, and reimagine a new audience and/or purpose. This approach—where you carefully borrow and repurpose content—succeeded in helping students negotiate and purposefully use multiple semiotic modes but offered little more (e.g., it did not allow for reflection on literacy practice and development).

Also, securing enough A/V equipment to send students into the wild to create new content can be a logistical nightmare; and, frankly, training students to use higher-end equipment is a bit out of our area of expertise, leading to the teaching *of* technology rather than teaching *with* technology. We wanted to go to a place where students already felt comfortable, where they knew the lay of the land.

Like DeVoss, Cushman, and Grabill who see an infrastructural framework as an important invention space for teachers, we wanted to develop an experience in which students are asked to explicitly interact with the networks and technologies that support their literacies and identities, many of which are connected to the devices in their pockets (16). We wanted to place a sustained focus on just how interwoven mobile technology and literacy can be.

Thankfully, every day in our classes, students are using high-powered, multifunctional design and production suites that fit in their pockets and that are loaded with fodder for stories and reflection. They are creating memes, sending Snapchats, orchestrating Vines, and so much more. It occurred to us that the path of least resistance—and the path accommodating the most traffic—was right in front of us: the digital mobile device (i.e., the smartphone or tablet), the very device we sometimes loathe to see swiped and tapped beneath our students' desks. In the end, what we desperately wanted to create, and what is chronicled in this chapter, is a deeply experiential assignment that allows us to "profess less and learn more" (Eldred 120) and to provide a genuine exigency based on self-inquiry.

According to the Pew Research Center, as of 2014, 91 percent of American adults owned cell phones,with nearly two-thirds being smartphones. Among that number, 98 percent of adults aged eighteen to twenty-nine owned a mobile device of some kind. But those figures tell only part of the story about the proliferation of mobile technologies. Increasingly, mobile devices are infiltrating more and more facets of our literate lives. As examples, according to Pew, in 2014 30 percent of smartphone owners accessed educational content or took classes through their phones, 62 percent used their phones to research information regarding their health or an illness, and 40 percent used their phones to access governmental information.

More than simply providing evidence that people use their phones to access various types of information, these data tell us that mobile devices provide ready access to an array of discourse communities and sites of literacy. Swiping between information about the Magna Carta (school), basal cell carcinoma (health), and land use ordinances (government), in many ways, encapsulates our literate lives as we increasingly interact with our world through a series of swipes and taps that serve as a gateway to a vast, networked world.

And Pew's list doesn't include the music, art, and culture that we all access through places like Rap Genius, Tumblr, and YouTube, which serve as important and foundational places of literacy practice and development, places where students are sharing their own work and exercising their own interests.

We, among others, believe that drawing deliberate and sustained attention to these sites, sponsors, and agents of literacy is exactly what the literacy narrative, at its best, seeks to do, and there are perhaps no better material manifestations of this interconnectivity than the smartphone and tablet.

To better understand the theoretical backbone of this approach, we survey relevant literature on three fronts: identity texts and their relevance to the writing classroom, artifacts and their inventive power, and multimodal composing and its place in the twenty-first-century classroom.

Identity Texts as Windows to Cultural and Literacy Narratives

The first assumption this project makes is that mobile devices are identity texts.

Literacy scholars have long studied "identity texts"—material objects dense with semiotic and cultural meaning. Take for instance Kirkland and Jackson, who examined the role clothing played in youth constructing cool, masculine identities (290). Along with that, Wohlwend found that, for young girls, toys became rich identity texts used to address issues of gender and consumer expectations by allowing children to create, revise, and layer new meanings and identities onto traditional gendered media narratives ("'Are You Guys *Girls?*'" 19).

In this way, identity texts are complicated in their origins and dissemination. In many cases, identity texts are commercialized and normalized messages passed onto consumers and redistributed in hegemonic and uncritical ways. According to Wohlwend:

> identity messages circulate through merchandise that surrounds young consumers as they dress in, sleep on, bathe in, eat from, and play with commercial goods decorated with popular-culture images, print, and logos. The constant transmitting of identity messages immerses children in products that invite identification with familiar media characters and communicates gendered expectations about what children should buy, how they should play, and who they should be (New London Group, 1996). ("Damsels" 2)

Mobile devices are dense with these types of messages—from games to news sources to commercial apps; these items reflect our positionality in the world.

But identity texts affect more than just children. We are always already negotiating a series of signs and symbols systems that, in some way, represent various facets of our lives: gender, sexuality, socioeconomics, interests, etc. As we discussed earlier, these identity texts are nested in any number of places accessible from and housed within the mobile device.

This project shines a bright light on those icons, symbols, and requisite sponsors and sites by asking students to index and mobilize these symbols and icons in meaningful and reflective ways.

Wohlwend uses Rowsell and Pahl's idea of sedimentation to talk about the ways identities are cast through these various texts. She describes the ways various discourses layer on top of one another to create dense and multivalent identities (447). Our belief is that mobile devices themselves are sedimented with many cultural and literate artifacts baked into various layers of time and place. More important, students can greatly benefit from the quasi-anthropological experience of excavating, examining, and reassembling these artifacts in meaningful ways.

An Artifactual Approach to Literacy Narratives

The second assumption this project makes is that as identity texts, mobile devices are the perfect artifacts for analysis in literacy narratives.

The project of crafting literacy narratives from the contents of student phones and tablets draws significant inspiration from Halbritter and Lindquist, who document a new approach to the traditional literacy narrative that focuses less on formal literacy practice and pays more attention to the artifacts, sponsors, and sites of literacy development, broadly conceived (172–74). And while their project represents a longer-term research methodology that takes place over four stages, the process of focusing on artifacts, sponsors, and scenes—especially those that are less explicitly related to traditional definitions of literacy—is transferrable across pedagogical and infrastructural contexts. Of particular generative and inventive power is the use of artifacts to spur conversations about literacy scenes and sponsors.

Using artifacts as a starting point in understanding literacy practices and development is significant because they offer physical (or digital) links between identity and experience. Halbritter and Lindquist write that "artifacts have great inventive power in eliciting narratives of experience" (189). They, too, cite the work of Pahl and Rowsell, who explain that "objects carry emotional resonance, and these infuse stories." Artifacts "uncover people and epistemologies," so that researchers may discover participants' "embodied understandings of the world" as these are related to "the sensory nature of place and space, and artifacts as performed and expressed in stories (11)" (qtd. in Halbritter and Lindquist 189). To that, we might add that the reflective space of a literacy narrative also provides the *writer* autoethnographic space to understand their own cultural milieu and taken-for-granted practices, values, and norms in a new way. This is particularly true when students see just how much of their lives are indexed in networked environments through binary code on their mobile devices.

On a more practical level, an artifactual approach has the effect of limiting the scope of student compositions. It's been our experience that when asked to write in the literacy memoir/narrative genre, students tend to survey their entire life from birth to present. Part of this certainly can be attributed to students being asked to write in a new genre, one in which sustained focus on a singular event or place is not only acceptable but preferred, but artifacts help students anchor their stories in the concrete rather than heavily abstracted. Also, having students begin with a series of observations, hunches, and raw connections can serve as a valuable experiential lesson about the writing and invention process.

Seeing the mobile device as the ultimate identity text, a nexus to the many spheres of cultural influence and discourse communities we all interact with on a daily basis, is not a new stance. In his book, *Where the Action Is*, computer scientist Paul Dourish brought attention to how computing—specifically within wireless networks and with mobile devices—is not merely an action that people engage in. Rather, computing serves as a medium that facilitates what users do. In this way, computing (and, by extension, mobile devices) offers an infrastructure that allows users to build, shape, and share their identities across different contexts and different scenes. Fortunati noted that mobile phones have the unique characteristic of following us into multiple spheres of our lives (e.g., work, school, and home), making them particularly interesting for thinking about things like literacy, discourse, and identity (97). And those observations were made before the advent of smartphones, which have become repositories for many types of identity-related data: music, photos, videos, text messages, etc. We believe mobile devices are the perfect subject and venue for literacy narrative work because of this omnipresent quality.

Multimodality and Identity

As much as this assignment is about asking students to use the processing power of their mobile devices to weave together images, sound, and words into meaningful texts, it's also a metalinguistic experience that requires students to appreciate and appraise the many modalities with which they communicate on a day-to-day basis. This combination of reflection and production, we hope, is what makes this assignment a useful response to the ongoing call for multiliterate classrooms where students develop the capacities and willingness to transmit, negotiate, and revise the messages that make up our globalized, pluralized, and networked worlds (New London Group 60).

In her review of the terms multimodal and multimedia, Claire Lauer refers to Kress and Van Leeuwen's argument that all modes "can be operated by one multi-skilled person, using one interface, one mode of physical manipulation, so that he or she can ask, at every point: 'Shall I express this with sound or music? Shall I say this visually or verbally?'" (2). Multimodal texts are characterized by the mixed logics brought together through the combination of modes (such as images, text, and color). When students begin asking these types of questions, we're doing well because they are exercising the infinitely transferable skill of appraising the affordances and disaffordances of various communication modalities.

Not surprisingly, with this array of compositional options, scholars have found that multimodality has the effect of increasing engagement and improving outcomes. Vasudevan, Schultz, and Bateman examined the composing practices of fifth-grade students and found that giving them the opportunity to produce multimodal texts gave way to what they call new "authorial stances" or literate identities (442). These authorial stances gave students the platform to engage and participate in the classroom space in ways that print-based texts did not allow. They also found that multimodal composing allowed students to "draw on their knowledge, experiences, and passions nurtured in their home communities to tell new stories and become more deeply engaged in the academic content of school" (443). These stories, like many, were anchored in artifacts: photographs, newspaper clippings, etc., which serve as inventional spaces and jumping off points.

We believe similar empowerment and engagement can be produced through a project where students engage with the texts that matter most to them, the texts that fill up their memory cards and cloud accounts.

Three Phases

Through the affordances of mobile technologies, we believe our project synthesizes all of the aforementioned concepts and theories of literacy narratives, multimodal composition, and identity in productive and scalable ways. This idea of scalability is where we see this assignment gaining the most traction as it can be applied and used in many different scenes and within a variety of scopes. For instance, we have had the opportunity to teach this assignment to multiple audiences, including pre-service teachers, urban youth, and first-year writing students at both a large, land grant university and a community college—all with varying needs, expertise, and access regarding mobile technologies—and in multiple venues, including writing classrooms, workshops, and national conferences. To effectively teach for and with these audiences, we've built an assignment that we believe is amenable to the pedagogical needs of all teachers hoping to engage students in multimodal composition practices.

To execute this assignment, we've split it up into three phases: (1) foundation building, (2) composing and making, and (3) critical reflection.

Foundation Building

The first phase is rooted in inquiry and modeling. The inquiry begins with a few simple framing questions: What does your mobile device mean to you? What do you *do* with your mobile device? What are the connections between mobile technology and literacy? With these core questions planted, modeling the process of analyzing one's literacies, identity, and use of technology begins.

Most education scholars would agree that knowing how to use different instructional technologies is only strengthened by the ability to demonstrate or perform the application of such technology, not just provide a summary of its functions. This distinction is imperative when teaching digital mobile storytelling because it offers a place where you can share your own story to students as well as the chance to build a story alongside them.

With this in mind, we start the assignment by modeling what kind of story can emerge using just a mobile device by showing a screenshot of our phone's homescreen and/or a photo album on a projector or screen.

We begin asking questions like "What stands out to you? What can you tell just from this screen?" Then we ask follow-up questions and invite students to "rhetorically analyze" our homescreen and photo stream. Based on the apps, images, and other things they see (and the arrangement of those artifacts presented on the screen), ask them how they can begin to draw conclusions about the owner of this phone. How does this device, which is often not thought of critically as a storytelling device, tell a story about the owner?

In staging the first phase, it's important to move from generalized questions to questions that drill into discourse and literacy. One way to do this is by asking students to identify a discourse community that you might belong to based on the content of your device. For example, students in the past have commented on the prominence of sports-related apps on Mike's phone, which has led to generative conversations about the types of knowledge and literacies attached to that cultural milieu: the attention to data and statistics, the constant banter and speculation, and even just the volume of content produced through and about sports, which results in constant push notifications and habitualized "checking the score."

Composing and Making

You can limit the horizon of possibilities as much or as little as makes sense for your particular pedagogy. As an example, you may want to focus on literacy sponsorship, in which case it might make sense to limit the scope and nature of the final product to an examination of a single person or sponsor. Conversely, you can ask broader questions like the one we begin this chapter with: How did you end up in this place at this moment? Or you can focus more explicitly on a discourse community to which the student belongs by asking them to share what makes that culture unique. Then, situate the second phase of the assignment by asking:

- How can we cull, curate, and copy images, videos, sound, etc., and apply it to a new mode?

- How can we combine existing materials to create a rich dialogue between the many ostensibly disparate media we own and consume on a daily basis?

- Ultimately, how can we take existing materials—materials that we carry with us every day—and transform them into a powerful story with a beginning, middle, and end?

By answering these questions, not only will students begin to construct a narrative from seemingly mundane objects on their phones, but they can start to apply that process to that of multimodal writing, by drawing and reflecting on crystallized aspects of their identities and experiences via mobile technologies.

At this point, it's necessary to direct attention to their own mobile devices and their associated artifacts. Ask them: "What kind of story can you tell using only the material you have on your phone?" Remind students that these stories do not need to be an accurate portrayal of who they are, but can be copied and transformed into new contexts and for new purposes—essentially underscoring the multiple, sedimented layers of identity that encompass them as humans. Also, remind students to be purposeful in their decisions to add pictures, songs, etc.—an important element of multimodal composition. Ask them, "What does the inclusion of particular images add to the overall rhetorical purpose of your video? How can you tell your story in the most effective way?" Answering such questions will strengthen their ability to analyze any writing situation for its rhetorical success.

After building the foundation and outlining expectations for the students, it's important to then demonstrate how students can switch from thinking to making. In our experience, we've had success using the free movie editing software Splice (available only on iOS; a good alternative is VidTrim, available in the Android marketplace) to create the digital stories.

It's been our experience that instruction in the particulars of the various software platforms needn't be too sophisticated or long-winded. Since most video-making apps follow iMovie's object-oriented lead, the interfaces are fairly intuitive.

After students have a good sense of how to maneuver the app, let them work individually (or in groups if they do not have a smartphone) to create their stories. It is at this point where outcomes can splinter off into different avenues, depending on the learning goals set. For instance, students can create stories using their past experiences as the starting point, or they can craft new experiences and build a story of their present self. With this infrastructure in place, this assignment can be used in whole, or in part, depending on the pedagogical goals set out by the instructor. Although we have described its use through the span of a class session, we've had experiences teaching this assignment as a series of workshops, or as a thought exercise leading into a more substantial writing project. The process of simply flipping through one's phone with an eye toward discourse, literacy, sponsors, and sites is an important and useful exercise in examining the sometimes invisible ways we engage with our world and, more often than not, leads to more interesting, precise, and critical written examinations of literacy and culture.

Critical Reflection

Crucial to the utility and longevity of this assignment is the last phase in the project, where we ask students to engage in systematic reflection. Giving students the space to reflect on their choices throughout the writing process pushes them to think beyond the purview of their mobile devices, making them better equipped to make sound decisions as multimodal writers and writers in general. Such questions can be oriented toward the volume and nature of the artifacts themselves. What did students learn about their use of mobile technologies? How do they understand the link between mobile, digital technology and literacy now?

Ultimately, the sequence of this project emphasizes that the fidelity of the final outcome (whatever it looks like) is not as important as the critical thinking skills involved in the process of multimodal composition and the ability to confidently and successfully evaluate their mobile devices to make new meaning and to provide new contexts for the things they carry with them every day.

Conclusion

We hope to instigate conversations about the interplay of mobility, technology, and literacy, which themselves can be facilitated, inspired, and reimagined with and through mobile technologies in fruitful and lasting ways—ways that live far longer than the battery life of a phone or tablet. As a digital mobile storytelling device, cell phones can be a rich and generative identity text, ripe with artifacts steeped and layered in fragments of ourselves, which can be excavated and critically examined to write powerful multimodal literacy narratives. And as more and more of our lives are preserved in the binary code of social media and other digital spaces, these narratives will become only more complex and necessary.

Works Cited

DeVoss, Dànielle Nicole, Ellen Cushman, and Jeffrey T. Grabill. "Infrastructure and Composing: The *When* of New-Media Writing." *College Composition and Communication* 57.1 (2005): 14–44. *JSTOR.* Web. 2 Feb. 2016.

Dourish, Paul. *Where the Action Is: The Foundations of Embodied Interaction.* Cambridge: MIT P, 2001. Print.

Eldred, Janet. "To Code or Not to Code, or, If I Can't Program a Computer, Why Am I Teaching Writing?" *College Composition and Communication* 58.1 (2006): 119–25. Web. 2 Feb. 2016.

Fortunati, Leopoldina. "The Mobile Phone: An Identity on the Move." *Personal and Ubiquitous Computing* 5.2 (2001): 85–98. Web. 2 Feb. 2016.

Halbritter, Bump, and Julie Lindquist. "Time, Lives, and Videotape: Operationalizing Discovery in Scenes of Literacy Sponsorship." *College English* 75.2 (2012): 171–98. Web. 2 Feb. 2016.

Kirkland, David E., and Austin Jackson. "'We Real Cool': Toward a Theory of Black Masculine Literacies." *Reading Research Quarterly* 44.3 (2009): 278–97. Web. 2 Feb. 2016.

Kress, Gunther R., and Theo Van Leeuwen. *Multimodal Discourse: The Modes and Media of Contemporary Communication*. London: Arnold, 2001. Print.

Lauer, Claire. "Contending with Terms: 'Multimodal' and 'Multimedia' in the Academic and Public Spheres." *Computers and Composition* 26.4 (2009): 225–39. Web. 2 Feb. 2016.

New London Group. "A Pedagogy of Multiliteracies: Designing Social Futures." *Harvard Educational Review* 66.1 (1996): 60–92. Print.

Pahl, Kate, and Jennifer Rowsell. *Artifactual Literacies: Every Object Tells a Story*. New York: Teachers College, 2010. Print.

Pew Research Center. "Mobile Technology Fact Sheet." *Pew Research Center*. Pew Research Center, 27 Dec. 2013. Web. 25 July 2015.

Rowsell, Jennifer, and Kate Pahl. "Sedimented Identities in Texts: Instances of Practice." *Reading Research Quarterly* 42.3 (2007): 388–404. Web. 2 Feb. 2016.

Vasudevan, Lalitha, Katherine Schultz, and Jennifer Bateman. "Rethinking Composing in a Digital Age: Authoring Literate Identities through Multimodal Storytelling." *Written Communication* 27.4 (2010): 442–68. Web. 2 Feb. 2016.

Wohlwend, Karen E. "'Are You Guys *Girls*?': Boys, Identity Texts, and Disney Princess Play." *Journal of Early Childhood Literacy* 12.1 (2012): 3–23. Web. 2 Feb. 2016.

———. "Damsels in Discourse: Girls Consuming and Producing Identity Texts through Disney Princess Play." *Reading Research Quarterly* 44.1 (2009): 57–83. Web. 2 Feb. 2016.

INDEX

Note: A "t" following a page number indicates a table; an "f" indicates a figure.

Remix assignments, 208–9
Reynolds, Nedra, 145, 179, 180
Rhetorical analysis. *See also*
 Critical analysis
 with apps, 52, 57–65
 arrangement, 55
 classical canons of, 54–55
 defined, 53
 delivery, 56–57
 invention, 55
 key terms of, 58f
 memory, 56
 style, 55–56
Rhetorical exigence, 58f
Rhetorical situation, 58f
Rhetorical skills, as outcome of
 mobile initiatives, 2–3,
 159–61
Rodrigo, Rochelle, xii, 1
Roemer, Marjorie, 134
Rossing, Jonathan P., 119
Rowsell, Jennifer, 211, 212
Rubrics
 for app design project, 76f
 for audio essay with QR code
 project, 42f, 47
 for rhetorical analysis of apps
 project, 61–62f
Rummy Rush (game), 90

Sandlin, Jennifer A., 179
Scanlon, Eileen, 39
Scharber, Cassandra, 5, 17
Schmidt, Christopher, 69, 95,
 191–92
Schreyer, Jessica, xii, 39, 96
Schultz, Brian D., 179
Schultz, Katherine, 214
Schultz, Lucille, 134
Schwartz, John Pedro, 17, 95,
 114, 135, 184
Sedimentation, 211–12
Selfe, Cynthia L., 23, 34, 37,
 101, 151, 161
Séror, Jérémie, 173

Sharma, Sue Ann, 198
Sharples, Mike, 121–22
Shazam app, 64–65
Shipka, Jody, 133
Shuler, Carly, 172
Situated learning, 196–97
Skitch app, 108, 109–10
Smith, Aaron, 149
Social contexts
 and mobile gaming project,
 88–91
 of mobile technology use, 23,
 24, 32–33
"Spatial shock," 181
Splice app, 217
Stake, Robert E., 24, 30
Stranz, Adam, 95
Street, Brian, 33
Students. *See also* Access
 on digital portfolios, 144–45
 everyday vs. academic writing,
 95
 as receptive to mobile learning,
 121
 use of mobile technologies, for
 academic purposes, xi
Style, 58f
 as rhetorical canon, 55–56

Takayoshi, Pamela, 136, 151
Tardiff, Mike, 97
Taylor, Josie, 121–22
Teachers
 feedback of, via mobile videocaptures, 170–71, 173–75
 and mobile technology's pedagogical challenges, xi
 as users of mobile technologies, 164–65
Technology literacies project,
 122–30
TED app, 64
Terms of service policies
 assignments and activities,
 86–88

EDITOR

Claire Lutkewitte is an associate professor of writing in the College of Arts, Humanities, and Social Sciences at Nova Southeastern University. She teaches a variety of undergraduate and graduate courses, including basic writing, college writing, advanced composition, writing with technologies, teaching of writing, and research methods. Her research interests include writing technologies, FYC pedagogy, writing center research, and identity studies. She is working with colleagues on a two-year, grant-funded national study that investigates how students transition out of their graduate programs in writing and into assistant professor positions at colleges or universities. She has published in several peer-reviewed journals and has published two books, *Multimodal Composition: A Critical Sourcebook* and *Web 2.0: Applications for Composition Classrooms*.

CONTRIBUTORS

Soni Adhikari was an English teacher and lecturer in Nepal, and she is pursuing her second master's degree in English, focusing on writing studies. Her interests include second language writers, comparative literature, and the use of new media in the classroom.

Ann N. Amicucci is director of first-year rhetoric and writing and assistant professor of English at the University of Colorado, Colorado Springs. Her recent publications include "Responding with the Golden Rule: A Cross-Institutional Peer Review Experiment" with Kristen Getchell in *Teaching English in the Two-Year College*, "'How They Really Talk': Students' Perspectives on Digital Literacies in the Writing Classroom" in *Journal of Adolescent and Adult Literacy*, and "Multimodal Concept Drawings: Engaging EALs in Brainstorming about Course Terms" with Tracy Lassiter in *TESOL Journal*.

Jessie C. Borgman began teaching face-to-face in 2006 and has taught online since 2009. She works for four schools: two for-profit, a community college, and a four-year university. She has presented at annual conferences, including CCCCs, C&W, and TYCA. She is an expert panelist for the CCCC Committee for Effective Practices in Online Writing Instruction. She has published several book chapters, a piece in the *OWI Open Resource*, and has designed/authored a *Mercury Reader* textbook for her online first-year composition courses. Her research interests include online writing instruction, course design, genre studies, two-year colleges, and writing program administration.

Jason Dockter is a professor of English at Lincoln Land Community College, where he teaches composition classes primarily online. He recently completed his PhD in English Studies at Illinois State University with an emphasis on rhetoric/composition, with a specific interest in online writing instruction and multimodal composition. He has presented at the NCTE, CCCCs, and C&W annual conferences on such topics as first-year composition, developing and including multimodal composition projects in composition classes, and online writing instruction.

Moe Folk is an associate professor of digital rhetoric and multimodal composition at Kutztown University in Pennsylvania. He has a PhD in Rhetoric and Technical Communication from Michigan Technological University. His recent publications include a coauthored examination of technological professional development in *Computers and Composition Online*; an essay on visual rhetoric and multimodal style in *Carnivàle* and the *American Grotesque*; and a coedited book on evaluating Web information titled *Online Credibility and Digital Ethos*. He is the editor of the Disputatio section of *Kairos: A Journal of Rhetoric, Technology, and Pedagogy*.

Josh Herron works in online teaching and learning administration and teaches composition and communication courses. He has full-time and adjunct undergraduate teaching experience in a variety of modes at diverse institutional settings. He was a Mobile Learning Teaching Fellow while a full-time lecturer of English at Anderson University (SC) and worked with the composition committee to redesign the first-year writing program. He transitioned into the role of instructional designer and faculty development coordinator in the university's Center for Innovation and Digital Learning, which supports faculty and students in mobile, online, and blended courses and programs. He earned his MA in English (Teaching Composition) at UNC Greensboro and is currently completing his PhD at Clemson University in Rhetorics, Communication, and Information Design. Herron has presented nationally and regionally on innovative instructional practices, pedagogical research, and interdisciplinary scholarship.

Ashley J. Holmes is an assistant professor of English at Georgia State University. She is working on a book-length manuscript that argues for public approaches to pedagogy and administration based on comparative analysis of three case studies conducted within writing programs. Holmes has published articles in *Community Literacy Journal*, *Reflections*, and *English Journal*, and she is an assistant editor with the refereed open-access online journal *Kairos*.

Casey R. McArdle is an assistant professor in the Department of Writing, Rhetoric, and American Cultures at Michigan State University. He has worked with the National Writing Project and presented at numerous conferences, such as Computers and Writing and the Conference on College Composition and Communication. His research and publications center on the use of digital technologies and how they can be used to create knowledge-making spaces for students to collaborate via peer-to-peer learning. He is also a member of the Expert Panel for the CCCC Committee for Effective Practices in Online Writing Instruction.

Christina Moore is a special lecturer in writing and rhetoric at Oakland University in Rochester, Michigan. She also serves as media manager in the university's Center for Excellence in Teaching and Learning. Her scholarship focuses on project-based learning and best practices in teaching and facilitating online collaboration in the first-year writing classroom. She has completed grant-funded work on how to design online first-year writing classes that better retain their freshmen population.

Minh-Tam Nguyen is a PhD student in the Department of Writing, Rhetoric, and American Cultures at Michigan State University, focusing on digital rhetoric and technical writing. There, she taught first-year writing courses with an emphasis on the relationship between science, technology, and writing.

Randy D. Nichols is chair of the Department of Communications and Interdisciplinary Studies at Limestone College, where he teaches communications, digital literacies, critical thinking, and dynamic spatial narratives in the College's Professional Communication degree program. Nichols holds an MA in English literature from Rutgers University–Newark and a PhD in rhetorics, communication, and information design from Clemson University. He has presented at national conferences for the Popular Culture Association and the Conference on College Composition and Communication on his work in new media literacies. Nichols curates the "Smartphone Museum," an occasional, experimental, interactive, collaborative, multimodal compositional space/event that has exhibited at Limestone College's Teacher Cadet Conference and currently at the Cherokee History and Arts Museum. His latest Smartphone Museum exhibit, "Artifacts from the Future," opened in October 2015. He maintains a resource-sharing website for fellow researchers and educators at RhetoricSoup.com.

Jessica Schreyer is an associate professor of English and writing program administrator at the University of Dubuque. She teaches composition, journalism, environmental literature, and related writing courses in the language and literature department. She recently published an article in the *Journal of Basic Writing* and a book chapter in *New Media Literacies and Participatory Popular Culture Across Borders*. She is also on the editorial board for *JUMP: The Journal for Undergraduate Multimedia Projects*.

Ghanashyam Sharma is assistant professor of writing and rhetoric at Stony Brook University. A former English teacher and university lecturer in Kathmandu, Nepal, Shyam specializes in writing in the disciplines, teaching writing with technology, and cross-cultural issues in rhetoric and communication.

Mike Tardiff is an English instructor at Kennebec Valley Community College in Fairfield, Maine.

Melissa Toomey is a visiting assistant professor of English at the University of Cincinnati at Blue Ash. She has written articles such as "Balancing Graduate Studies with Writing Instruction," which appeared in *Teaching with the Norton Field Guide to Writing*. She currently teaches courses in rhetoric and composition, and her interests include social activist rhetorics, teaching feminist methodologies, and finding new methods for teaching with technology in the classroom.

Stephanie Vie is associate professor of writing and rhetoric at the University of Central Florida. She researches social media's impact on literate practices and is currently conducting several grant-funded national surveys of faculty members' attitudes toward social media in composition. She is a reviews coeditor for *Kairos: A Journal of Rhetoric, Technology, and Pedagogy* and a project director with the Computers and Composition Digital Press. Her work has appeared in journals such as *First Monday*, *Computers and Composition*, *Technoculture*, and *Computers and Composition Online*, and her textbook *E-Dentity* (2011) examines the impact of social media on twenty-first-century literacies.

Josephine Walwema is an assistant professor in the Department of Writing and Rhetoric at Oakland University, where she teaches courses in composition, technical and professional communication, and global and legal rhetorics. She has published in the *Journal of Writing and Pedagogy*, *The IEEE Transactions on Professional Communication*, and *Programmatic Perspectives*. She has reviewed for and presented at national and international conferences on approaches to teaching writing.

This book was typeset in Sabon by Barbara Frazier.
Typefaces used on the cover include Baskerville and Gill Sans.
The book was printed on 50-lb. White Offset paper
by Versa Press, Inc.